Irish Film

'No more stories about Irish mothers, priests, sexual repressions and the miseries of rural life': Brian J. O'Byrne in *The Fifth Province* (Irish Film Archive of the Film Institute of Ireland)

Irish Film

The Emergence of a Contemporary Cinema

Martin McLoone

 British Film Institute

For my parents,
John and Gretta McLoone

First published in 2000 by the
British Film Institute
21 Stephen Street, London W1P 2LN

The British Film Institute promotes greater understanding of,
and access to, film and moving image culture in the UK.

Copyright © Martin McLoone 2000

Cover design: Ketchup, London
Cover images: *The Butcher Boy* (Neil Jordan, 1997)

Set in Minion by Fakenham Photosetting Ltd, Fakenham, Norfolk
Printed in Great Britain by St Edmundsbury Press, Bury St Edmunds

British Library Cataloguing-in-Publication Data
A catalogue record for this book is available from the British Library
ISBN 0–85170–792–0 (hbk)
ISBN 0–85170–793–9 (pbk)

Contents

Acknowledgments

This book is indebted to the pioneering work of Kevin Rockett, Luke Gibbons and John Hill, the authors of *Cinema and Ireland* (1987). The present work revisits many of the issues that they first raised and, it is hoped, adds to and expands on the agenda that they so perceptively established back in the days when an Irish film industry was still struggling to be born. All three have been invaluable sources of advice in the intervening years. I am particularly indebted to my colleague at the University of Ulster, John Hill, for advice and encouragement over the years and for sharing innumerable curries as well as intellectual ideas. I benefited from a period of leave of absence at a crucial point in the book's gestation and am indebted to the Faculty of Art, Design and Humanities at the University of Ulster for supporting the project. My colleagues in Media Studies at UU kindly struggled on in my absence and I am grateful to them for easing the burden.

My thanks, too, to the staff at the Irish Film Centre in Dublin, especially Sunniva O'Flynn and Liam Wylie, for setting up archive viewing and to Emma Keogh for helping with stills. Ted Sheehy from *Film Ireland* gave me invaluable box office information and the staffs of both the Galway Film Fleadh and the Cork Film Festival were generous with their time and advice. A special thanks, in this regard, to Mick Hannigan.

Andrew Lockett and Sophia Contento at the BFI were helpful, supportive and above all patient.

A particular debt of gratitude is owed to the students of media studies at UU who have studied the emerging film industry in Ireland over the last decade and offered invaluable insight and comment on the ideas that developed into this book. Some of the material here appeared in earlier, shorter and more tentative form in other publications (occasionally, in less tentative form as well) and earlier discussions of some films appeared particularly in *Cinéaste*. My thanks to Gary Crowdus and the editorial board for their encouragement and support.

The book was supported by two grants from the Arts and Humanities Research Board, a travel grant that allowed me to get the research done and a research leave grant which gave me that invaluable commodity – time to write.

Finally, special thanks to Cindy Milner and our three daughters, Katie, Maeve and Grainne, for their love and support and for tolerating all the mood swings.

Introduction

In the autumn of 1999, Ireland's national broadcasting service, RTÉ (Radio Telefis Éireann) broadcast a five-part documentary series on Irish emigration called *The Irish Empire*. Earlier that year, two independently produced films of some significance were released that also dealt with aspects of Irish emigration, Desmond Bell's *Rotha Mór an tSaoil/The Hard Road to the Klondike* and Nichola Bruce's *I Could Read the Sky*. All three films are concerned to show the impact of emigration on Irish society at home, on the societies abroad that received large numbers of sometimes wretched and distressed immigrants and finally on the individuals themselves through a process of reclaiming lost or forgotten personal memories. The coincidence of these productions appearing within months of each other confirms a major trend in recent Irish historical and cultural studies. In the last ten years or so, there has been a growing interest in the consequences of Ireland's unusually large and persistent levels of emigration. Emigration (and deportation) had been a factor in Irish life from the eighteenth century on but had gathered pace in the Famine years of the 1840s and continued unabated down to the end of the twentieth century.

This renewed interest in emigration is not, however, merely a matter of academic or professional concern. It has impinged on popular consciousness in Ireland in a very personal and direct way. There are very few communities in Ireland which have escaped the effects of emigration and therefore there are few individuals today for whom emigration is not a matter of painful family memory. In her inaugural address in 1990, the newly elected President of Ireland, Mary Robinson, caught this popular mood and made it a theme of her seven-year term of office.

> My primary role as president will be to represent this state. But the state is not the only model of community with which the Irish people can and do identify. Beyond our state there is a vast community of Irish emigrants extending not only across our neighbouring island ... but also throughout the continents of North America, Australia and of course Europe itself. There are over 70 million people living on this globe who claim Irish descent. I will be proud to represent them. (quoted in McQuillan, 1994, p. 2)

Reclaiming personal memories of emigration: *I Could Read the Sky*

This renewed concern with Irish emigration has had the effect, in other words, of broadening and extending the very definitions of Irishness itself, from a narrow and purist notion of identity to a concept that has a global reach. The cultural impact of emigration, in Ireland and across the globe, on the diverse ways in which Irishness is now discussed has opened up both cultural and critical practice to a broader range of discourses than those traditionally associated with the imaginings of Irish nationalism. The result has been to reinvigorate and accelerate a process of cultural reimagining that had begun in the 1960s at the cusp of a programme of modernisation but which looked to have run its course in the 1980s. This accelerating and deepening cultural process dovetailed with a remarkable recovery in the Irish economy in the 1990s, which witnessed Ireland finally taking its place within the global marketplace, with all the opportunities and problems associated with this.

In the same period, Irish culture of all kinds enjoyed unprecedented success and acclaim in the international arena. In literature, Seamus Heaney's Nobel prize was merely the highpoint of a decade of continuing Irish success. In popular culture, Ireland's global success has been even more remarkable. Mainstream rock and pop music have been dominated by Irish acts and the global success of the show *Riverdance* has re-energised Irish traditional music and dance not only worldwide but also in Ireland itself. The Irish soccer team which reached the quarter finals of the 1990 World Cup in Italy was made up of a squad of players some of whom were native born and many others the sons, grandsons and even great-grandsons of Irish emigrants. In this way, the 'national' team went global with significant success, eloquently symbolising deeper cultural, social and ideological changes in Irish society as a whole.

Irish cinema emerged internationally in this period as well with Oscar success for *My Left Foot* (1989) and *The Crying Game* (1992) and a high profile and critical praise for a host of other Irish and Irish-related films. In a short period of time a number of strong Irish male leads emerged in Hollywood, including Liam Neeson, Pierce Brosnan, Gabriel Byrne, Stephen Rea and Aidan Quinn (whose own childhood spent between Ireland and the USA seems to symbolise, in a peculiarly appropriate form, both the widening definition of Irishness and the interconnectedness and hybridity of the emigrant experience). A recognisable, low budget indigenous cinema also appeared during these years and, as was to be expected, provided another cultural expression of the changing context in Ireland.

This book, therefore, is about contemporary Ireland and the cinema which it both produces and inspires. It adopts a broad strategy that considers cinema in a wider cultural, social and historical context. It is concerned to look at the way in which Irish society has had an impact on the cinema as well as the way in which the cinema has reflected back on Irish society. Especially of interest is the legacy of emigration and the broadening definitions of Irishness that a renewed interest in this has helped to promote. Such definitions, the book argues, are imagined and constantly reimagined in the cultural arena, subject to wider economic and social forces. One key site for such a process is the cinema and diasporic definitions of Irishness especially have played a key role in the development of cinematic genres and stereotypes in the cinema in general. This diasporic imagination, however, has always existed in a complicated relationship to the native and a key theme in the book is the way in which these have interacted down the years. Crucial in this regard is the nature of the native imagining that came to dominate culture and society in Ireland itself in the twentieth century.

Chapter One, therefore, looks at the legacy of Irish cultural nationalism as it developed in the late nineteenth and early twentieth century. It does so by mobilising the formulation devised by Benedict Anderson that the 'nation is an imagined political community and imagined as inherently limited and sovereign' (Anderson, 1983, p. 14). This process of 'imagining' is the key to understanding the cultural dimension of nationalist movements everywhere. The chapter aims to map out the key cultural precepts that underpinned Irish nationalism in its formative phase and to indicate the ways in which this has interacted with cinema in Ireland.

Central to the argument of Chapters Two and Three are the traditions of cinematic representation that dominated in the period down to the 1960s, largely the result of the British and American film industries. These images of

Ireland, whether the romantic evocations of rural Ireland or the sombre narratives of political violence, interact in surprising ways with the major paradigms that were bequeathed by Irish nationalism itself, sometimes neatly dovetailing with official attitudes and at other times inspiring a hostile response to their more outlandish stereotypes. It cannot be argued that these films constitute an element of Irish national culture but in the absence of indigenous images from Ireland they have circulated in culture generally as markers of 'Irishness'. As such, they have been as influential at the point of consumption in Ireland as they have been elsewhere and, as will be argued later, this cinematic tradition has become one point of departure for the films that have latterly been produced in Ireland itself. Furthermore, such is the force of generic convention and audience expectation that the recurring motifs of this cinematic tradition are apt to reappear in contemporary representations as well. It is only to be expected, then, that a study of contemporary Irish cinema should be concerned with those 'outsider' images that Ireland has inspired, rather than actually produced, and that have constituted such an influential cinematic tradition.

In Chapter Two, the emphasis is on romantic images of Ireland as they have been encapsulated in two influential films, Robert Flaherty's *Man of Aran* (1934) and John Ford's *The Quiet Man* (1952). The argument here is that neither film is actually about the Irish themselves. Flaherty was more interested in capturing visually an elemental tale of humanity's epic struggle against nature while Ford was more concerned with diasporic Irishness than he was with the real Ireland that he used for location shooting. In the end, Flaherty's romantic primitivism captured well the prevailing ideologies of Irish-Ireland nationalism while Ford's film offers a vision of Ireland based upon a self-consciousness about Irish-America and its illusions. Chapter Three, on the other hand, is concerned with the darker aspects of cinematic Ireland, the world of political violence and personal obsession. Following a long tradition of representing political violence in Ireland as an atavistic fault of the Irish themselves, this cinematic tradition ends up denying the historical, social and political roots of such violence. In both chapters, traditional representations are discussed in relation to contemporary films which, it is argued, perpetuate or recycle to some extent the dominant myths and representations of tradition.

Chapter Four outlines the major social and economic changes that have occurred in Ireland over the last forty years or so and maps the impact that these have had on cultural debate in general. The argument here is that Ireland emerged from a period of relative economic stagnation and cultural isolation to embrace the global capitalist economy with enthusiasm and increasing success. A new prosperity that resulted from massive inward investment and a strong commitment to the European Union has had inevitable consequences for the way in which Irish cultural identity is imagined. The basic cultural tenets of Irish nationalism, discussed in detail in Chapter One, began to be revised and this in turn has given rise to a considerable internal debate that has touched all aspects of culture and cultural production. The chapter attempts to detail the different stages that modernisation went through and to map on to these the developing cultural debate about Irish identity. The context is crucial for understanding the nature of contemporary indigenous cinema in Ireland as well as the changing images of cinematic Ireland generally.

In Chapter Five, the slow emergence of narrative film-making in Ireland since the 1970s is described and discussed in a national and an international context. In particular, the changing national climate, especially in relation to state funding of film production and its cultural infrastructure, is considered against conflicting notions of what constitutes a national film culture. Central to the argument here is that as commercial cinema, represented by Hollywood, established a near-global monopoly during the 1980s and 1990s, the developing film industry in Ireland was affected profoundly. The space for a more adventurous and politically challenging cinema narrowed considerably as a result and the formal and thematic adventurousness of the emerging Irish cinema of the 1970s and early 1980s gave way to a more industrially organised commercial cinema that was increasingly dependent on dominant cinematic conventions. This chapter also revisits and reconfigures the idea of a 'First, Second and Third' Cinema typology, first developed in the 1960s to describe national and radical cinemas' relationship to dominant Hollywood forms. Here it is appropriated to describe the intensely complex and contradictory position that Irish film and films about Ireland now occupy within the considerable shadow of Hollywood. In particular, it is mobilised to consider the relationship of low-budget indigenous cinema to that of Irish and non-Irish directors who work in or on the margins of the mainstream and who have returned to Irish themes over the years.

The rest of the book looks more closely at contemporary films themselves and attempts to explicate recurring themes and issues against the historical, cultural, national and international contexts described in the earlier chapters. Thus Chapter Six considers in detail the 'first wave' directors of the 1970s and early 1980s and argues that their more challenging aesthetic amounted to a cinema of 'national questioning' that mirrored the changing nature of Irish society while tapping into a radical trend in film-making that was characteristic of the time. In these films, there is a double critique. On the one hand they offer a sometimes bitter, sometimes ironic critique of the myths of nationalist Ireland and yet they presage as well the problems that modernisation was beginning to throw up. A characteristic of this early period of film-making is the films' concern with questions of form. This early cinema, in other words, was rich in a kind of formal experiment that is largely absent from the films of the 1990s, now operating out of a more commercial film culture.

Chapter Seven considers the importance of short film-making in Ireland and locates in this arena much of the potential and many of the problems that are writ large in bigger-budget feature film production. The short film was often the only option available for indigenous film-makers in the absence of a funding infrastructure and remains an important element in the funding framework today. And yet, here too, we can see the effect of the commercialisation of the cinema globally. There is a tension, in other words, between what might be called a national or indigenous address and mainstream commercial values. Certainly, the short film provides a space removed from the exigencies of commercial film-making that would allow for an adventurousness in both form and theme and yet, even here, the desire to succeed in the global marketplace has meant that all to often the films end up aping commercial imperatives.

Chapter Eight looks more closely at the films of the 1990s, the period of the so-called 'Celtic Tiger' economy. The chapter teases out the main themes and issues of these films and links them to the nature of Ireland's changing society. What is particularly noteworthy about these films is the preponderance of oedipal themes played out against a background of incomplete families and displaced or ineffectual fathers. A recurring motif is that of child-abuse and incest, as if the films replay in symbolic form some deep, half-remembered national trauma. The family, in political discourse as much as in cultural convention, is often a metaphor for the nation and, viewed through this prism, the films offer some suggestive clues as to the nature of this trauma.

Chapter Nine considers in more detail how contemporary Irish cinema looks at issues of cultural identity and in particular, at the influence of American popular culture on the way in which the Irish negotiate national uncertainties. In this chapter as well, the question of emigration to the USA is an important theme, given the plethora of low-budget film-making which has recently addressed itself to these issues. One contradiction in particular is noteworthy. Just as Ireland begins to mould its political destiny more in line with Europe, its 'special relationship' to America seems to assume greater importance. The more European Ireland gets politically, in other words, the closer its imaginative axis is drawn to America, the culture most influenced by its emigrant population.

Chapter Ten, on the other hand, is concerned with the unresolved tensions at home, between Ireland's nationalist imaginings of the past and its embrace of capitalist modernity in the present. This is particularly the case with images of rural and urban life and especially with the ideological accretions of landscape and the west of Ireland. Contemporary cinema suggests that Irish culture is still obsessed with coming to terms with its rural past but has still not found

Irish 'inbetweenness': from Dublin to the Arctic Circle in *The Disappearance of Finbar*

an accommodation imaginatively with its urban present. The unresolved tension here is ultimately a political one. Having abandoned the imagined community of nationalism for an ideology of national progress, there is a sense of displacement about contemporary Irish life that increasing affluence only exacerbates. A sense of belonging is still a deep, subconscious need but while Europe is embraced as a mechanism for economic and social progress, it does not offer an emotional sense of collective identity. Ireland now inhabits a cultural space somewhere between its nationalist past, its European future and its American imagination. This space, though culturally rich in potential, can be, at the same time, a lonely, displaced and unsettling in-betweenness that so far has failed to offer either emotional commitment or a new imagining of collective identity. Irish cinema's ambivalence about its rural past and urban present is a reflection of this uncertainty about its sense of belonging.

Chapter Eleven offers a particular reading of Neil Jordan's *The Butcher Boy* (1997) as a way of summarising the themes of the book overall. The film again uses the metaphors of the dysfunctional family and child-abuse/-neglect to comment on the family of the nation. Thus, home-grown forms of repression are linked in the mind of the protagonist to a changing social world and the considerable influence of foreign popular culture. In the film, these themes are woven into a complex and contradictory narrative that compresses the whole cultural ferment in Ireland into a film of deep significance and startling visual richness.

A final point to note is that this book is concerned, in the main, with fictional representations of Ireland and documentary traditions are mentioned only in passing as they impact on recurring themes. This is not to deny the importance of documentary film-making in Ireland as it has developed, on and off television, over the years. Many of the important issues discussed in this book were introduced into Irish consciousness by documentary films and the importance and innovative practice of Irish documentarists is a matter of record, even if this remains, so far, largely under-researched and sparsely written up. Given the scope of this present study, it was impossible to give documentary film-making the space it deserves.

I hope that this gap in Irish film studies will be filled before too long.

Chapter 1
Nationalism, Popular Culture and the Cinema in Ireland

Just after he was assassinated in 1922, the writings and speeches of Michael Collins, subject of Neil Jordan's 1996 biopic, were published in a short book called *The Path to Freedom*. These writings give an insight into the man himself and at the same time illuminate the character that emerges from Jordan's film. In a short essay on 'Distinctive Culture', for example, Collins sets out his vision of independent Ireland which he locates in the peasant women of Achill Island:

> … impoverished as the people are, hard as their lives are, difficult as the struggle for existence is, the outward aspect is pageant. One may see processions of young women riding down on Island ponies to collect sand from the seashore or gathering turf, dressed in their shawls and in their brilliantly coloured skirts made of material spun, woven and dyed by themselves, as it has been spun, woven and dyed for over a thousand years. Their simple cottages are also little changed. They remain simple and picturesque. It is only in such places that one gets a glimpse of what Ireland may become again, when the beauty may be something more than pageant, will be the outward sign of a prosperous and happy Gaelic life. (Collins, 1922/1968, p. 99)

It might seem difficult reconciling the brutal and brilliant military strategist of history with the writer of such romantic and essentially regressive sentimentality. However, these two versions of Collins were born of a political culture capable of nourishing and sustaining both without contradiction. Jordan was aware of this. The hard man of urban guerrilla warfare in Jordan's film is appropriately played by Liam Neeson who has made a screen career out of portraying 'gentle giants', physical men with a deep and sensitive vulnerability (most famously in Steven Spielberg's *Schindler's List* [1993]). As Jordan himself says about the Neeson persona, 'He could bury his grandmother in concrete and you would still sympathise with him' (Jordan, 1996, p. 17).

The culture that could contain the dewy-eyed romanticism of Collins with a brutal genius for war was the cultural nationalism of late nineteenth- and early twentieth-century Ireland. Writing of cultural nationalism in general, John Hutchinson has observed that the primary aim of nationalists is 'the moral regeneration of the historic community … the re-creation of their distinctive national civilization'. Typically this aim has always followed a certain pattern, involving the establishment of 'informal and decentralized clusters of cultural societies and journals, designed to inspire a spontaneous love of community in its different members by educating them to their common heritage of splendour and suffering'. This cultural activity is designed to achieve a broad set of results. Hutchinson continues that nationalists 'engage in naming rituals, celebrate national cultural uniqueness and reject foreign practices in order to identify the community to itself, embed this identity in everyday life and differentiate it against other communities' (Hutchinson, 1987, p. 15).

The process that Hutchinson here describes is an echo of Benedict Anderson's influential formulation of the nation as 'an imagined political community and imagined as inherently limited and sovereign' (Anderson, 1983, p. 15). It is cultural activity, of the kind referred to by Hutchinson, which brings this community into being and helps to maintain it against attack or threat. The irony is that the sense of national identity that emerges through this cultural activity becomes embedded so deeply in the common-sense experience of the community that the process of imagining is itself disguised or suppressed. This can result in a very essentialist definition of identity, one that is affirmed but rarely interrogated, narrow rather than embracing and pure rather than multifaceted. National culture is removed from history and rendered as a mystical process. It becomes a timeless entity or a deep essence, the rich achievement of a particular genius, that may have been suppressed at times in the past (thus Hutchinson's notion of 'splendour and suffering') but which has a fundamental (often a 'God-given') right to exist or to be reasserted in a sovereign political state, through violence and armed struggle, if necessary.

In contrast, Anderson and Hutchinson suggest a more materialist definition of a concept that is so notoriously elusive and ethereal. National identity for them is *constructed*, not given or handed down in the inner spirit of the community. It is the product of human endeavour, artefact not nature; thus all national identities are ultimately cultural identities. National identity is contained in history, economics, ideology and class and though it often works hard to disguise its historical specificity, it can only be understood in terms of the material factors that have brought it into being and which continue to shape it. It is above all else, a product of modernisation. In the classical literature on nationalism, whether Marxist or not, the desire for self-sufficiency is seen to be the central economic impulse that has motivated nationalism everywhere.

Nationalism aims to establish the political conditions free from colonial or imperialist exploitation in which native capitalism under the control of the native bourgeoisie might flourish, essentially a modernising movement (Kedourie, 1960; Nairn, 1977; Anderson, 1983; Gellner, 1983; Hobsbawm, 1990). If the ultimate political aim of nationalist movements is the establishment of a sovereign state, the justification for this is found culturally in the clearly defined nature of the community this state must serve. The 'inherently limited and sovereign' nature of the imagined community, therefore, requires substantial cultural work to establish what it is not, as much as what it is. Thus a process of sifting and selection, of inclusion and exclusion, is constantly being applied despite the nation's supposed transparency or its apparent stability through time and space.

National identity exists, in other words, in a dialectical relationship between some notion of 'us' and the 'other' and this in turn can give rise to seemingly fixed binary oppositions. For small nations the crucial dialectic is often the relationship between the centre and the periphery and, as we shall see in the case of cultural nationalism in Ireland, this can have important ideological implications. Of course, the imagining of the nation is a centralising process and as well as disguising class, gender and regional differences it can also create internal oppositions, differently constructed notions of 'us' and the 'other' out of the very differences it has attempted to suppress. These internal minorities themselves often begin to construct an alternative imagining through their own versions of 'splendour and suffering', giving rise to national subcultures that exist in an intensely ambivalent relationship to the central imagining. Nationalisms everywhere, therefore, have had to work hard to contain oppositions between capital and labour, the country and the city, women's rights and patriarchy or the tensions that arise from ethnic or religious minorities from within.

Cultural Nationalism in Ireland

If these theoretical propositions are applied to cultural nationalism in Ireland they illustrate quite well the way in which a specific set of assumptions about the nature of Irish identity came to dominate the cultural agenda and are implicit in Collins' vision of a 'happy Gaelic life'. Promulgated originally in the nineteenth and early twentieth centuries, these definitions of Irish identity were influential in shaping the political and social culture of independent Ireland. The influence of cultural nationalism has waned considerably in recent years but its legacy still carries major cultural force in contemporary Ireland. Thus cultural nationalism and its ingrained preferences and prejudices has inevitably had immense consequences for the cinema in Ireland. In fact, it is impossible to understand the nature of contemporary cinematic debates in Ireland without first considering in detail how cultural nationalism has had an impact on the traditions of cinematic representation and has moulded aspects of contemporary Irish sensibility. Six fundamental principles that underlay cultural nationalism in the early twentieth century are of particular interest:

- Irish identity was seen to be *unique*;
- the Irish were seen to constitute an *historic* nation, one of the oldest in Europe;
- this Irish nation was seen to be essentially *Gaelic* in culture and *Irish-speaking* in language;
- this Gaelic culture was essentially *rural*;
- Irish identity was closely linked to the *Catholic* religion;
- the Irish nation, therefore, should aspire to *self-sufficiency*, both economic and cultural.

The Uniqueness of Irish Identity

Irish cultural nationalism asserted a kind of primordial uniqueness for the Irish nation and a lot of cultural endeavour in Ireland in the late nineteenth and early twentieth centuries went towards establishing this uniqueness. Of course, there is nothing surprising in this, given that uniqueness is the basic characteristic of national discourse everywhere. It is, as Anderson has pointed out, one of the many contradictions about nationalism – the universality of nationalism as a socio-cultural concept as against the 'irremediable particularity of its manifestation'. Thus, despite the fact that nationalism is found everywhere, each nationalism sees itself as *sui generis* (Anderson, 1983, p. 14). What is particularly interesting about the way in which the uniqueness of Irish identity was constructed is how it was defined against its 'other'. Whatever its positive attributes, crucially Irish identity was not British.

In 1892, for example, Douglas Hyde, later to become President of Ireland under the constitution of Eamon de Valera, delivered a famous lecture entitled 'The Necessity for De-Anglicising Ireland'. This later became the rallying cry for the Gaelic League, one of the most influential of those cultural societies identified by Hutchinson, and the main platform for what was known as 'Irish-Ireland' nationalism. Hyde's opinion was that 'within the last ninety years we have, with unparalleled frivolity, deliberately thrown away our birthright and anglicized ourselves ... ceasing to be Irish without becoming English' (Hyde, 1892/1986, pp. 153–170). He urged, therefore, the rejection of all things English or British and his sentiments were adopted over the following years in a series of campaigns designed to rid Ireland of the most popular forms of British culture. The aims of Maud Gonne's women's society the Daughters of Erin, for example, included '... to discourage the circulation of low English literature, the singing of English songs, the attending of vulgar English entertainments ... and to combat in every way any English influence' (Goldring, 1975/1982, p. 14). Thus blatant and residual anti-Britishness and a fear and distrust of popular forms of culture, including, of course, the cinema, continued to be an element of Irish national sensibility throughout the twentieth century.

There is, however, an important but often-neglected caveat to this anti-Britishness and it is alluded to in Hyde's original lecture. As he saw it in the 1890s, the urgent need for 'de-Anglicising' Irish culture was that the Irish had actually embraced so much Britishness already, especially in the previous century, that the national culture was in danger of losing its historic uniqueness. The adoption of the English language and the decline of Gaelic symbolised a deep schizophrenia in the Irish, according to Hyde. 'It has always been very curious to me how Irish sentiment sticks in this half-way house – how it continues to apparently hate the English and at the same time continues to imitate them' (Hyde, 1892/1986, p. 154). If the defining element in cultural nationalism was 'Irish-Ireland' it is important to remember that 'Anglophone' Ireland has remained a defining characteristic of Irish culture as it is lived in day-to-day experience. As we shall see, this continues to be one of the country's competitive advantages in the remarkable economic success of the 1990s and is held to be a key advantage for its developing film industry in a world dominated by English-speaking Hollywood.

The Historic Nation

Cultural nationalism asserted the historic longevity of the Irish nation – the fact that it pre-dated English or British involvement in Ireland and that it could only reassert itself by separation from the British state ('a nation once again', as Collins implied). This long history included, of course, both a long history of artistic achievement and a history of suppression under British rule ('splendour and suffering' again but also the splendour of the suffering). The emphasis on history has inevitably resulted in the valorisation of tradition and the past at the expense of the new and the modern, giving Irish nationalism a paradoxical radical conservatism. As we have seen, the literature on nationalism in general has stressed that it is essentially a process of modernisation, an inevitable path towards economic development that has been a characteristic of capitalist development universally. It is surely ironic, then, that this path so often leads backwards into a dim and distant past. Again, Anderson has pointed out another of nationalism's paradoxes here – 'the objective modernity of nations to the historian's eye vs. their subjective antiquity in the eyes of nationalists' (Anderson, 1983, p. 14). The central dialectic here is that between tradition and modernity and is a recurring theme in Irish cinema (the most complex exploration is again by Neil Jordan, this time in *The Butcher Boy* [1997]).

However, in a cultural climate in which the interpretation of history (and its inevitable reinterpretation) is so crucial to the foundational myths of both nation and state, it is hardly surprising that history itself is often the dynamic for heated debate. Thus *Michael Collins* (1996), dealing as it does with an important period and an emblematic personality in recent history, inevitably found itself at the centre of intense scrutiny and in many ways, it came to symbolise the deep cultural schisms of contemporary Ireland (discussed in Chapter Eleven). Many cinematic portrayals of the Irish down the years have been set in contentious historical periods or have dealt with similarly central personalities and events, and the context in Ireland governs how these have been received or how they might be read. This is particularly so with those films that might be described as 'heritage movies', for example, 'the Big House' cycle that includes Robert Knights' *The Dawning* (1989), Pat O'Connor's *Fools of Fortune* (1990) and Deborah Warner's *The Last September* (1999). In these cases, the films' careful evocation of a 'heritage' Ireland of the Anglo-Irish Ascendancy is skewed by the facts of history and the triumph of nationalism. Thus the context in Ireland reconfigures the debate about heritage in interesting and unexpected ways (Hill, 1999b; Barton, 1997).

The Gaelic Nation and the Irish Language

Irish national identity was constructed as essentially Gaelic in culture and Irish-speaking in language. This was, in fact, the main argument of Hyde's famous and highly influential lecture and it dominated cultural nationalism throughout the revolutionary period and well beyond the foundation of the Irish Free State in 1922. Arguably, it is the one characteristic in cultural nationalism of this period that still carries a powerful charge in contemporary Ireland (though equally, its essentialist assumptions are also the most controversial aspect in contemporary cultural politics). The ethereal nature of Hyde's conception of Irish identity is characterised by his allusion to the 'dim consciousness' of ancient Ireland, 'which is one of those things which are at the back of Irish national sentiment' (Hyde, 1892/1986, p. 156). He urged Ireland to recover its Gaelic past – the language, music, games, dress and mindset of the ancient Gael – and the influence of his vision of the past did much to perpetuate the hostile aversion to modern popular culture in 'official' nationalist Ireland down to the 1960s.

The revival of this Gaelic culture was to have mixed results in independent Ireland. Arguably, in Gaelic sports and in traditional music and dance, the revival was spectacularly successful and in these areas the distinctiveness of Irish identity is internationally acknowledged. The revival of the Irish language is another matter altogether.

From the foundation of the Irish Free State in 1922, Irish was established as 'the first official language' and the speaking of Irish became compulsory for all civil servants and other key state employees (including teachers). Irish became a compulsory part of the school curriculum and in all outward manifestations of the new state (in its bureaucracy, for example, but even in its street names) Irish was asserted as primary in a bilingual policy. The revival of the language was an important objective of state broadcasting when this was inaugurated in 1926 and remained a fundamental principle of state policy down to the present. In this regard the policy was a dismal failure and, by the end of the 1980s, the number of native Irish speakers was only about one-tenth that of 1922 (Lee, 1989, p. 673). Even so sympathetic a commentator as Lee has argued that the language policy was ineffective, self-defeating, self-deluding and hypocritical (Lee, 1989, pp. 658–74). Irish may have been designated 'the first official language' of the state but fewer and fewer of the Irish people knew how to speak it. In this way, the question of the Irish language in the overall construction of Irish identity continues to be a matter of bitter and protracted controversy. Its relevance to the study of Irish cinema is particularly complex.

For a start, indigenous Irish cinema, like Irish broadcasting, is overwhelmingly an Anglophone cinema. Despite the intentions of the language revival movement, the Irish language has come close to extinction. Now there are simply too few native speakers to justify wholesale investment in an Irish language cinema (in 1999, *The Irish Times* estimated the total number of native Irish-speakers to be about 20,000). Certainly, after many years of lobbying, a state-financed Irish language television station was finally established in 1996 (now called TG4) and this, in partnership with RTÉ and the Irish Film Board, has funded short film-making and the occasional feature. However, film-making in the Irish language remains a marginal activity and the debate about film being an expression of 'national culture' as well as an 'industry' has done little to change the situation. This raises interesting questions about Irish cinema's relationship to the international industry, itself overwhelmingly Anglophone because of the dominance of Hollywood.

In one way it might be argued that Irish cinema has a potential commercial advantage over non-English speaking cinemas with its relatively easy access to the huge market in the USA. The success in America of Jim Sheridan's *My Left Foot* (1989) and Neil Jordan's *The Crying Game* (1992) is attributable, at least in part, to the fact that these were English-language films rather than subtitled foreign fare. The potential to strike gold in the US market remains a significant factor in the production of films in Ireland – the commercial 'holy grail' that has haunted British film production for many decades. There might, of course, be a cultural price to pay for pursuing this objective, as Bob Quinn has suggested. 'Ireland has long been a figment of the American imagination', he argues. 'Reciprocally now, Irish film-makers see America as their only salvation'

(Quinn, 1999, p. 73). The cultural price can be quite specific as well, according to Kevin Rockett. He argues that the price paid by Jim Sheridan for American financial backing of his second film, *The Field* (1990) was that the action was changed from the 1960s to the 1930s and an American actor (Tom Berenger) was imposed in the key role of the returned emigrant. In the original play on which the film is based this character returns from England and Rockett feels that because of both changes important cultural, political and ideological meanings are lost (Rockett, 1994, p. 139).

However, the question of Irish language and nationality is most significant and most controversial when applied within a 'cultural imperialism' discourse and here the virtual abandonment of the language by the Irish themselves appears particularly problematic. In an overview of language revival strategies since 1922, Lee argues that the failure to revive everyday speaking of Irish is the fault of successive governments and the inadequacies of the Department of Education. 'What might have been a noble chapter in the history of the new state became instead a sordid one,' he asserts. He is so scathing about the failure of the language policy because he is so sympathetic to the language itself. For him, to be in possession of an indigenous language is still a marker of nationality and experience elsewhere (Sweden, Denmark, Finland, Holland) has shown that maintaining the indigenous language while embracing the 'international' language of English in a genuine bilingual culture is an important aspect of European modernity. In the case of Ireland, while there are undoubtedly great advantages to being 'native' speakers of English, there is also the danger that Irish culture is now uniquely vulnerable to Anglo-American dominance. 'When the language of those countries dominates international communications networks and global mass culture, then a tiny country, shorn of her own linguistic defences, is peculiarly vulnerable to inundation ...' (Lee, 1989, p. 667). This is the classic argument of the cultural imperialism thesis and the language question merely poses the general issues it raises in a particular manner.

It is important in this regard to note that the threat to Irish cultural distinctiveness is no longer seen to emanate from the 'old enemy', Britain, but from Ireland's 'special relationship' to America. The Irish language lobby in Ireland was one of the first cultural groups to realise this. On 2 September 1977, Conradh na Gaeilge invited American Marxist and long-time proponent of the cultural imperialism thesis, Herb Schiller, to deliver a lecture in which he outlined the parameters of what he called 'New Modes of Cultural Domination'. He noted the problems facing English-speaking Canada, where in many cities and communities the people are far heavier viewers of American television than of their own. One of the reasons for this is the lack of a language barrier. The Irish language, therefore, should be regarded as priceless. 'In their mother tongue the Irish people have a powerful defence mechanism against cultural domination' (Schiller, 1978, p. 23).

Lee and Schiller have recast the language question in terms of a tension between the 'public' discourse of international or global culture and the 'private' discourse of national consciousness. However, it is still the case that the supporters of the language revival are inclined to offer a protected private space only for Irish rather than allow it to take its place and assert its presence in wider public discourse. The fate of two of the most important films in the Irish language is instructive here.

George Morrison's *Mise Eire* (1959) and *Saoirse?* (1961) are two remarkable documentaries tracing the years of the War of Independence and the Civil War in Ireland from 1916 to 1922. The films integrate a range of period documents – archive film, still photographs, drawings, cartoons and printed documents – into a narrative in Irish that is further embellished with a justly celebrated original score by Sean O'Riada. The films are of their time in terms of their fairly uncritical nationalist sentiment (though *Saoirse?*, dealing with the Civil War, is inevitably a more bitter and less triumphant film than its predecessor). Yet formally both films are remarkably ahead of their times in their use of archive material (it was often said in Ireland during the ensuing decades that these two films were as close as the country had come until then to establishing a national film archive). O'Riada's scores for the films, blending Irish traditional idioms with orchestral arrangements, were prescient of much musical exploration that was to follow. However, these two important films have not had the international exposure that their achievement has merited and it is fair to say that they have not been seen by indigenous Irish audiences to the extent that they might. The reason for this is that the films were produced by the Irish language and cultural body, Gael Linn, which has consistently refused to strike subtitled prints. Where the films have been seen over the years, the exhibitors have had to distribute a written summary of the narration. This, it could be argued, only exasperates the 'private discourse' of the Irish language and has severely curtailed the impact that the films could have made, especially in Britain and America, where they have a particular cultural resonance.

The essentialist, purist and protective tendencies in the Irish language lobby have proved to be self-defeating in the past. The language policy of TG4 is more plural today than these essentialist formulations would have allowed and the success of Welsh-language cinema like *Hedd Wyn* (1992) and *Gadael Lenin* (1993) indicates that there is potential for a cinema in minority languages. The problem remains attracting financial support for Irish-language films and then assessing the opportunities and negotiating the dangers that lie in its interface with global culture.

The Rural and the Urban

In its fundamental principles, cultural nationalism defined Gaelic Irish identity as essentially rural in character and the culture of nationalist Ireland was correspondingly anti-urban and anti-industrial in its imaginings. The implications of this are quite profound. For one thing, this rural imagination followed logically from the anti-British assumptions of Hyde. If Britain at this time was the most urban and most industrial society in the world, it is hardly surprising that cultural nationalism should emphasise its own rural 'otherness'.

Of course, the economic and social realities of Ireland in the early twentieth century gave this emphasis a certain legitimacy. Ireland was relatively undeveloped in comparison to the more powerful nation states of Europe or to the USA and even by 1921 over 50 per cent of its working population was employed in agriculture. With so great a proportion of the population living directly on the land, and in smallholdings, it was hardly surprising that its average income per capita was only two-thirds that of industrial Britain. (For some historians, however, the comparison with Britain, the great imperial power, is invidious. Lee, for example, argues that in comparison to many other economies in Europe, especially Eastern Europe, in 1921 Ireland was relatively developed and its standard of living certainly no worse [Lee 1989, p. 71].) The Irish economy was a rural economy and its culture was predicated on this fact. What is perhaps surprising is that in its idealism, as demonstrated in Collins' vision, Irish cultural nationalism was opposed to the kind of industrial and urban development characteristic of most other nationalist movements committed to a process of regeneration. In fact, successive Irish governments made no serious attempt to encourage industrial growth until the end of the 1950s (Sweeney, 1998).

In political terms, the result was a low profile for the kind of class politics that defined political culture elsewhere in Europe. Labour movements are primarily associated with the urban industrial working-class, and since this was so relatively undeveloped outside of the north-east corner around Belfast, it is hardly surprising that the left–right split that characterises political culture elsewhere has been subsumed under the totalising impulses of nationalism. 'Labour must wait,' as de Valera so grandiloquently expressed it. *The Catholic Bulletin* of November 1913 put hostility to the labour movement into the Irish-Ireland context:

> For the past twenty years the Gael has been crying … for help to beat back the Anglicisation he saw dragging its slimy length along – the immoral literature, the smutty postcards, the lewd plays and the suggestive songs were bad, yet they were merely puffs from the foul breath of a paganised society. The full sewerage from the *cloaca maxima* of Anglicisation is now discharged upon us. The black devil of Socialism, hoof and horns, is amongst us. (Lyons, 1979, p. 96)

This commitment to a rural economy was, in a real sense, a flight from modernity itself, understandable, perhaps, if modernity was associated only with the colonial exploitation of British imperialism, as it inevitably was in post-Famine Ireland. But, as *The Catholic Bulletin* so vituperatively feared, other versions of modernity were on offer and, as we shall see, other versions of Irish identity were in circulation. The reasons for the failure to develop along alternative routes, or even the extent to which these were viable options at the time, is another debating point in contemporary Ireland.

The cultural implications, however, of this nationalist commitment to a rural identity are immense. For a start, Ireland had, of course, its great urban centres, especially Dublin and Belfast, and one significant consequence was the almost total elision of the Irish city from nationalist culture. For most of the nineteenth and twentieth centuries this culture exuded a preference for a romantic as opposed to a realist aesthetic and this remains a considerable ideological and aesthetic issue for cultural studies in Ireland (Gibbons, 1996). In the twentieth century, the social realism that is characteristic, for example, of British film and television, is relatively absent in Irish culture. Even in the age of television, the socially committed, intensely realist drama associated with British television in the 1960s was extremely rare, the Prix Italia-winning *A Week in the Life of Martin Cluxton* (1971) being one accomplished exception (McLoone, 1984, pp. 65–8).

The irony in all this is that Ireland produced one of world literature's great urban novels in Joyce's *Ulysses* and his short story collection, *Dubliners*, was to provide John Huston with the inspiration for his last film, *The Dead* (1987). The Irish city began to make its cinematic impact only relatively recently, therefore, in the early work of some indigenous film-makers in the 1970s and early 1980s, and then more publicly in the 1990s with the success of *My Left Foot* and the various adaptations of Roddy Doyle's novels (Alan Parker's *The Commitments* [1991] and Stephen Frear's T*he Snapper* [1993] and *The Van* [1996]).

The reverse, of course, is true for representations of rural Ireland. Romantic images of rural life have predominated cinematic portrayals of Ireland and can be traced back to the first American films ever shot on location outside the USA – the romantic one- and two-reelers made by Sidney Olcott's Kalem Company in Killarney in the 1910s (Rockett, Gibbons and Hill, 1988).

The importance of Irish landscape in these representations cannot be overstressed. The preponderance of landscape in dominant cinematic representations of Ireland may well, as in the case of Olcott, have had an economic logic at base (satisfying the nostalgic yearnings of the large Irish immigrant audience in the USA) but it also has greater ideological significance. As Luke Gibbons has argued,

> The point of drawing attention to [the] interpretation of nature as a symbolic
> field is to underline the case for treating landscape in romantic images of
> Ireland not merely as a picturesque backdrop, but as a layer of meaning in its
> own right, a thematic element which may reinforce or cut across the other
> levels of meaning in a text. (Gibbons, 1988a, p. 210)

Landscape is loaded with political and ideological significance in Ireland. As we
have seen in Collins' vision of the west of Ireland, landscape is the chosen
environment for nationalist Ireland's own self-image, the residue of all that is
perceived as pure and essential in Irish identity. Such is the ideological power
of this notion that it reappears in contemporary cinema and finds full
expression in Mike Newell's *Into the West* (1992), scripted by Dubliner Jim
Sheridan, and John Sayles' *The Secret of Roan Inish* (1994), both of which vindicate the authentic experience of the west at the expense of the alienating
character of the city.

In outsider images of Ireland, landscape and its changeable climate are also
linked closely to the personality and character of the Irish people itself, and this
is most obvious in John Ford's *The Quiet Man* (1952). However, it reappears
with considerable regularity over the years and Gibbons traces the inexorable
linkage of character and landscape in films as diverse as *Luck of the Irish* (1948)
and *Ryan's Daughter* (1970). In the former, this relationship is quite explicit.
One character chides returned Irish-American Stephen Fitzgerald for his faith
in Irish roads actually leading somewhere. 'Don't be so sure about Irish paths.
Irish paths are whimsical – like the Irish character.' When Stephen follows the
path anyway, it is entirely predictable that it should lead him into a wood
inhabited by an overweight leprechaun who then becomes the agent in rescu-
ing him from the alienating world of US capitalism (Gibbons, 1988a, pp.
227–8).

Romantic interpretations of the landscape are not, therefore, the preserve of
the Irish nor are they to be found only in relation to Ireland. The romantic sensibility emanated originally from the European urban intelligentsia as an
aesthetic response to urbanisation and industrialisation and many of the
peripheral parts of Europe were similarly subjected to an artistic 'tourist' gaze.
An understanding of the deeper levels of meaning in romantic images of Ireland needs to go beyond their appropriation by cultural nationalism in Ireland
and to consider these broader historical roots as well (Gibbons, 1988a, Slater,
1993). In Chapter Ten, we will consider recent cinematic images of the country
and the city in more detail and tease out the ideological and aesthetic implications for contemporary Ireland of this divide.

Interestingly, many contemporary commentators have noted that, if there is
a flight from realism and modernity in Irish culture, ironically there has also

been a determinedly modernist/avant-garde tradition in Joyce, Beckett and Flann O'Brien. This considerable anomaly seems to be at odds with the dominant conception of Irish culture that emerges from a study of cultural nationalism and offers some interesting perspectives to assess the whole nationalist project. As we shall see, during the 1980s, as the process of modernisation stalled, the presence of this tradition was much commented upon, almost as if the cultural trajectory of Ireland involved a flight into postmodernity before economic and social modernity had itself been achieved. Such anomalies and such peculiarities are central to contemporary cultural debate and have an impact on debates about the cinema in interesting ways (Deane, 1991; Eagleton, 1995; Gibbons, 1996). These issues will be discussed in more detail in Chapter Four.

Catholicism and Irish Identity

An important characteristic of Irish cultural nationalism was the close association of Irish identity with the Catholic religion. Again, this was only to be expected in a construction of Irishness that depended on establishing its difference from Englishness/Britishness. One of the defining characteristics of the Irish was their popular adherence to the faith in spite of, or because of, the suppression of Catholicism attempted at various stages by a hostile Protestant government in London. This popular Catholicism did not, of itself, guarantee that nationalism in Ireland would be aligned so closely to the Catholic church. One factor here is surely the decline of nationalist sentiment among Irish Protestants following the 'evangelical revival' of the 1850s. This was especially so among northern Presbyterians who had given birth to Irish republicanism in the revolutionary years of the 1780s and 1790s and had provided some of the intellectual leadership to the Young Ireland movement in the 1840s. As the Rev. Ian Paisley, self-confessed inheritor of the Ulster evangelical revival of 1859, has noted, 'The revival of 1859 strengthened Ulster in her stand against Roman Catholic agitation and without doubt laid the foundation which enabled Ulster under the leadership of Lord Carson to preserve her Protestant position' (Paisley, 1959, p. 202).

In fact, the Catholic church had always been wary of the secular and democratic impulses behind the revolutionary movements and actively discouraged its flock from getting involved. Indeed, throughout the eighteenth and nineteenth centuries, the church was particularly opposed to the secret agrarian societies that periodically emerged in the wake of land grievance and agitation. According to Tom Inglis, it was government awareness of this fact that changed London policy in regard to the Catholic church and allowed the church to build a power-base among the Irish people that would be consolidated in the post-Famine period. 'By the middle of the eighteenth century,' Inglis argues,

> English politicians began to realise that the attempt to abolish Catholicism in Ireland through persecution had failed. ... It was at this stage that a tentative power alliance began to be formed between the English State and the Catholic Church. As long as the Irish could be prevented from bloody rebellion and become civil and disciplined, it did not matter so much who produced the results. (Inglis, 1987, p. 111)

From the mid-nineteenth century on, the church, in the form of its clergy and lay intellectuals, played an important ideological role in the formation of Irish nationalism and through its control of education and health, and in its professionalised bureaucratic structure, it became the main conduit for propagating nationalist ideals to the mass population. Inglis stresses the 'rigorist' nature of Irish Catholicism – ironically, almost puritan in its teaching on morality – and contends that this rigorism was 'constituted by a systematic discipline, surveillance and sexualisation of the body' (Inglis, 1987, p. 138). Sexuality was controlled and shame and guilt became aspects of Irish morality. In particular, Inglis goes on, '... the sexual moralisation process became centred on gaining control of women's sex. ... It was only when it was controlled that the refined, delicate nature of women could be revealed' (Inglis, 1987, p. 150). Inglis likens this process to the Protestant puritan code by which women's sexuality was defined and regulated in Victorian Britain and for a similar purpose of reconstituting women as desexualised mothers. He locates a number of key economic and social imperatives in Ireland behind this strategy. First, the industrialisation of cloth production ended the economic power that women had held in the home through spinning and weaving. Second, the shift from tillage to pasture farming gave rise to a new powerful tenant farmer class in rural Ireland that was concerned to consolidate the farm by refusing to subdivide it among competing offspring. This in turn required that the offspring postpone marriage, not marry at all and remain permanently celibate or emigrate. The regulation, therefore, of sexuality outside of marriage became important and here the church played the key role by cementing an ideological and social partnership with the Irish mother that gave her a new and powerful role as the moral authority in the home. The desexualised and overbearing Irish mother became a dominant stereotype in films about Ireland and was to play an important ideological role in the assimilationist thrust of early American genre cinema, as we shall see in Chapter Two.

The model that the church promoted was characterised by a special devotion to Our Lady. 'The chaste, modest and humble virtues of Irish women and mothers grew apace with their penitential devotion to Our Lady ... an ideal-type figure that was fecund and female and yet remained virgin and pure' (Inglis, 1987, pp. 187–214). The chaste maidens by the seashore in Collins'

Penitential devotion to Our Lady: Sinéad O'Connor in *The Butcher Boy*

vision of the new Ireland is one cultural manifestation of this process (and perhaps Julia Roberts' surprisingly prim portrayal of Kitty Kiernan in *Michael
Collins* is another). The casting of Sinéad O'Connor as Our Lady in *The Butcher
Boy* was surely a mischievous riposte by Neil Jordan to the dominance of this
ideal-type, but a highly successful one in terms of the film's overall discourse
on religion and sexuality. The impact of Catholicism on the representation of
women and sexuality in Irish cinema generally is, as we shall see, a key critical
concern and is the focus of Pat Murphy and John Davies' *Maeve* (1981) and
Margo Harkin's *Hush-a-Bye Baby* (1989).

The ideology of self-denial implicit in this devotion to the Virgin Mary also
had the effect of giving cultural nationalism a particularly ascetic character
where simplicity, poverty and sexual celibacy were venerated. This is superbly
realised in *Michael Collins* by Alan Rickman's portrayal of a cold and remote de
Valera. In the jailbreak sequence Jordan plays with this aspect of the de Valera
persona. As they make their escape, Collins throws a woman's fur coat around
de Valera to disguise his prison uniform. 'What's this?' he asks. 'Your fur coat,'

Collins replies, 'Pretend you're a tart.' As he and Collins bundle the bemused de Valera into the getaway car, Boland asks, 'Fancy a cuddle, love?' In general terms, therefore, the confluence of rural mythology and Catholicism gave cultural nationalism a particularly confessional and moralistic character, strongly anti-secular, profoundly anti-materialist and politically and economically conservative. The legacy of this more ascetic sense of Irish identity, with its high moral tone and cult of self-denial, is an important element in cinematic images of Ireland and has been a theme in a contemporary cinema that has attempted to probe this legacy and reimagine Irishness in opposition. Frank McCourt, in his literary autobiography, *Angela's Ashes*, has famously encapsulated the bitter and ironic tone of much contemporary Irish culture in relation to its Catholic past. 'Worse than the ordinary miserable childhood is the miserable Irish childhood, and worse yet is the miserable Irish Catholic childhood' (McCourt, 1996, p. 11).

Self-sufficiency

A final characteristic of cultural nationalism with interesting implications is its aspiration towards self-sufficiency (as in 'Sinn Féin' – literally, 'We Ourselves', but usually rendered as 'Ourselves Alone'). This is, of course, a key component of nationalism universally and remains the central political plank in the sovereignty of the imagined community. We have noted that nationalism has been characterised in most academic study as essentially a modernising process

'... the miserable Irish Catholic childhood ...': the family in *Angela's Ashes*

which has allowed native capital to consolidate political power and to push forward a process of economic and social change (Kedourie, 1960; Nairn, 1977; Anderson, 1983; Gellner, 1983; Hobsbawm, 1990). As we have seen, though, the paradox in Irish cultural nationalism was its romantic flight from modernity and the character of the state that emerged from its success reflected this. Self-sufficiency was predicated on the primacy of the rural economy (Collins' shawls and skirts 'spun, woven and dyed by themselves'). The new state, under the careful bookkeeping of W. T. Cosgrave, proved to be penny-pinching and parsimonious in its careful management of the economy. Later, under the influence of de Valera's economic nationalism, state policy was committed to a protectionist economic strategy that took it out of mainstream capitalism until the late 1950s (Lee, 1989, pp. 56–168). The undoubted hardships that protectionism visited on the rural poor and the cattle-farmers that formed the bedrock of the nationalist movement were vitiated by the fact that the policies were directed against the old enemy, England. Self-sufficiency meant self-sacrifice and national expectations were kept modest. 'Frugal comfort', as the ascetic de Valera expressed them (Brown, 1981, p. 146).

However, self-sufficiency also extended to culture. If an economic wall was built around the economy using tariffs, then an attempt was made to build a cultural wall around society using censorship. One of the first acts passed by the Free State Dáil was the Censorship of Films Act, 1923. In 1929, the Censorship of Publications Act was passed. The operation of these two acts resulted in the most extensive and most punitive censorship regime in Europe and represents, in many ways, the most inglorious chapter in recent Irish history. And yet, this regime was the logical conclusion of the idealism of Irish cultural nationalism. If there was a steady opposition to censorship from a vocal intellectual lobby over the worst years from the 1920s to the 1960s, nonetheless, the regime operated with popular and well-nigh unanimous support. The consensus forged around the basic tenets of cultural nationalism – the church, national and local politics, cultural and sporting bodies, education and the Irish media – was rarely challenged and managed to create a complacent and conservative society that drifted out of mainstream European culture for nearly four decades.

It is significant as well that this consensus included both opposing camps from the Civil War, distinguished in the years that followed only by the zeal with which they pursued the aims of cultural nationalism. Through various changes of government the consensus held firm. John Whyte described the situation cogently:

> Mr Cosgrave refused to legalise divorce; Mr de Valera made it
> unconstitutional. Mr Cosgrave's government regulated films and books; Mr de

Valera's regulated dance halls. Mr Cosgrave's government forbade propaganda
for the use of contraceptives; Mr de Valera's banned their sale or import. In all
this they had the support of the third party in Irish politics, the Labour Party.
The Catholic populace gave no hint of protest. The Protestant minority
acquiesced. The only real opposition came from a coterie of literary men
whose impact on public opinion was slight. (Whyte, 1971, pp. 60–61)

This consensus represented an alliance of forces that was forged in the years
leading up to independence. It had specific agreed and understood class and
social priorities, despite the internal strife that resulted in the Civil War. The
new world that emerged from independence was, in F. S. Lyons' estimation, 'not
for Wolfe Tone's men of no property but for business, for the shopocracy, and
for the farmer-owners of the rising generations' (Lyons, 1971, p. 685).

Cultural Nationalism and Popular Culture

As we have seen, the cultural climate engendered by cultural nationalism was
hostile to most forms of popular culture. Since these were, by and large, the
products of 'foreign cultures' (British to begin with but increasingly, as the
1930s proceeded, American as well) various campaigns against popular culture
could be couched in nationalist terms as well as founded on moral grounds.
The earliest attacks on popular forms of culture were orchestrated by the Irish
Vigilance Association against the British popular press (in general the Sunday
papers, but especially the *News of the World*). The Association was set up in 1911
and controlled by members of the Dominican Order. It engaged in a campaign
against newspaper-sellers as well as buyers and lobbied and agitated throughout the country in a series of letter-writing campaigns. Association volunteers
handed out literature to Mass-goers on Sundays, urging them to boycott the
'evil literature' on sale outside the church gates (Adams, 1968, p. 15). The
Association does not seem to have met with much success before independence
but in consort with various other religious and cultural groups, it was instrumental in creating the draconian censorship code ultimately embodied in the
1929 Censorship of Publications Act (Brown, 1981, p. 69). This resulted in the
banning of a host of major international writers from Faulkner, Hemingway
and Bellow to Proust, Sartre and Moravia. Irish writers suffered particularly,
including Joyce, Beckett, O'Casey, Frank O'Connor, Sean O'Faoláin, Liam
O'Flaherty, Brian Moore, Edna O'Brien and John McGahern among many
others (Adams, 1968).

Another form of popular culture that was subjected to an intermittent but
intense campaign throughout the 1930s and 1940s was the dance music of the
time, often dismissed under the generic name of 'jazz'. The medium in question here was Irish radio, established in 1926 as a response to the increasing

popularity in Ireland of British broadcasting. The same combination of nationalism and moralism was at play here as well (one prominent government minister, Postmaster General, J. J. Walsh, described the BBC as 'British music-hall dope and British propaganda'). The fact that dance music was alien was bad enough but it was also the occasion of sin or lustful desire, especially in the dance halls and ballrooms of rural Ireland. Furthermore, the more this music was allowed on radio, the less time there was for Irish traditional music and song. What is remarkable about the anti-jazz campaign was that the most vigorous opponents were the church, the Gaelic Athletic Association (GAA, ostensibly a sporting body), local councillors and individual members of the Labour and Fianna Fáil parties, a particularly telling example of the protectionist consensus in operation at the time (McLoone, 2000).

The history of the cinema in Ireland during the period of cultural nationalism's hegemony has been well documented by Kevin Rockett (Rockett, 1988). Needless to say, the protectionist and nationalist fervour of the times was visited on the cinema with the same moral ardour as on other forms of popular culture. The Dáil sat late through the night in 1923 to pass the Censorship of Films Act ('under cover of night', as Adams puts it), one of the first major pieces of legislation enacted under the new regime and Kevin Rockett estimates that between 1924 and the late 1980s about 3,000 films were banned outright and over 8,000 were cut (Rockett, 1988, p. 53).

It is worth noting here, as well, the influence of Irish Catholicism on cinema censorship in the USA itself. The establishment in 1922 of the Hays Office as an industry body for self-regulating the content of cinema had proved ineffectual as far as an increasingly confident Irish Catholic lobby was concerned. The adoption by the Hays office of a production code drawn up under the guidance of Irish-American Catholics and imposed by the Irish Catholic lobby group, The Legion of Decency, was to prove much more effective (Curran, 1989, pp. 48–52; Black, 1997). The Production Code was administered by one of the founding figures of the Legion of Decency, Joseph Breen and drawn up by a Jesuit priest, Rev. Daniel Lord. By 1934, the Irish Catholic ethos had secured considerable control over Hollywood at the production stage. As Curran notes, 'Although there was scattered opposition to the Legion of Decency's imposition of "Catholic" standards on the general public, it was minimal in the 1930s ...' (Curran, 1989, pp. 50–51). And Gregory D. Black muses on the same topic. 'For more than three decades, from 1934 to the late 1960s, the Catholic church, through its Legion of Decency, had the power that modern Christian conservatives ... and countless politicians of all stripes can only dream about – the power to control the content of Hollywood films' (Black, 1997, p. 1).

The fact that the church in Ireland felt it necessary to censor American films even further says much about the conservative nature of Irish Catholicism at home. Adams argues that the reason there was so little opposition to film censorship was the fact that film had not yet found its place as an artistic medium and therefore there was little opposition from cultural and artistic quarters (Adams, 1968, p. 17).

This may well be the case and yet Rockett has shown the important role film played in the nationalist cause in the run-up to independence. The films of Kalem in the 1910s, shot on location in Killarney, carried a strong pro-nationalist message. The 1910 film, *Rory O'More*, for example, offers a short narrative that is almost a perfect template of cultural nationalist ideology. The film is set in the past and concerns the heroic struggle for Irish freedom of a small rural community fighting against the might of the English redcoats and coping with the treachery of an informer from within. The hero, Rory O'More, takes refuge from the English among the beautiful hills and lakes of his small rural community, which are lovingly photographed by director Sidney Olcott. Strategically placed insert captions tell the audience where the location is – the Lakes of Killarney, the Gap of Dunloe. These intrude on the narrative to such an extent that it is difficult to judge which is the hero – the man or the landscape (Gibbons, 1988a, p. 223). The narrative, such as it is, brings together the dominant players and motifs of Irish nationalism – rural life, the fight for freedom, the beautiful colleen, the romantic landscape and the parish priest. The other caption inserts tell the story well enough: 'If to love Ireland be a crime then I am guilty'; 'Fr. O'Brien has a plan'; 'The Priest's sacrifice'; 'Escape to America'. It is hardly surprising that the Kalem films register another first in the history of cinema – the first instance of direct political censorship when the British authorities put pressure on the American authorities, who in turn put pressure on Kalem to tone down the pro-nationalist bias of their Irish location films (Rockett, 1988, p. 9).

Ireland's first major indigenous production company, the Film Company of Ireland, made a number of prestigious and highly successful feature films in the period from 1910 to 1920, all of which were consciously devised to help the nationalist cause. Especially of interest were *Knocknagow* (1918) and *Willy Reilly and his Colleen Bawn* (1920), both of which enjoyed considerable commercial success as well as achieving admirable artistic standards. There was a close relationship between the Film Company of Ireland and the nationalist cause. The themes of their films were strongly nationalist in tone but the Company's personnel consisted of individuals with strong affinities to Sinn Féin. Chief among these was John MacDonagh, the director of *Willy Reilly*, whose brother was Thomas MacDonagh, one of the executed leaders of the 1916 rising. It might have been assumed, therefore, that film would have continued to develop under independent rule, but this did not happen. Rockett locates three reasons for the lack of development: the consolidation of the industry internationally in Hollywood, the insularity of the nationalist movement in its perception of popular culture and the enormous economic difficulties facing the new state. The silent period, he argues, 'represented an initial important phase in indigenous fiction film-making that in volume, quality and relevance … was not to be emulated to the 1970s' (Rockett, 1988, p. 46).

Certainly, the weakness of native capital was a major contributing factor. One of the remarkable facts of the first twenty years of Irish independence was the amount of state intervention in the economy, an attempt to compensate for this weakness. A host of state enterprises was established to try to kick-start various aspects of the economy or to provide basic amenities that otherwise might have been developed by a more vibrant private enterprise. Between 1927 and 1939, nineteen such state bodies were established covering electricity supply, agricultural credit, transport, peat and turf production, milk and sugar production and tourism (Lyons, 1971, p. 608). This amounted to a form of 'state socialism' quite out of character with the conservative, Catholic ethos of society as a whole and was the result of economic necessity. Another area of state control that is significant was broadcasting. Although the original plan for a broadcasting service envisaged Irish private enterprise financing and managing a national service, the combination of protectionist nationalist sentiment and an awareness of the weakness of Irish capital meant that eventually a state service was established in 1926. This was probably Europe's first public service broadcasting system, pre-dating the incorporation of the BBC by one year (McLoone, 2000).

The architect of the original White Paper on broadcasting in 1924 and the Minister responsible for seeing the service through to its inauguration in 1926 was the Postmaster General, J. J. Walsh. He had been a director of the Film Company of Ireland before independence and might have been expected to lobby vigorously on behalf of a film industry. However, Walsh was strongly committed to private enterprise as much as he was to Irish-Ireland ideology and therefore was unlikely to support any moves for state intervention to help bring about a film industry. Rather, the speedy passage of the Censorship of Films Act in 1923 by the government of which he was a member was more representative of 'official' Ireland's attitude to the cinema and here the insularity and xenophobia of nationalist culture was the most significant factor. It was not until 1958, with the establishment of the Ardmore Studios, that substantial government investment in film was to be secured. The history of this facility, however, makes sad reading (Rockett, 1988, pp. 95–126). Established more as a job creating facility than as a genuine attempt at promoting indigenous production, it remained for most of the period down to its closure in 1982 essentially a facility for foreign companies to take advantage of Irish locations. This would not have been so bad if there had been a significant 'trickle down' effect in the training of Irish personnel and support for Irish production, but this never happened. Undoubtedly, the studios facilitated many international films of quality (and many more of no cultural significance) but by the end, 'there was recognition … that Ardmore was not going to lead to the establishment of an Irish film industry … [nor was it] a panacea for indigenous film production' (Rockett, 1988, p. 114).

Film going in the 1920s to the 1960s was pursued in Ireland much as it was elsewhere in the English-speaking world, as a mass entertainment dominated by American, and less comprehensively by British, productions. The Irish saw their films (those that were not banned outright by the censor) under the regime of Irish-Ireland stricture – often heavily cut to a point where general family audiences could view them. It represented the 'infantilisation' of the people, where a strongly authoritarian and paternalistic ethos regulated imagination and desire (McLoone, 2000). However, the Irish people still attended the cinema in great numbers, the young still listened to popular dance music on the radio and went to the dance halls, if not exactly to dance with the devil, then certainly to enjoy 'the devil's music'. They did so in the face of continuous clerical and other official disapproval and herein lies one of the conundrums of Irish-Ireland culture. There was often a great disparity between the image and the reality of Catholic Ireland – a popular hypocrisy at the heart of a seemingly solid consensus. Terence Brown quotes Neil Kevin's interesting description of the small town of Templemore, Co. Tipperary in 1943 that is at odds with the dominant ethos and culture of the times. Kevin argues that the overwhelming majority of the people in Ireland were in step with the rest of the English-speaking world and that this fact 'is not deducible from the literature that is written about Ireland' (nor we might add from the cinema portrayals of Ireland that emanated from Hollywood and Britain).

> Modernized countryside has not yet become 'typically Irish' in print, though, out of print, it certainly is. The country town with a wireless-set in the houses of the rich and poor, with a talkie-cinema, with inhabitants who wear the evening clothes of London or New York and dance the same dances to the same music – this town has not yet appeared in Irish literature but it is the most typical Irish town. (Brown, 1981, pp. 89–90)

This description of small-town Irish life undoubtedly reflected a reality of sorts, driving the Irish-Ireland zealots of church and state to ever-greater efforts. However, the description could only fit the rural population that had actually stayed in Ireland. Emigration, especially to the USA, was, of course, a factor in the development of many European states in the nineteenth century (Italy, Germany, Poland, or the Nordic countries) but in proportion to the overall population, emigration out of Ireland was unique. In addition, the Famine of the 1840s meant that Ireland suffered a catastrophe of such magnitude that the haemorrhage of its population was akin to a national trauma that still hangs heavy over cultural debate even today. Emigration had continued unabated since the horrendous years of the Famine and its aftermath so that by the early 1920s, on the eve of independence, 43 per cent of Irish-born men and women were living abroad (Brown, 1981, pp. 19–20). Such was the economic and cultural stagnation of rural Ireland, inevitably mass emigration remained a factor of Irish life. The high rate of emigration continued after independence right down to the 1960s, reaching a high point in the 1950s, during which decade four out of every five children born in Ireland between 1931 and 1941 emigrated (Lee, 1989, p. 379). These are truly astounding statistics that certainly mark Ireland out as unique in one way at least. Today, there can be no other country in the world where the population is less than half of what it was 150 years ago. If the cause of this 'mass eviction process' (Lee, 1989, p. 384) was the abject failure of the rural utopia being constructed by the Irish-Ireland political, professional and clerical elite, there was a great reluctance on their behalf to accept responsibility. Popular culture in general and the cinema in particular were identified as the real culprits. In 1937, for example, Bishop MacNamee of Ardagh and Clonmacnoise responded to growing worries about the increasing number of young women from rural Ireland who were emigrating:

> ... they are lured perhaps, by the fascinations of the garish distractions of the city, and by the hectic life of the great world as displayed before their wondering eyes in the glamorous unrealities of the films ... it is not the least of the sins of the cinema to breed a discontent that is anything but divine in the prosaic placidity of rural life. (Rockett, 1980, no page numbers given)

The gap between image and reality was not, therefore just a matter of popular hypocrisy among the Irish people. In their reluctance to acknowledge for four decades their own failure to provide economic well-being the ruling elites of the nationalist consensus were guilty of the greater hypocrisy. As the 1950s drew to a close, it was inevitable that something needed to be done to address the stagnation of Irish life. The solution was the wholesale abandonment of some of the cherished principles (and personalities) of cultural nationalism and the consequent beginning of a period of national reimagining (detailed in Chapter Four).

However, this reimagining has had to respond to the general legacy of cultural nationalism and the dominant representations of Ireland and the Irish that it gave rise to. The failure to develop an indigenous film industry coupled with the fact of such massive emigration meant that most cinematic portrayals

of Ireland emerged from outside of the country itself. These cinematic traditions continue to exert a considerable influence and to understand better the
cinematic context for contemporary film-making in Ireland, it is important to
explore these traditions in more detail.

Chapter 2
Traditions of Representation: Romanticism and Landscape

The huge Irish diaspora in the USA was to become an important element in the emerging audience for popular cinema. It was the economic potential of this ethnic audience that brought the Kalem Company to Killarney in the 1910s, the first American company to shoot on location outside of the USA. The significance of the Irish diaspora for popular cinema, however, goes beyond its substantial presence in the emerging popular audience. Joseph M. Curran and Lee Lourdeaux have both pointed out the enormous contribution of Irish-Americans to early Hollywood production, either as actors (Lillian Gish, Mary Pickford and Colleen Moore), as directors (Mack Sennet, Rex Ingram, Leo McCarey and John Ford) or in other areas of general crafts (Curran, 1989, pp. 3–72; Lourdeaux, 1990, pp. 48–65). As a result a large number of Irish-themed films were produced in Hollywood in addition to the general presence in genre cinema of a range of recognisably Irish stereotypes. Kevin Rockett, for example, identifies over two thousand films with an Irish theme since 1900, only a very few of which were made in Ireland itself and these mostly in the last twenty years (Rockett, 1996). Therefore, in the absence of countervailing indigenous images for most of the twentieth century, the stereotypes of the Irish that have populated American and to a lesser extent British cinema have registered as markers for a general 'Irishness'.

The Primitive Image

It is no surprise that the overall judgment on this 'outsider' tradition of representation has been negative. In the most persuasive study, Rockett, Gibbons and Hill have concluded that it amounted to a 'disabling' set of representations 'which has tended to sustain a sense of cultural inferiority'. Furthermore, this inferiority stemmed from the vision of a relatively primitive Ireland when compared to the sophistication of the metropolitan culture which produced it. 'For whether it be rural backwardness or a marked proclivity for violence, the film-producing nations of the metropolitan centre have been able to find in Ireland a set of characteristics which stand in contrast to the assumed virtues of their own cultures' (Rockett, Gibbons and Hill, 1988, pp. xi–xii).

Thus two dominant trends are identified in this tradition of representation. On one hand, Ireland has been represented as a kind of rural utopia, bathed in a romantic sensibility that ignored the urban centres and elided the poverty and stifling lack of opportunity in rural Ireland that prolonged emigration in the first place. Certainly, as we shall discuss, this vision of rural backwardness was often a 'benign primitivism' that was used to show up the urban inadequacies of the developed world and to suggest a sense of escape from the worst aspects of urban, industrial modernity. But it was a particular ideological construction that owed more to the culture of the centre than to the realities of life on the periphery. On the other hand, Ireland was also presented as a society torn asunder by violence and internecine strife, where a proclivity to violence was seen as a tragic flaw of the Irish themselves. This again was often presented as the result of ignorance and a lack of progress. John Hill has argued that the romantic view of Ireland was more generally a characteristic of the American cinema, representing the nostalgic imaginings of the Irish-American diaspora, while the darker vision of a strife-torn Ireland was more characteristic of the British cinema, the result of Britain's close political, economic and military involvement in Ireland itself (Hill, 1988, pp. 147–8).

It must be said, though, that this Irish proclivity to violence manifests itself in two ways. Hill focuses on the representation, especially in British cinema, of political violence in Ireland and here the atmosphere is one of fatalism, gloom and pessimism. This has become a major theme again recently as contemporary cinema, Irish and non-Irish, has attempted to address itself to the politics of Northern Ireland. We will look at these films separately in Chapter Three and discuss in detail how they respond to the tradition of representation that is the focus of Hill's argument. However, violence in the form of general brawling and fisticuffs is a characteristic of Irish stereotypes in general and forms a key element even in the benign utopias of romantic pastoralism (as, for example, in John Ford's *The Quiet Man*). Here, communal brawling is presented as an amiable trait, fuelled by communal drinking and as much a part of Irish sensibility as poetry, music and imaginative leaps of fantasy. The concern here, therefore, is with this romantic tradition, considering both the way in which it reflects the prejudices and imaginings of metropolitan culture and the way in which it interacts with the imaginings of Irish nationalism itself.

The two most interesting and most controversial films in this tradition are Robert Flaherty's *Man of Aran* (1934) and John Ford's *The Quiet Man* (1952). These films are particularly interesting because their success with audiences for over half a century has meant that, more than any other cinematic vision of Ireland and the Irish, it is these which have stood as markers for a general

'Irishness'. Flaherty's film enjoys the greater critical reputation, even if it is considerably less popular with audiences than Ford's. Indeed, Ford's bucolic knockabout has gained a whole new lease of life since its release on to video in the mid-1980s so that by 1990, it had sold almost 200,000 copies in the UK alone (McNee, 1990, p. 10). However, it has also come to be seen as the epitome of 'paddywhackery' and its popularity, especially among Irish audiences at home and abroad, is often the occasion of some acute national embarrassment. In other words, the relationship of these two films to the metropolitan culture that produced them and to the Ireland which they represent is very different and their place in contemporary cultural debate is more complex than the received wisdom might suggest.

In the imaginings of Irish cultural nationalism, we have identified a key opposition as that between 'tradition' and 'modernity' and noted a central paradox about Irish nationalism. Despite the fact that, like all nationalisms, it was essentially a modernising process, it nonetheless rejected urban and industrial modernity in favour of a romantic rural conception of the future. It may well be a paradox but if we consider the notion of the 'primitive' that underlies the contrast between tradition and modernity, we can discover the cultural dynamics that brought this about.

In the conflict between tradition and modernity, primitivism seems to look both ways. Writing about the role of British ethnography in the construction of an imperialist sense of national identity, Annie E. Coombes discusses a curious and revealing aspect of the Franco–British exhibition held at the White City, London, in 1908 (Coombes, 1991, pp. 189–214). This was one of a series of International and Colonial exhibitions that were mounted as both popular entertainment and popular education. For Coombes, they were also celebrations of European (especially British) civilisation and its superiority over the primitive colonial cultures whose artefacts were on public display. These artefacts were often displayed in reconstructions of 'typical' villages inhabited by the colonial subjects in their native lands. Professional performers from the countries represented acted out the native culture of these villages. The curious aspect of the 1908 exhibition was that, as well as the construction of primitive villages from various African and Asian countries, the exhibition contained both a 'typical' Irish and a 'typical' Scottish village.

This might strike us today as rather contradictory. After all, the purpose of the exhibition was to celebrate and reinforce British superiority, not to admit that primitivism could exist close to the heart of the most powerful empire in human history.

But as Coombes points out, these villages performed an important ideological function. On one hand, the European 'primitive' provided a kind of historical and teleological perspective that actually reinforced the difference and distance between Europe and its colonies. Even European 'primitivism' was inherently superior to that of the colonised races represented at the exhibition and this was evident to the general public in the vastly more 'advanced' culture presented in the Irish and Scottish exhibits. And, of course, the relative primitivism of its Celtic periphery only reinforced the high achievement of the Anglo-Saxon centre. Furthermore, as far as the construction of a particular 'British' sense of identity was concerned, the Irish and Scottish villages confirmed the rich folk tradition upon which the 'national' culture was being constructed and helped to reinforce the illusion of a homogeneous British culture (Coombes, 1991, pp. 106–7). This is a primitivism, in other words, that validates, and is in turn validated by, a specific form of modernity, that of imperial Britain.

These villages, of course, might also have performed another function, one associated with a Rousseauesque romantic sensibility. They can also look back at this imperial progress with a more critical gaze, suggesting in their authentic folk traditions, in their organicism and closeness to nature, the price that has been paid for such progress. The 'primitive', then, has two faces – the uncivilised beast and the noble savage or, in Lewis P. Curtis' terms, the 'ape' or the 'angel' (Curtis Jr., 1971/1997). As Curtis has shown, these images of the Irish long pre-date the cinema and find their most graphic form in the cartoons and illustrations of Victorian popular journals, reflecting the progress of nineteenth-century political tensions between Britain and Ireland. Thus the stereotypes of the Irish that grew out of British involvement vacillated between these two extremes, the negative pertaining at times when the political tensions between the two islands were at their most acrimonious.

The more positive (or at least less negative) face of Irish primitivism continued to coexist with, and develop alongside, the Neanderthal Irishman. The version of Ireland that presented the country as a potential Garden of Eden, populated by a simple, musically gifted, loquacious and happy (if quarrelsome) peasantry, bore as little resemblance to reality as did the ape-man brute, but it was an important aspect of European romanticism throughout the nineteenth century. The Celtic periphery of Europe continued to provide intimations of the sublime for this romantic sensibility as a response to the increasingly urban and industrial nature of modernity and progress. Also, it is significant that two years after the White City exhibition, the Kalem Company was in Killarney making one- and two-reel fictions that reproduced the 'typical' Irish village for very different ideological reasons than that identified by Coombes. In the Kalem films, the village was the centre of resistance to British 'civilisation' and the rural simplicity of the Irish was constructed as national difference rather than as imperial homogeneity. Similarly, the romantic primitivism of much of the writings of cultural nationalism is designed to achieve a break, not continuity with Britain. Thus, in the ideological struggle over Ireland, symbolised on one side by the White City exhibition and on the other by Michael Collins' idealised peasant women, the myth of the primitive was mobilised for opposing political aims.

The irony is, then, that metropolitan romantic primitivism became internalised in Ireland itself. The combination of a rural utopia, a simple but moral peasantry and the intimations of the sublime perfectly suited the religious/political alliance that fuelled Catholic nationalism towards the end of the nineteenth century. Thus, an image of the Irish that grew out of the romantic imaginings of metropolitan intellectuals and antiquarians was mobilised in the long struggle for national determination and then turned against the imperial centre that had produced them in the first place. There is nothing unique about this process, of course. The idea of the nation is itself a product of the kind of modernity that imperialism and colonialism promoted and is implicit in the racial selection and categorisation characteristic of imperial culture such as that represented at the White City exhibition. Furthermore, the search for the individuality that marked out one nation from another is a product of the romantic sensibility more generally, one that created the utopianism of the 'primitive' as one response to modernity. In this way, the images and language of the coloniser became the weapons to overthrow him and the imaginings of the centre became internalised at the periphery.

This process did not end with nineteenth-century nationalism. As we shall see, the stereotypes of the Irish promulgated by WASP America were similar in their ideological thrust to those in Britain. One way of looking at their appearance in American genre cinema, therefore, especially that of John Ford is to view them as a weapon in Irish-America's response to WASP prejudice. Contemporary Nigerian novelist Chinua Achebe, writing about a symposium he attended in Dublin in 1988, notes a similar response in colonial literature today. 'We (Africans) chose English not because the British desired it, but because, having tacitly accepted the new nationalities into which colonialism had grouped us, we needed its language to transact our business, including the business of overthrowing colonialism itself in the fullness of time' (Achebe, 1990, p. 32). In accepting and promoting a romantic rural sense of Irish identity, therefore, cultural nationalism ironically accepted one of the great stereotypes of Ireland produced by imperialism. In doing so, it came to reject not only the imperial definition of urban, industrial modernity but also the very notion of modernity itself. Cultural nationalism's own version of the Irish future was predicated on the Rousseauesque critique of modernity that lies below the surface of the primitive image and found its perfect cinematic expression in *Man of Aran*.

Man of Aran and Ascetic Nationalism

When *Man of Aran* opened in Dublin in May 1934 it was a national event attended by de Valera himself and members of his cabinet (Rockett, 1988, p. 71). The enthusiastic reception accorded to the film in Ireland was summed up by nationalist historian and close supporter of de Valera, Dorothy Macardle, who saw in its portrayal of the heroic struggle of the Aran islanders nothing less than the rehabilitation of the Irish people in the eyes of the world (Gibbons, 1988a, p. 195). Interestingly, Macardle pinpoints with uncanny accuracy the traditions of representation that are discussed here, demonstrating just how enduring they are and how deeply embedded they have been in culture generally. 'We have become almost resigned', she writes, 'to being traduced in literature, whether under the guise of the comic "Paddy" of Victorian music halls, or the drunken swindler of some Irish farces or the "gunman" of more sombre writers today' (Gibbons, 1988a, p. 195). *Man of Aran*, she argues, was a proud and truthful riposte to these stereotypes. In her railing against negative representations of the Irish, one can detect here her distaste not only for British caricatures but also for the less flattering portrayals of the Irish in the native writings of Synge and O'Casey. However, in her haste to dismiss these, she has missed the point about Flaherty's particular vision of the Aran Islands.

Flaherty's film has long been at the centre of controversy precisely because of its ambivalent relationship to objective reality and the impression that it gives, not of myths being challenged but of myths being reinforced. These controversies have been well documented by various critics over the years (Calder-Marshall, 1963; Murphy, 1978; Gibbons, 1987; Barsam, 1988). In hindsight it can now be seen that the political and cultural context of the early 1930s dictated the reception of the film to the point that it exposed rather starkly the paradoxical nature of Flaherty's nineteenth-century romantic sensibility. First, the film became the focus of an aesthetic debate about the nature and social purpose of the documentary form itself, and this clouded the film's reception, especially in Britain. Second, the political thrust of this debate was heightened by the depression and by the rise of fascism in Europe, both of which occasioned an international anxiety about the relationship between culture and politics generally. Third, in Ireland, the film arrived just as the de Valera government was reinvigorating the ideals of cultural nationalism and it provided an almost perfect cinematic expression of the ascetic romanticism that lay behind this whole project.

As far as the debate about the documentary form was concerned, Flaherty was, in a sense, the victim of John Grierson's patronage. Grierson had originally coined the word 'documentary' in reference to Flaherty's *Moana* (1927). As he himself said, he used the word originally as an adjective. However, he initiated a debate in Britain about the nature of the word as a noun, one that came to signify a certain kind of non-fiction film that had defined working methods and an overtly social purpose. Grierson's continuing support for Flaherty brought the latter's particular cinematic vision into the ambit of this debate. It is hardly surprising, therefore, that the politically committed film-makers and critics who clustered around documentary film-making in Britain at the time should find Flaherty's high romanticism particularly problematic. Murphy traces the development of this controversy as it smouldered in C. A. Lejeune's review in the *Observer* and caught fire in the pages of *Cinema Quarterly* in articles by Ralph Bond and David Schrire (Murphy, 1978, pp. 70–74). Schrire described the film as 'evasive documentary' that avoided all the important social and political issues in favour of an anachronistic portrayal of the 'noble savage' and his struggle against nature. The film is thus condemned for what it avoids – social relationships, capitalist exploitation, evictions, the class struggle, the whole reality, in other words of 'man's struggle with man'.

The film also raises serious issues about Flaherty's method and those aspects of Aran life that he chose to include. The British documentary movement was committed to an aesthetic practice that interfered as little as possible with the objective reality of life as the camera found it, faithfully recording the social relationships and the ordinariness of lived experience. Although Flaherty had pioneered the method of participant observation that Grierson in particular so admired, his insistence on staging and recreating his own reality was seen as a travesty. Thus the two centrepieces of *Man of Aran* – the building of a field on the barren rocks and the shark hunt – were practices that had long since died out. Even the family in the film, central to Flaherty's depiction of the struggle for existence on the island, was constructed around the need for photogenic faces and one of the locals who worked on the film, Pat Mullen, described many other instances of Flaherty's blatant manipulation of reality (Mullen, 1934).

Much of the controversy, therefore, has centred on questions of content (both what was included and what was avoided) but the meaning of *Man of Aran* depends as much on film form (in other words on *how* we see as much as on *what* we do or do not see). In the field-making sequence, for example, Flaherty shows the tedious process of laying out a field on the barren rocky landscape of the island. There is a realist's attention to detail in these scenes. First, the islanders must collect what little soil is available to them by scraping it out from rock crevices with their fingers. This is then laid out on beds of seaweed gathered and carried back-achingly from the beach to the rocky plateau above. If necessary, a flat surface for the plot is hacked out from the rock through a combination of brute force and sheer determination. However, the characteristic shooting and framing of the sequence imposes a certain judgment on the characters and their lifestyle which is anything but realist. Flaherty uses a combination of low-angle shots and high, panoramic shots of the people against landscapes and seascapes. Often the characters are framed against the skyline, sometimes in silhouette. We can see this clearly in the soil-gathering sequence in general but in the rock-breaking scene in particular. The Man (Tiger King) is captured in a low-angle shot, the camera looking upwards at him, framing him against the sky as he lifts the boulder above his head. There is a series of rapid edits, showing the action from a number of perspectives in a montage that emphasises the character's physical strength and determination. The combination of shooting style, framing and editing works to heroicise the Man and to give an epic dimension to his rather mundane tasks. Similarly, we see his wife (Maggie Dirrane) carrying a basket of soil or seaweed over the barren landscape, heroically framed on the horizon against this same elemental skyline.

In another sequence at the end of the film, the family has just rescued the fishing nets from the sea and the Man himself has narrowly escaped drowning in the tempestuous waters. As the three characters walk away from the shore, they pause on the edge of the cliff and look back at the crashing waves. Flaherty edits a series of low-angle shots of the human characters framed against the skyline with contrasting shots of the thunderous waves. The way in which he does so again imposes a meaning that is highly romantic and in the political terms of the documentary debate, extremely reactionary. The first shot shows all three characters framed in this typical manner. When we return to the human characters after the first sea shots, we get a low-angle shot of the father himself. On cue, he turns his head slightly to offer a perfect profile of his chiselled good looks, framed against the skyline by the 'tam-o'-shanter' headgear which Flaherty insisted that the characters wear. As with the rock-breaking sequence we get here a perfect realisation of Stakhanovite virility. More shots of the crashing seas follow this stylised, monumental pose before finally cutting to a low-angle shot of the son (Michael Dillane) in similar pensive pose. The sequence ends with a three-shot again of the family, walking home against the majesty of the sky, fragile human beings tenuously holding on to a cultural space against the awesome power of nature. The main ideological impact of the sequence, however, is to suggest continuity between father and son – implying that the father's struggle will eventually become the son's and that this elemental existence is set to continue in an unending cycle. It is hardly surprising that Flaherty's stylised heroics would appear so reactionary to a group of filmmakers and critics committed to social change and to a form of non-fiction film that would facilitate this.

To achieve his epic vision of the 'noble savage', Flaherty took considerable liberties with the objective reality of life on Aran as he found it. However, even if everything he showed was objectively true the film could still be dismissed as stylised romanticism because of its visual style and editing. As Luke Gibbons

Stylised, monumental poses: the family in *Man of Aran*

has argued, 'The mythic element in *Man of Aran* is best exemplified by the manner in which the everyday grind of work and production is desocialised and
transformed into a heroic struggle between humanity and nature.' He quotes
the critic Peter Marinelli's description of this kind of 'romantic pastoral' as a
view of nature 'which begins with the individual figure, concentrates upon his
hard lot in life, and then magnifies him, almost insensibly, into a figure of titanic
proportions, an emblem of general Humanity' (Gibbons, 1988a, p. 201). That
is exactly what Flaherty does in *Man of Aran*, so that the life depicted is mag-
nified 'almost insensibly' through camera angle, framing and editing. In this
regard it is surprising that for critics, it is Flaherty's style that rescues the film
from opprobrium. Barsam, for example, agrees that Flaherty's subjective view
of reality – 'his making-it-up' – has its basis in romanticism, thus 'idealizing the
simple, natural, and even non-existent life'. However, he specifically exempts
Flaherty's visuals from this judgment, arguing rather surprisingly that Flaherty
also 'achieves a realistic image through location shooting, straight cinematography, and fidelity in editing to temporal and spatial actuality' (Barsam, 1988,
p. 116).

  Location filming in itself does not guarantee objective reality or authenticity and Flaherty's cinematography and editing are most certainly not concerned
with the exigencies of found reality, even by his own admission. For Flaherty,

the shot itself was the important thing and how this shot might fit in later was of secondary importance. His editor John Goldman claimed that Flaherty had no sense of the rhythm of the film, the timing of shots in a sequence or their cumulative effect. The film was in his head, regardless of the reality around him (Murphy, 1978, p. 28). In this regard, C. A. Lejeune's famous comment that the film was 'a sealed document, the key to which was still in Flaherty's mind' seems apposite (Murphy, 1978, p. 71). Of course, Flaherty's defenders also point out that the concerns of the British documentarists were not those of Flaherty and that he should not be criticised because he chose to make a different kind of film. Rather, his achievement should be judged on the basis that he set out to tell a universal human story about humanity's relationship to nature, especially the elemental struggle between 'Man and the sea'.

Barsam also offers in defence of the film the observation that 'however much Flaherty may have distorted reality, it was not with the deceptive, propagandistic intentions of a film such as Leni Riefenstahl's *Triumph of the Will* (1936)' (Barsam, 1988, p. 116). This observation is significant because it raises one of the more serious accusations levelled at *Man of Aran* – that its celebration of heroic elemental humanity at the expense of real social and political issues amounted to nothing less than fascism. This judgment followed the film's success at the 1932 Venice Film Festival when it won the top prize for the best foreign film, 'the Mussolini Cup'. The ideological considerations that would come to dominate the early Venice festivals were intimated at that year's festival when Gustav Machaty's Czechoslovakian entry *Extase*, featuring the infamous nude shot of Hedwig Kiesler (Hedy Lamarr), was condemned for 'bringing adultery, eroticism and crime against maternity to the screen' (Pickard, 1980). Against this, Flaherty's vision of a pure and noble humanity must surely have impressed. Riefenstahl herself was to win the Mussolini Cup in 1938 for *Olympia*, her documentary about the 1936 Berlin Olympics, which elicited an angry response from the British and American delegates, who dismissed her film as blatant Nazi propaganda. All of this evidence is circumstantial and it does seem harsh today that Flaherty should have had to contend with the implication that his film displayed a fascist sensibility. He was certainly no fascist but his essentially nineteenth-century sensibility, his anthropological instincts and his celebration of a Rousseauesque primitivism made him vulnerable to the charge in the heated political context of the 1930s. (Flaherty is quoted as saying that he was an explorer first and only a film-maker a long way after [Barsam, 1988, p. 4].) The particular confluence of his aesthetics and that of the fascist art of the times seems to give the claim some legitimacy.

In a famous essay on Leni Riefenstahl, Susan Sontag did attempt to define what fascist aesthetics are and her, admittedly tentative, conclusions provide an interesting codicil to the debate on *Man of Aran*. Riefenstahl had made two notorious Nazi propaganda films for Hitler in the 1930s, *Triumph of the Will* in 1936 and *Olympia* (1938). In the 1970s, she attempted to reinstate her artistic credentials through the publication of a number of photographic studies and Sontag was reviewing her book on the Nuba tribespeople of Sudan. She took the opportunity to look again at Riefenstahl's career and to consider whether or not there was something in her work that might be considered inherently 'fascist'. Admitting the difficulty of definition that this posed, she nonetheless argued:

> National Socialism – or more broadly, fascism – stands for an ideal, and one that is persistent today under other banners: the ideal of life as art, the cult of beauty, the fetishism of courage, the dissolution of alienation in ecstatic feelings of community, the repudiation of the intellect, the family of man (under the parenthood of leaders). (Sontag, 1975, pp. 42–3)

Man of Aran is certainly guilty of most if not all of these traits and it is a measure of the apolitical nature of Flaherty's vision that he was unaware of the problem inherent in his nineteenth-century primitive sensibility. Even removed from the political hothouse atmosphere of the 1930s Flaherty's film still provides a suggestive insight into the implications of a concerted romantic gaze – one that evacuates the material reality of existence and denies the complexity of human culture in the pursuit of an idealised essence. Worrying still is the generally enthusiastic reception accorded the film in Ireland at the time.

Man of Aran was promoted and largely accepted in Ireland as a realistic portrayal of life in contemporary Aran and part of the huge attraction of the film for audiences at the time was precisely its so-called realism. Translated into the Ireland of the early 1930s, this realism had a profoundly nationalist dimension. As we have seen, Macardle saw in the film a realistic response to the romantic or hostile stereotypes of the past. For the critic of the *Derry Journal*, *Man of Aran* provided 'Irish realism at last – a grim, sad realism that grips at the heart of the nation' (Review, 23 May 1933). How can such a heroic romanticisation have been mistaken for realism? Luke Gibbons offers one possible explanation for a general misrecognition of the film. He usefully points out that the pastoral genre has in fact two romantic variations. Following the art critic Erwin Panofsky, Gibbons refers to these as 'soft' and 'hard' primitivism. Soft primitivism is the romanticism that is most obvious, 'a golden age of plenty, innocence and happiness – in other words, civilised life purged of its vices'. Hard primitivism is more problematic, in that it casts a romantic eye on the less attractive aspects of landscape and rural life – it 'conceives of primitive life as an almost subhuman existence full of terrible hardships and devoid of all comforts'. This, as Gibbons points out, is a perfect description of *Man of Aran* (Gibbons, 1988b, pp. 198–201).

The problem, though, is that at the time of its release in Ireland in 1934, the film was received as a realistic representation of the Aran Islands, its hard prim- itivist romanticism mistaken for a slice of social realism. The image of the islanders that the film promoted no doubt dovetailed with the prevailing ethos of Irish nationalism at the time and seemed to offer visual credence to de Valera's own vision of an Ireland of frugal self-sufficiency. But if the romanti- cism of Flaherty's film can be mistaken for realism on one hand and stands accused of fascism on the other, what does this say about the conception of the nation that saw its own image in the film?

In the 1930s, Ireland, like most European democracies, had its own vaguely fascist movement, here known as the Blueshirts. This grouping grew out of elements of the old IRA that had accepted the Treaty in 1922 and had fought the Republicans in the Civil War. But by 1934, de Valera had effectively outmanœu- vred and crushed them. A more interesting question is how close to fascism was Irish nationalism in general in the 1930s, given its romantic idealism, its close- ness to authoritarian religion, its veneration of folk tradition and its flight from urban, industrial modernity. Lee's judgment is that certain preconditions nor- mally conducive to successful fascist movements did exist and that, despite its opposition to the Blueshirts, it was de Valera's Fianna Fáil party that harnessed that potential. It exuded 'some isolated resemblances' to fascism in its rhetoric – some of the more strident versions of integral nationalism, its commitment to ideas of an agrarian utopia and a charismatic leader (Lee, 1989, p. 182). However, a general historical judgment is that de Valera's main achievement was in secur- ing for democracy a state that had been born out of an anti-imperialist war, had then endured a bitter and even bloodier civil war and continued to labour under severe economic problems for decades. Despite its church-driven anti-commu- nism and the general support for Francoist Spain, Ireland remained a deeply conservative country that managed to avoid the drift towards full-blown fascism.

The legacy of *Man of Aran* and the dangers inherent in its romantic excesses are, however, deeply significant for the development of indigenous film-mak- ing. The myths embodied in Irish landscape and the ideological constructions of the west of Ireland – the way in which a particular form of Irish identity was imagined, in other words – have provided one important theme in recent Irish cinema. Thus, one of this new cinema's main projects has been to demytholo- gise rural Ireland and to question the ascetic nationalism that underpinned it.

Irish Ethnicity, American Cinema and *The Quiet Man*

In James Cameron's *Titanic* (1997) there is an elaborate sequence which con- trasts the privileged world of the first-class passengers on the upper decks with the simplicity of the steerage-class emigrants below. Bohemian artist Jack (Leonardo Di Caprio) has just inveigled his way into a first-class dinner party with the family and friends of Rose (Kate Winslett) and witnessed at first hand the selfish individualism of the moneyed classes. Afterwards, at a secret assignation with Rose, Jack declares: 'Let's go to a real party!' The scene cuts to a boisterous drinking and dancing party below decks where wildly exuberant emigrants whirl and stumble to the strains of an Irish traditional group (identified as 'Celtic Storm' in the credits). In the dress and physical features of the exuberant passengers we can read the visual clues of a disparate ethnicity – Irish, Scottish, Italian, Nordic, East European and Jewish. Under the cultural leadership of the Irish (the music, the dancing, the 'black beer'), this motley assembly has gelled into a community of mutual interest, self-supporting and intensely democratic. There is, it must be admitted, something rather contrived and faintly absurd about the scene, where cultural and linguistic differences have seemingly been magically whisked away in a frenzy of communal celebration. However, there is more at stake here than merely a contrast between poverty and wealth.

The party below decks does not represent real ethnic groups in a supposedly real setting. Rather, the scene operates as a semiotic display of Hollywood ethnicity. The very stereotypes that allow us to read the ethnicity of the steerage passengers work only because these are cinematic stereotypes, long ingrained into the fabric of American genre film and absorbed into the consciousness of audiences skilled at registering their narrative and ideological significance. The contrast that the film sets up is, therefore, as much about ethnicity as it is about class – the communal and public world of ethnic diversity juxtaposed to the stifling and individualistic world of WASP privilege. Rose herself notices the regulation of the self and the body that WASP culture involves. In the first-class dining room a little girl is instructed by her mother in the decorum of eating, being shown how to sit at the table properly and how to arrange her napkin in the correct manner. The physical pleasure of eating is wrapped in layers of convention, reduced to a display of refinement and delicacy. In one of the numerous confrontations with her own mother, Rose's protests are literally stifled as her mother pulls hard on the corset that entombs her body. Rose's body, of course, is later revealed to Jack (and the audience) both as an object of artistic beauty and desire and as the conduit of her released sexuality.

Rose's sexual and social release is presaged in the party scene where she abandons herself to the communal rituals of the emigrants. She joins in the dancing and drinking and even matches the physical prowess of the arm-wrestling men. She performs a pain-inducing toe-point that, removed from the bourgeois world of ballet, is here reinscribed as a feat of physical endurance every bit as impressive as that of the men. In other words, she has entered an extremely physical world, where the body is celebrated and consumption and sensuality – the pleasures of the flesh – are accepted aspects of a public communal culture. Rose's journey of self-discovery is one in which she moves inexorably away from the suffocating world of WASP culture and finds sexual and emotional fulfilment in the new democratic culture of the diverse ethnic groups which will form the backbone of twentieth-century America. Cameron's epic can, therefore, be read as a metaphor for the decline of English bourgeois culture (and its American WASP representatives) and the rise of a more communal, multi-ethnic, egalitarian and democratic culture of the new America – the end of Europe's nineteenth and the real beginning of America's twentieth century. This is cinematic myth, of course, the dominant ideological world-view of much of Hollywood genre cinema, encapsulated in Hollywood's formative years by the Westerns of John Ford and the populist cinema of Frank Capra. If Cameron's celebration of ethnic culture resembles anything then it resembles the communal rituals that are such a feature of Ford's cinema. These rituals in Ford are a kind of punctuation, the grammar of ordinary communal life that nonetheless forms the basis of a successful and fulfilling civilisation. As Joseph McBride has observed, 'Ford's favourite device for heightening the meaning of the commonplace was the ritual' (McBride and Wilmington, 1974, p. 28). In the cinema of John Ford, as in *Titanic*, the Irish are at the centre of such communal rituals.

This emphasis on a cinematic ethnicity is important for an understanding of the ideological significance of Irish stereotypes in American cinema. As we have seen, American culture in the nineteenth century was replete with the same kind of stereotypes that dominated British perceptions of the Irish. These stereotypes had a long history in the USA itself and by the beginning of the twentieth century, they had sunk deep into American culture. Interestingly, Grady McWhiney locates them in the (WASP) North's enduring stereotypes of the ante-bellum South and traces them back to what he argues is the profoundly Celtic influence in the South. By 1850, he has estimated that as much as 50 per cent of the population of the South were descendants of what he calls the pre-modern Celts of Britain (Ireland, Scotland, Wales, Cornwall and the uplands of England). This gave the South a particular cultural profile (summed up in the word 'Cracker', a pejorative name for Southerners) that allowed the WASP North to begin to identify itself in its difference. Thus, many of the stereotypes that would later become associated with the Irish were used to describe the ante-bellum South. Among these, McWhiney identifies indolence, drunkenness, gambling, high consumption of tobacco, lack of hygiene, propensity to violence, and a love of leisure that was filled with music-making and dancing. The WASP work ethic and attention to cleanliness (of body and mind) and its rules of etiquette stood in contrast to this litany of social evils (McWhiney, 1988).

During the nineteenth century (both before and after the Famine) the Irish were the largest white immigrant group in the USA and again in the North, where they mostly settled, these stereotypes began to emerge as particularly Irish traits. Dale T. Knobel traces the development of both anti-Catholic and anti-Irish stereotyping in the period down to the 1860s and noted a number of phases that this went through. The pattern though was consistent. This rhetoric, he found, was as much about Anglo-America and its attempts at self-definition as it was about the Irish. He quotes a mid-century observer who wrote: 'More incongruous elements it would be difficult to bring together than the jolly, reckless, good-natured, passionate, priest-ridden, whiskey-loving, thriftless Paddy, and the cold, shrewd, frugal, correct, meeting-going Yankee' (Knobel, 1986, p. 27). By the end of the century, Knobel contends that Anglo-America had already begun the process of accepting the Irish 'as honorary Saxons', although the stereotypes, both negative and amiable, continued to feed into all aspects of American popular culture.

In its quest for self-definition during the course of the nineteenth century Anglo-America's need to mark its difference from the Irish was motivated by its own sense of cultural superiority. A whole array of negative and sometimes vicious anti-Irish imagery was the result. This sense of cultural superiority is the ideological imperative that Rockett, Gibbons and Hill located in dominant cinematic images of the Irish in the twentieth century (Rockett, Gibbons and Hill, 1988, pp. xi–xii). However, in the case of *Titanic*, the Irish are, if anything, presented in a more favourable light than the dominant WASP culture, representing as they do, a communal spirit of earthy democracy so obviously lacking on the upper decks. It is here that the full force of Hollywood ethnicity – a semiotic system of the admirably ordinary – comes in to play. In *Titanic*, of course, WASP culture is represented on screen in all its stifling and repressive awfulness, personified in the grotesque caricatures of Rose's mother and fiancé. In many of the films discussed by Rockett, Gibbons and Hill, the supposedly superior metropolitan culture operates off screen – the civilised values that it embodies being all the more significant by being unrepresented. However, it is possible to come to a different conclusion about dominant representations of the Irish by considering them through the filter of ethnicity in America (rather than as stereotypes of the Irish at home) and by being sensitive to the ideological role of stereotypes in genre cinema in general. What is at stake here, then, is not the representations of Ireland and the Irish at home but of the Irish diaspora abroad, a parallel sense of cultural identity which is as much about 'American-ness' as it is about Irishness.

In his useful study of ethnicity in American cinema, Lee Lourdeaux comes to just such a different conclusion. For Lourdeaux, what is significant about Irish (and Italian) immigrants is their Catholic religion and the particular cultural characteristics which this signifies in the largely WASP culture of early twentieth-century America. Central to his analysis is the project of assimilation, the desire of the immigrants to assimilate into American culture and society but also the desire of ethnic film-makers to highlight precisely those virtues that the immigrant embodies and which Anglo-America sadly lacks. In other words, it is assimilation that works in both directions. As he argues:

> Among the various ethnic Catholics working in Hollywood, it was the Irish and the Italians who had the most lasting impact. Irish and Italian film-makers would change the values, if not the surface signs, of Hollywood products. In movie theaters nation-wide, this surface acculturation was actually a reciprocal assimilation that allowed Anglo-American moviegoers to take what they wanted from ethnic cultures. (Lourdeaux, 1990, p. 14)

Lourdeaux works on an ethno-religious basis to trace the process of assimilation and to map out the role of ethnic film-makers in both allaying the fears of the Anglo-American audience and in inducting this audience into the virtues of ethnic culture. He locates three characteristics of Catholic culture which form the basis of this reciprocal assimilation – communion, mediation and sacramentality. Sacramentality is the most elusive of these virtues. 'Catholics, unlike Protestants,' Lourdeaux argues, 'do not feel compelled to choose between the world and God; rather, God's revelation is mediated through the world.' Thus, in the case of John Ford, when he directs what Lourdeaux describes as confessional narratives 'and lingers on Western landscapes in long, worshipful shots he adds his Irish-American vision to America's cult of the West' (Lourdeaux, 1990, pp. 18–19). In this way, Ford's Irish-American identity and his Catholicism are deep structures in all his films, not just in his overtly Irish films, giving a coherence and a particular ideological consistency to his whole work. Whatever about the virtue of sacramentality as a critical tool for understanding films, the other two Catholic traits identified by Lourdeaux, communion and mediation, perfectly encapsulate the stereotypical world of Irish ethnic identity in Hollywood cinema and are the key registers in Ford's poetry of the ordinary.

Communion is the most obvious and is found most abundantly in the community rituals of Ford's films. In its contrast to the individualism of the Protestant ethic and the culture of WASP America, this spirit of community emerges as the most desirable trait of the Hollywood Irish. Like the party scene in *Titanic*, there is sometimes something slightly absurd in Ford's use of ritual – formal communal rites performed in inappropriate, even vaguely sacrilegious settings – and yet these are the markers of a common humanity that will rescue Ford's communities from the wilderness. In *The Searchers* (1956) Mrs

Jorgensen (the ethnic mouthpiece and moral centre of the film's isolated Western community) says, 'We be Texicans and a Texican ain't nothing but a man way out on a limb.' When society is way out on a limb, the ethnic Irish, representing the communal instincts of a host of other ethnic groups, will bring those essential traits of communion to bear. Drinking parties and communal brawls thus play an important ideological role in Ford's cinema. The dance in the unfinished church in *My Darling Clementine* (1946), the wedding held in the bar in *The Searchers*, or the spontaneous communal singing and debates about parliamentary procedure in an Irish pub in *The Quiet Man* (1952) are all part of the same ideological universe. They are not just important to the narratives of Ford's films but are crucial ideological interventions into dominant Anglo-American culture generally, the attempt to encourage WASP America to adopt the positive social values that they embody. These rituals only work within the narrative and on audience perceptions because they rely on stereotypes and genre conventions and here the third trait of Catholic culture that Lourdeaux identifies, that of mediation, is particularly significant.

The figure of the Catholic priest, a central genre convention in many films about Irish-Americans, symbolises mediation most clearly. The priest is, of course, the mediator between God and the individual, but in genre cinema he is also a social mediator, the figure of authority who will ensure that the physical and ebullient Irish can be regulated and brought under some kind of social control. The Irish cop performs the same role and the whole process of mediation within the Irish community that he embodies is reassuring to an Anglo-American audience suspicious and fearful of the riotous inner-city districts of the Irish immigrant. 'To WASP Americans, the Irish were famous both for their saloons and for the sobering figures of the parish priest, the street cop and the strict straw boss. For all these reasons, Hollywood elected the Irish to serve as role models of assimilation for other immigrants' (Lourdeaux, 1990, p. 48).

However, as we have seen in our discussion of Catholicism in Ireland, the Irish retained a puritan, rigorist form of their religion that celebrated the community of the church while condemning overt sexuality and wrapping the body in layers of guilt. This is the WASP trait in the Irish that was utilised most effectively for allaying Anglo-American fears (and so, for Lourdeaux, unbridled sensuality in genre cinema became the preserve of the Italians). In this worldview, the Irish mother became a central force for mediating social and sexual order and this was carried to America with the diaspora. The special devotion to the Virgin Mary (the great intercession between the church and God) was instrumental in imposing a particular role model for Irish women. It is hardly surprising, therefore, that in Hollywood genre films the Irish mother was so often presented as the primary mediator within the family and the community.

(Thus, for example, Mrs Jorgensen in *The Searchers* is an ethnic stereotype whose genesis is the Irish mother.) A paradoxical stereotype of Irish woman-hood thus emerged – a strong-willed, independent woman nonetheless committed to conservative social values. This woman had two manifestations – the mother (often a widow) and the feisty but highly moral colleen (the older and the younger self, the mother and the daughter). The radical conservatism implicit in these cinematic representations is crucial for understanding the complexities of Irish-American cultural identity and for assessing the impact of genre stereotypes of the Irish in general.

In fact, we have noted the paradox already as a major characteristic of Irish cultural nationalism itself. Kevin O'Higgins, one of the ministers in the first government of the Irish Free State, was to boast that he and his colleagues in government were the most conservative revolutionaries who ever lived (Fanning, 1983, p. 52). The spirit of the Irish nationalist revolution is often referred to by Yeats' famous oxymoron 'A terrible beauty is born', but in reality, the oxymoron 'radical conservatism' is more appropriate. In film criticism, it has often been noted that Ford is a similarly paradoxical artist. Joseph McBride, for instance, notes that while Ford has often been accused of being a conservative, nevertheless typical Ford characters rebel against intolerant and unjust conditions in their own communities. Ford's obsession with justice created an odd mixture of the anarchist and the authoritarian 'which makes his work equally attractive to those on both extremes of the political spectrum' (McBride and Wilmington, 1974, p. 21).

The same contradiction and tension can be observed in the character of Ford's most famous Irish colleen, Mary Kate (Maureen O'Hara) in *The Quiet Man*. Many feminist critics have praised her as a strong-willed and independent woman who refuses to sleep with her husband until he publicly fights for the dowry that symbolises her economic independence. For Janey Place, this portrayal is almost 'revolutionary' in screen representations of women while, for Brandon French, Mary Kate is a good example of a tendency in 1950s cinema to show the female character 'on the verge of revolt' (Place, 1979, p. 196; French, 1978, pp. 13–22). Yet in the end, Mary Kate returns to the kitchen to prepare the supper for her husband, accepting a traditional wifely role despite all the thunder and bluster of her earlier revolt. (Maureen O'Hara was to play the other side of the duality of Irish stereotypical women when she returned to the screen after a long absence in 1991 to play the widowed mother who still regulates her son's sex life in Chris Columbus' romantic comedy *Only the Lonely*.)

If the articulation and the rearticulation of Irish stereotypes in Hollywood genre cinema played an important role in the assimilation of the Irish into mainstream American society, it has to be remembered that the cinema was not the only, nor even the most important, social force in this assimilation. The labour unions by the turn of the century were largely Irish institutions, but the early unions, headed largely by native or British-born Protestants, according to Noel Ignatiev, should be regarded 'as institutions for assimilating the Irish into White America' (Ignatiev, 1995, p. 103). The racial definition here is crucial, because the Irish paid a price for economic and social integration. Coming from their native country, with the experience of poverty, discrimination and repression and a history of organised resistance, they quickly learned the benefits of organised resistance in America to capitalist exploitation of their labour. The Irish involvement in early labour agitation was crucial to the developing labour movement and was an understandable and radical response to the appalling conditions under which the immigrants of the nineteenth century laboured. But the price was that the Irish had to learn to become 'white', to recognise that, whatever their ethnic differences to the native Anglo-Americans, their white skins allowed them the opportunity of integrating with the dominant culture eventually, a possibility denied to even the free blacks of the North. In organising general labourers and the industrial workers of the factories the Irish consigned black Americans to the sub-wage economy of the shoeshine and street huckster. Ignatiev describes the process by which the Irish took over the New York docks in the 1850s, fighting black workers on the job and eventually driving them out by threatening employers with industrial action if they attempted to re-employ them. The longshoremen's union that the Irish established eventually became a model of mixed-ethnic unity, provided that these ethnicities were white. Ignatiev's caustic judgment is that the Irish 'showed they had learned well the lesson that they would make their way in the U.S. not as Irishmen but as whites' (Ignatiev, 1995, p. 121).

Thus, we have another example of the contradictory position of the Irish in America. When viewed within the history of white America, their story is one of exemplary radicalism. Facing the considerable disadvantages of a despised and feared minority, consigned to the most inhuman and exploitative jobs in the labour market, they organised and rebelled, eventually gaining acceptance within the dominant culture and ultimately changing this culture itself in radical and irrevocable ways. Within the context of a racially divided society, on the other hand, this success appears to be at the expense of other racial minorities, especially the Afro-American but also, to some extent, other minority racial groups such as the Asians and native Americans. The later films of John Ford often exude pathos and sadness about the decline of radical idealism in America and this is true in a general way. However, given the importance that Ford attached to the gallery of Irish stereotypes that populate his films and especially the ideological role that these played in a process of mutual assimilation, it is tempting to see these late films as an attempt also to come to terms with the downside of the Irish success story. This is most obvious in *The Last Hurrah* (1958), his satire on Irish-American politics and in particular the kind of politics represented by the famed Tammany Hall political machine that, at the time of the film's production, was about to help deliver Catholic Ireland's first American president. In a less obvious way, we can see Ford's changing attitude to ethnic America in *Sergeant Rutledge* (1960), where a Ford *alter ego*, Cantrell (Jeffrey Hunter), defends the black soldier (Woody Strode) accused of raping and murdering a white girl. The film locates the problem of racism within white America (now including the assimilated Irish) and the stereotypes of the black soldiers (brave, noble, and intensely loyal but also lonely, isolated and displaced) are here operating as the ideological models of a new project of assimilation. The romanticised heroism of the black soldiers (and the innocence of Sergeant Rutledge himself) is unequivocal in the film, as if Ford felt it necessary to present the black man in terms acceptable to the white audience. This, according to McBride and Wilmington, was 'perhaps a necessary first step towards integration, both of society externally and of the neurotic American psyche' (McBride and Wilmington, 1974, p. 174).

This judgment could also apply to the Irish stereotypes that populate all of Ford's films. He did not create the gallery of boisterous rogues, drunks, rebels and feisty females which recur in his films – these came ready-made from the prejudices of Anglo-American culture (Knobel, 1986). However, he used them skilfully to allay the fears of a neurotic America that gave rise to them in the first place and then elevated the radical conservatism implicit in them to promote a more democratic and more communal popular culture. These stereotypes are of, and about, America, not Ireland and to the extent that they were about assimilation, they were enabling in the strict sense of the word, rather than disabling. Given Lourdeaux's astuteness in tracing the trajectory of Irish stereotypes in genre cinema generally and in Ford's films in particular, it is somewhat surprising, then, that he misses the significance of *The Quiet Man* and misreads the film so completely.

The Quiet Man: Parody and Playfulness

Lourdeaux dismisses Ford's most famous and the most popular film about Ireland as 'little more than sentimental Irish faces and stereotypical fisticuffs' (Lourdeaux, 1990, p. 109). His religious approach to Irish stereotypes here lets him down, for he rightly finds little in *The Quiet Man* that adheres to the kind of confessional or Passion-play narratives which he seeks to locate in Ford's work. The film, he argues, is 'uncertain and unfocused' but this is only true if one is looking for the kind of rigid structure or narrative coherence that is the hallmark of much of Ford's cinema. (For example, in *The Searchers*, arguably Ford's greatest film, a systematic narrative structure is built upon a series of arrivals and departures, plots and characters that suggest parallels and a repetition of stylised visual compositions.) The point about *The Quiet Man* is precisely its rambling, structure-less nature. It is, in fact, an 'anti-structure', because it is the one film in Ford's work that carries on a dialogue with his own narrative structures – a contrast between illusion and reality and a discourse on the illusion of illusion.

The opening sequences, for example, seem to establish Ireland as a mysterious, pre-industrial rural paradise. Eccentric characters more inclined to leisure than to work and more attuned to Nature than to Culture people this benign primitivism. The extended joke at the beginning of the film concerns the whereabouts of 'Innisfree', the ultimate destination of the returning Irish-American, Sean Thornton (John Wayne) and allows the director to establish the ambience of an illogical land and an equally illogical people. There is much emphasis on the beauties and pleasure to be found in Ireland (fishing in particular) and on the slower pace of life to be found in this strangely attractive land (the train is three hours late 'as usual' and the locals seem more keen on arguing among themselves than hurrying towards any resolution of the dilemma). In fact the dilemma is resolved through an equally mysterious and illogical means. With no narrative explanation, Michaeleen (Barry Fitzgerald) appears, as if by magic, and carries Sean's bags off with a knowing wink, 'Innisfree this way!'

However, it is worth noting a device Ford uses in this sequence to raise questions already about the nature of the representation that we are witnessing. As Sean follows Michaeleen out of the station, we see the pony and trap that will carry him to Innisfree through the window of the waiting room. This shot is held for a few seconds, a frame within a frame, giving the impression of a picture postcard of this most traditional mode of transport. In many ways, this sums up the view of Ireland that is being constructed for the audience – a postcard Ireland steeped in tradition and somewhat removed from the pressures of the modern world. The point is re-emphasised as the pony and trap disappear under the railway bridge (travelling towards the traditional world) and the train moves over the bridge in the opposite direction (towards the modern world that it symbolises). However, the frame within a frame is repeated later in the film when the drunken villagers bring Mary Kate's furniture to the newly-weds' cottage. Sitting drunkenly on the back of the cart, one of the villagers holds an empty picture frame in front of his face, one of the many throw-away references in the film to the process of representation itself and a further alert to the audience that this particular representation is not all that it seems to be. If it is a picture-postcard view of Ireland then the emphasis seems to be on the postcard and on the frame as much as on what is contained within. This is an important emphasis for understanding how the film works and how it invites its audience into the illusion it creates.

The extended Irish joke at the beginning of the film is used to establish a contrast between tradition and modernity, between the rural world and the industrial, between the primitive and the modern. The implications of this contrast are reinforced in the scenes that follow as Sean travels to Innisfree. In his conversation with Michaeleen, Sean clearly establishes a value judgment on the merits of modernity and tradition. He tells Michaeleen that he has come from Pittsburgh, where 'the furnaces are so hot a man forgets his fear of Hell'. In a scene later in the film, Sean confesses that for him, 'Innisfree is another word for Heaven'. He has left the urban Hell of the USA to find peace and harmony in the rural tranquillity of Ireland and the film's cinematography, shot on location in the west of Ireland, emphasises this basic romantic perspective. We now seemingly have a clear set of contrasts underpinning the representation of Ireland that the film proposes and can tabulate them thus:

IRELAND	USA
TRADITION	MODERNITY
RURAL	URBAN
NATURE	CULTURE
LEISURE	WORK
HEAVEN	HELL

The basic characteristics of Ford's benignly primitive view of Ireland have now been established. The rest of the film plays out the difficulties posed for Sean's 'modern man', who must woo and win the love of Mary Kate's 'woman of nature and tradition', amid this seemingly illogical, comical world of an Ireland out of step with the rest of the modern world. The characters of this world are a collection of outrageous stereotypes, prone to drinking, singing and brawling, and familiar from many of Ford's non-Irish films. In his earlier films and in the formative years of Hollywood genre film in general we have suggested that these stereotypes played a crucial role in a process of mutual assimilation *in America*. What then are they doing in a film about Ireland itself?

To understand this, let us consider the sequence in which Sean stops his journey on a bridge to look down on the little thatched cottage (White O' Morn) in which he was born. As he surveys the beauty of the scene, with the cottage and the valley bathed in sunlight, he recalls the words he heard from his mother as a child ('It was a lovely little house, Seaneen, and the roses!'). There is clearly an implication here that Sean's perspective on Ireland is that of the nostalgic Irish-American – a fantasy made real by the imaginings of the exile. Michaeleen certainly attempts to inject a little realism into the proceedings. As Sean is immersed in his thoughts, admiring his first sighting of the family ancestral home, Michaeleen mutters to him, 'Ah, it's nothing but a wee humble cottage.' There is a contrast here between Sean's fantasy Ireland and Michaeleen's reality. As if to emphasise the point, the audience sees the cottage, in all its sunlit splendour, in a point-of-view shot as if through Sean's eyes, and yet when we see Sean on the bridge, he is framed against a dark and brooding background. Indeed, many critics over the years have pointed out that this backdrop is actually a painted studio set and its obvious falsity is contrasted to the point-of-view shots that were filmed on location in Ireland itself. It is open to conjecture quite why Ford chose to edit together in this sequence location shots and obvious fake studio shots (see, for example, Gibbons, 1988b, pp. 223–6). However, the result is a visual underpinning of the contrast between Sean's imagined Ireland and Michaeleen's more realistic comment.

The other sequence that raises these issues is the scene in which Sean first sees Mary Kate. Luke Gibbons is one of many critics who has discussed this extraordinary scene in detail:

> Here, in John Ford's most memorable evocation of the pastoral ideal, we see a radiant Mary Kate driving sheep through a primeval forest in luminous sunlight, a perfectly realised image of woman at home with nature. Such is the visual excess of the spectacle that Sean is led to question its authenticity: 'Hey, is that real. She couldn't be.' (Gibbons, 1988b, p. 200)

Again, Michaeleen tries to introduce the reality principle: 'Nonsense, man! It's only a mirage brought on by your terrible thirst.' Michaeleen's comment is, of course, an allusion to his own need for alcohol and another play by Ford on the stereotypical notion of the drunken, if amiable, Irishman. However, it is tempting to read this comment metaphorically as well. The real thirst is in fact Sean's, almost as if his own desire to realise his mother's idyllic Ireland has wished Mary Kate into existence. Not only is Mary Kate the embodiment of 'woman at home with nature', she is also the embodiment of 'Mother Ireland' herself, mystically appearing to satisfy Sean's longings. Again, we see her from Sean's point of view and Ford chooses to shoot her entrance and exit to emphasise this. Shot from a low angle, framed against the sky, she seems to materialise out of the bottom of the frame and disappear in similar fashion. What we are seeing here, in other words, is a vision of Ireland that was sustained by the Irish-American community that Ford was brought up in and the romantic excesses of this vision are attributable to the power of the exile to embellish memory with fantasy. The recurring theme music on the soundtrack of the film is built on snatches from the song 'The Isle of Innisfree', which captures the exile's condition:

I've met some folks who say that I'm a dreamer,
And I've no doubt there's truth in what they say,
Sure a body's bound to be a dreamer,
When all the things he loves are far away.

The problem though is that the exile's romanticism is subject not only to a reality principle provided by Michaeleen (as if this could carry much weight anyway) but also to a self-referential dialogue about the illusion itself. If we consider another key moment in the film, we can see how this self-referential dialogue works within an almost avant-garde disdain for classical narrative structure. The morning after Sean and Mary Kate have finally consummated their marriage, Sean is informed by Michaeleen that she has left for the Dublin train. A medium close-up of Sean smoking ends with him throwing the half-smoked cigarette away and ordering, 'Michaeleen, saddle my horse!' This gesture of decisive masculinity has been repeated throughout the film to the point of parody and by this stage has become a recurring joke within the film. However, the scene ends with a shot of Michaeleen collapsing in laughter, repeating the phrase 'Saddle my horse' with incredulous glee. He then begins to hum the recurring theme of the soundtrack, breaking classical narrative con-

Irish America's dreams and illusions: Maureen O'Hara in *The Quiet Man*

ventions. Postmodern critical insights now allow us to better express exactly what is going on here. The decisive masculinity that is being ridiculed is a very precise one – the Western persona of John Wayne that Ford had himself helped to create in the first place. In other words, it is an example of the film's *inter-textuality*, the constant referencing and parodying of other Ford films and characters that permeate *The Quiet Man*. In this way, the film is clearly part of the reassessment of his own myths that characterise the later films, a reassessment of what Wollen has called the 'Fordian system' (Wollen, 1972), including that array of genre stereotypes and situations that formed the backbone of the assimilation project. This reassessment is not quite in the manner that many critics, including Wollen, have identified.

John Hill, for instance, has pointed out the critical orthodoxy that sees Ford's film as a flight from America to rediscover the idealism in Ireland that failed to materialise in the American west, an attempt to relocate these Western values to a pre-modern Ireland and hence the force of the Ireland/America contrasts we located earlier. However, this reading only works if one takes the film at face value and it is surely difficult to do so given the self-conscious play within the film itself. Hill acknowledges the problem and notes that 'the very values of community which it celebrates are, at the same time, revealed as no more than illusion' (Hill, 1990, p. 733). The problem, though, is that the film does not deal with the idealism of the west, Irish or American, but deals with cinematic stereotypes of a particularly Hollywood (and Fordian) kind. It is hard to locate in the film either the melancholy or the disillusionment that would sustain this orthodox reading. Certainly, the negative experiences of the USA which drive Sean back to Ireland are referred to in the film and the expressionistic flashback to the fight in which Sean accidentally killed his opponent is an extraordinary visual intrusion into the bucolic play of the film as a whole. And Gibbons has drawn attention to the intimations of death that permeate the film (Gibbons, 1988a, pp. 239–40) though these are undercut by being further plays on illusion and reality. Rather, what we are presented with is another trajectory altogether and in many ways a more subversive one – comic ridicule and playful anarchy. When the Rev. Playfair and his wife see the cottage that Sean has prepared, she opines, 'It looks the way all Irish cottages should look and so seldom do. And only an American would think of painting it emerald green.' If Ford's more sombre later films are replete with melancholy and disillusionment, here his own cinematic imagination is self-consciously pummelled through parody. Just as the Irish stereotypes that permeate his early and mid-period films are about America and American-ness, not Ireland, so too with *The Quiet Man*. This is not a film about Ireland, real or imagined, but a film about the Irish-American imagination. It is not an unself-conscious recreation of a pre-modern (or pre-lapserian) rural idyll but a postmodern play on the cultural conventions of just such a vision. And herein lies the problem for many critics of the film.

The vision of Ireland that the film creates is, in fact, enticing. The dream is attractive and, at face value, its benign primitivism is thoroughly seductive. Thus, its enormous popularity with audiences through nearly five decades is highly suspect and personal enjoyment always seems to be tinged with guilt. In this regard, James MacKillop's relief is almost palpable when he writes '… I am content in saying that the film is not the piece of trash that I myself thought it was in the years I avoided seeing it out of expected embarrassment' (MacKillop, 1999, p. 179). And that is the final postmodern irony of the film – it allows us to enjoy its artifice without feeling guilty that we are colluding in prolonging outrageous stereotypes. Ford's imagined community of the Irish worked to offer important cultural and ideological support at a key point in the assimilation of the Irish diaspora in the USA. As the parody and playfulness of *The Quiet Man* comes to a close with a bow and a curtsey from his large cast of Irish stereotypes, it is almost as if Ford is declaring that this project is now finished and that he no longer needs them. In his later major films, Ford sought to reimagine a now assimilated white America, especially in its relationship to other racial groups and the mood is considerably less playful and self-conscious than in *The Quiet Man*. The subversive comedy that so lightens the film flows from the fact that, rather than sustaining a myth, Ford attempts to undermine it from the inside.

In what is certainly the most perceptive analysis of the film, Luke Gibbons elaborates this point. Cultural identity, he argues, is a construct whose artifice becomes apparent 'in proportion as it attempts to cancel out social difference'. Thus, to counter the controlling myths of this artifice, it is not to some notion of 'an essential, indubitable truth' that we should look (and certainly not if this truth is Michaeleen's) but rather to a strategy that can demonstrate 'the contrived, *imposed* nature of these myths'. Gibbons cautions against seeing the strategy of internal subversion as some kind of template for indigenous filmmakers, 'as if endlessly quoting from the past could ever meet the needs of present-day film production' (Gibbons, 1987, p. 241). The point is well made, given that the controlling myths which Ford undermines are largely his own (and Irish-America's) and not the national imaginings of Ireland itself.

The point is doubly well made, however, when we consider the tradition of representation that *The Quiet Man* seems to epitomise. Despite the specific historical and cultural context of assimilation in the USA, the regularity with which this tradition re-emerges at different times and in other contexts raises again their negative or disabling potential. In one of British cinema's most popular successes of 1999, Kirk Jones' *Waking Ned* (American title: *Waking Ned Devine*), the whimsical and amiable ambience of the village of Tullymore and its resourceful residents is captured in lovingly composed aerial shots of the landscape, confirming that this tradition of Irish imagery is not, like Ned Devine himself, going to die peremptorily at the onset of sudden wealth. The fact that the film was shot on location in the Isle of Man and not in Ireland raises interesting questions about funding incentives and authenticity but also indicates one of the problems with this form of Celtic mist whimsicality. If one progenitor of *Waking Ned* is *The Quiet Man*, then another is surely the tradition that stretches from Alexander Mackendrick's *Whisky Galore* (1949), through Vincente Minelli's *Brigadoon* (1954) and down to Bill Forsyth's *Local Hero* (1983). *Waking Ned*, in other words could just as easily have been set in Scotland (and given the amount of money involved in the lottery win at the centre of the film's narrative – nearly £7 million – then it would have made more sense that the lottery in question be the British, rather than the Irish one).

The problem with a film like *Waking Ned* is that it lacks any degree of self-consciousness or internal subversion that might rescue it from the charge of 'paddywhackery'. The mythical rural community that is created, with its wily and resourceful inhabitants, stands unproblematically for an authentic organic community that outfoxes the po-faced representative of urban modernity. The film's celebrated leads, two old men on an outrageous scam to defraud the national lottery, certainly add an original element to the story (no doubt achieving in the process a significant blow against the ageism of much contemporary cinema). However, the set of oppositions that the film sets up – between tradition and modernity, between Tullymore and Dublin – are almost exactly the same as those we located in *The Quiet Man*, but without the latter's ironic self-subversion as compensation.

The Quiet Man is often seen as the pinnacle of arch, Irish whimsy and here we have argued that, in the context of Ford's overall work and the ideological imperatives of the Irish diaspora in the USA, there is more at stake in the film than mere stage Irishness. However, the tradition that it is linked to is no less influential or potentially disabling as a result, especially to an Ireland that has changed massively in recent years. The internal subversions of Ford are not a template for undermining this whole tradition. Indigenous film-making would need to find its own way towards reimagining Irish cultural identity at home and at the same time, explore new avenues that might offer a challenge to this wider cinematic tradition.

Chapter 3
Traditions of Representation: Political Violence and the Myth of Atavism

In October 1982, a cartoon appeared in the London *Evening Standard* newspaper that was to gain a degree of notoriety among the Irish communities in Britain. A bemused English citizen walks past a large billboard advertisement for a new film. 'Emerald Isle Snuff Movies Present ...' the poster exclaims, '... The Ultimate in Psychopathic Horror – THE IRISH!' The poster is illustrated with some of the motifs of the horror film – severed hand, hacksaw, crucifixes over gravestones – and the common motifs of the simian Irish – a range of hulking, ape-like monsters representing both republican and loyalist paramilitary groups. The cartoon no doubt expressed British frustration at the seemingly intractable violence of Northern Ireland but was greeted with indignation and protest, especially from the Irish communities in Britain, which saw it as pandering to and exacerbating the anti-Irish prejudice with which they were already trying to cope (Curtis, 1984, p. 84).

This cartoon reminds us that the long and fractious relationship between Britain and Ireland has established a tradition of representation that continues to influence British perceptions of the Irish even today. Central to this tradition has been the representation of political violence in Ireland in the form of 'Paddy', the simian primitive – a violent and irrational character who came to represent the Irish as a whole. This tradition was consolidated in the nineteenth century, especially in humorous political journals like *Punch*, at periods when the political tensions between Ireland and Britain were most intense. Two distinct traditions were mobilised by British cartoonists to create these simian monsters. On one hand, the myth of Frankenstein was used to represent the political leaders of Ireland, accused of stirring up the beast of violence and then losing control of the monster they created. On the other hand, the misappropriation of Darwinian theory allowed the cartoonists to posit the Irish as a lower race in the evolutionary scale and a certain amount of bogus science was employed to give legitimacy to the theory of Anglo-Saxon superiority (Curtis Jr., 1971/1997). The result of these traditions was to absolve Britain from any responsibility for political violence in Ireland and to put the blame securely on the Irish themselves.

Return of the simian Irish: Jak cartoon

Elements of this tradition recur in cinematic portrayals of Ireland and are apt to dictate the way in which political violence is represented. The cinema itself has a long tradition of portraying political violence in Ireland, especially British cinema, which has returned to the topic time and again over the years. This cinematic tradition, from Carol *Reed's Odd Man Out* (1947) to John MacKenzie's *The Long Good Friday* (1979), has been well documented and analysed by John Hill (Hill, 1988, pp. 147–93). He finds in this tradition a recurring reluctance to deal with the violence as politically motivated. Rather the films have tended to portray the violence as essentially pathological – the fault of the Irish themselves. This tragic flaw in the Irish is the result of either their own innate proclivities, the workings of fate or the effects of nature and environment on the Irish psyche. The result is that Britain is absolved from any responsibility for the violence and the socio-cultural roots are denied. Even Irish films that have touched on the topic, such as Neil Jordan's *Angel* (1982) and Pat O'Connor's *Cal* (1984) have tended to reinforce this tradition of representation. It is, as Hill puts it, to exacerbate 'the bias against understanding'.

This is not to suggest that there is then a 'correct' interpretation of the conflicts that films about Ireland should be supporting. What it does imply, however, is that the ability to respond intelligently to history, and the willingness to engage with economic, political and cultural complexity, would need to be considerably greater than that which the cinema has so far demonstrated. (Hill, 1988, p. 184).

As Hill points out, the effect of this cinematic tradition is to reinforce the ideological assumptions of nineteenth-century imagery, even if the cinema has rarely reproduced its crudity. (He does refer to one film, *Old Mother Riley's Ghosts* from 1941, which comes close.) However, painfully troubled IRA men have often been played by major stars, like James Mason in *Odd Man Out* (1947) or John Mills and Dirk Bogarde in Basil Deardon's *The Gentle Gunman* (1952). These are, of course, a long way removed from the simian imagery that reappeared in the Jak cartoon in 1982, but the overall effect of the films is to reinforce the idea that the Irish are subject to some atavistic compulsion to violence. In the period since Hill's analysis, the cinema (Irish, British and American) has returned to violence in Ireland with more regularity. How have these films responded to the tradition that Hill identifies? The key here is to view the films against both this tradition and changing political circumstances in Northern Ireland in the last ten years. The focus is on the central question – how is political violence represented and what do the films say about the political relationship between Ireland and Britain?

Godfathers and Criminals

Political cartoons, like those of the nineteenth-century *Punch* or their contemporary equivalent like the Jak cartoon referred to, work through exaggeration and the grotesque, laced with humour or irony. The cinema, on the other hand, works through repetition and recognisable stereotypes. In fact, popular cinema has never been particularly interested in, or adept at, dealing with political situations, so it is hardly surprising that the great number of films down the years that have dabbled with Irish politics have tended to reinforce existing stereotypes. In the films that have dealt specifically with political violence in Ireland, the tendency has been to use dominant negative stereotypes to deny the politics of the situation and to blame the Irish themselves for their own proclivity to violence. This is the message of Carol Reed's 1947 film *Odd Man Out* or 1959's *Shake Hands with the Devil*, in which James Cagney reprises his psychopathic gangster persona in the guise of an obsessed and brutal IRA leader. The violence that he perpetuates is the result of both criminal and psychopathic inclinations (Hill, 1988).

Indeed, throughout the 1970s and the 1980s, the image of Francis Coppola's *Godfather* films was often invoked by British ministers to describe the activities of the paramilitaries in Northern Ireland, especially the IRA. This was in line with official policy, which was to criminalise their activities and deny republican prisoners political status. This policy was most openly challenged by republicans at the funerals of dead volunteers (including the ten republicans who, in 1981, died in prison on hunger strike protesting about the criminalisation policy). For republicans, it was important that these funerals reflected the military nature of their struggle – the coffin draped in the Irish national flag, the military beret and gloves on the coffin and the shots fired over the grave as a show of last respect. These were the international markers of honour and military respect and they were important correctives to the simian or Godfather imagery applied to their struggle.

For the government, army and police, it was equally important that these paramilitary trappings be denied and so each funeral was attended by a huge security operation designed to thwart any 'criminal' displays. These events became a macabre dance of death, a struggle to control the image of the struggle and it had the effect of reinforcing the closed circuit offered by the terrorist/freedom fighter paradigm – either these were the brute apes of a criminal conspiracy or the noble martyrs of a national struggle. For many people, then, it had become a priority to break open this closed paradigm and create a space in which the politics underlying the violence could be acknowledged and in which political activity could be pursued without resort to the gun and the bomb. It was time, in other words, for a real and meaningful political process. Ironically, it was imagery emanating from popular culture that hinted first at just such a process, some time before the idea entered mainstream politics.

In one of the more interesting examples of the British gangster movie, John MacKenzie's *The Long Good Friday* (1979), the stable world of London godfather Harry Shand (Bob Hoskins) is disrupted when the IRA move into his 'patch'. Shand is ultimately defeated precisely because the IRA are not criminals and therefore cannot be bought or frightened into submission. Their political motivation means that, in Don Corleone's phrase, they are not people he 'can do business with'. This reference to *The Godfather* is also picked up in Jim Sheridan's 1993 film *In the Name of the Father*, where the violence of the IRA, although extreme and brutal, is clearly differentiated from that of the ordinary criminal. Again the implicit suggestion is that, whatever the level of disgust with the violence itself, ultimately it is politically motivated and will only be stopped by a political process. The same message runs through *Loves Lies Bleeding*, a BBC television film, scripted by Ronan Bennett and transmitted in 1993 at a politically significant moment for Northern Ireland.

The most surprising source for this revision of the Godfather motif, however, was the British government itself. Throughout the decades of paramilitary violence in Northern Ireland, the government sponsored a series of television advertisements promoting a confidential telephone line which the public was encouraged to use to give the police information about terrorists. In the 1970s and 1980s, these advertisements followed the dominant imagery and portrayed the paramilitary groups as hooded, shadowy gangsters operating out of the dark alleys and mean streets of the city. However, in the summer of 1993, a new set of three advertisements appeared which moved the recurring imagery in two directions. First, aping mainstream cinema, the advertisements were presented as mini-narratives that showed the violence in a more graphic way, including slow motion shots of gory assassinations and murders. However, the impact of these new levels of explicit violence was heightened by the fact that the perpetrators were revealed without their hoods and their shadows and they turned out to be normal young men, after all, with normal human attributes, desires and grievances. They may have been as violent as the most savage of thriller movie villains but they were also as handsome as Hollywood stars and as normal as the young man living down the street.

There was an implicit suggestion in these advertisements that while the government could not, or would not, talk to psychopathic gunmen or bestial Neanderthals, it might talk to the ordinary young men who have resorted to violence in extraordinary political circumstances, if only they were prepared to renounce the use of force. It was no surprise, then, to many people in Northern Ireland when, a few months later, in November 1993 in a statement in Parliament, the government announced that it 'had opened channels of communication' with Sinn Féin, the republican movement's political wing (McLoone, 1993, pp. 34–6). The peace process was under way and the space between 'terrorist' and 'freedom fighter' was finally opening up.

The 'Cinema of the Peace Process'

There is, of course, no subgenre that is recognisably a 'cinema of the peace process'. However, the long (and, in its own way, seemingly intractable) peace process has had an impact on the films about Ireland that have emerged during the 1990s. The process that has marked a kind of 'endgame' to the violence in Northern Ireland has coincided with a number of factors that coalesce around these cinematic representations. If the peace process can be traced from 1993, then it is coterminous with the rebirth of Irish cinema following the new arrangements put in place earlier that year (and discussed in more detail in Chapter Five). The interest in Ireland from both the British and American industries has been maintained, partly as a result of the tax incentives put in place from the 1980s onwards which have made filming in Ireland so attractive and partly because of the high public profile that Ireland and things Irish have enjoyed generally during this period. It's now 'cool' to be Irish (Hailes, 1998). However, equally significant has been the collapse of the Soviet Union in the early 1990s and the subsequent need for American genre cinema to find new 'villains' to sustain the conventions of the thriller narrative. This has generally been achieved by settling on 'international terrorism' in general and the IRA in particular (or, more specifically, renegade elements within the IRA) as the new threat to American national security.

American Stories ...

At the end of Alan J. Pakula's *The Devil's Own* (1997), IRA man Frankie McGuire lies dying after a shoot-out with American cop, Tom O'Meara. His dying words are full of sombre irony. 'I told you,' he says, 'it's not an American story. It's an Irish one.' Presented with these characters, played as they are with typical male glamour and attractiveness by Harrison Ford and Brad Pitt and after an equally typical testosterone-fuelled narrative, we can be forgiven for thinking that Frankie has got this badly wrong. What we have witnessed, in fact, has been an all-American story with little or no relevance to the politics of Northern Ireland. *The Devil's Own* was one of a number of American films in the 1990s that used aspects of the Northern Ireland crisis to provide 'back story' for otherwise conventional thrillers. Perhaps it was one of the more cerebral of these, involving a conflict between two types of moral imperatives: O'Meara's decent Irish-American cop with a sense of honour, duty and justice and McGuire's commitment to the IRA (even if this is sometimes perilously close to a personal revenge campaign for his murdered father).

Tom O'Meara, played by Harrison Ford at his most attractively avuncular, exudes a staunch commitment to justice and to doing things 'by the book'. Frankie McGuire is a Belfast IRA man in the USA to buy missiles for his organisation who, through the sympathetic Irish-American network, is 'billeted' with O'Meara and his family. The necessary melodramatic element is provided, inevitably, by an oedipal sub-theme. In the opening scenes, against shots of Irish rural landscapes and seascapes, Frankie's father is assassinated in front of the child Frankie by (presumably) loyalist terrorists for being sympathetic to republicans. This violation of the family is a memory that is stirred for Frankie when he stays in the blue-collar comfort of Tom's family in New York. Meanwhile, surrounded by his wife and three daughters, Tom recognises in Frankie the son he has never had. 'Thank God to have someone else around here who pees standing up,' he mumbles on the evening of Frankie's arrival.

Despite his paternal concern for Frankie, Tom's moral conflict is initiated when Frankie brings his 'war' into the O'Meara home. This thinly disguised metaphor for the importing of the 'Irish story' into the USA is an example of genre cinema's struggle to find new villains in the aftermath of the demise of the Soviet threat. It is important then that Tom's all-round American decency is well established and that his pursuit of Frankie is presented as a moral, rather than as a personal, imperative. Frankie breaks the law in America and whatever his motivations for doing so, it is Tom's job to uphold the law. It is a variation, then, on the genre staple that 'a man's gotta do what a man's gotta do'. Frankie's motivations are more obscure. Certainly, his single-minded dedication to his 'job', largely gung-ho heroics with guns, is motivated by revenge for his father's death. The only political motivation expressed is his belief that in the nascent peace process the Brits want an IRA surrender. His quest to buy the 'stinger' missiles ('which drove the Russians out of Afghanistan', as the American supplier puts it) is a way of strengthening the IRA's bargaining position. However, in none of this do the complex politics of the Northern Ireland emerge. The shoot-out in Belfast is more back story and the contacts that Frankie makes in Noraid-type Irish-America are either, like Tom, completely honest and naive, or like Treat Williams' shady arms dealer, basically American criminals. Early in the film Frankie himself says of the situation in Northern Ireland, 'If you're not confused you don't know what's going on.' The film takes this glib nonsense at face value and considerably confuses its audience further.

Much of the controversy that the film generated, however, was not really about its politics as such, but about the fact that Brad Pitt plays the IRA man with considerable sympathy. He is probably the screen's most attractive IRA man ever and he is certainly the most smoothly efficient in the tradition of the American hero. In the scene set in contemporary Belfast Frankie, almost single-handedly, takes on and defeats 'half the fucking British Army' and in New York easily outwits and outguns mere American criminals who attempt to double-cross him in the deal over the missiles. The film's strength as a genre piece is that it sets in conflict two equally attractive American heroes, and in this central drama Ireland is largely irrelevant. As an example of the new villain, Frankie is ambivalent to say the least.

At its most crude, as, for example, in Stephen Hopkins' *Blown Away* (1994) the IRA renegade villain has involved breathing new life into James Cagney's psychotic gunman of *Shake Hands with the Devil* or Robert Beatty's unfeeling activist, Shinto, in *The Gentle Gunman*. However, in Tommy Lee Jones' portrayal of mad bomber Ryan Gaerity, intent on gaining revenge on his former disciple for landing him in prison, the cinema has created its ultimate psycho republican. The post-ceasefire world of the peace process demands that a clear distinction is drawn between this psychotic monster and his former IRA colleague, Jimmy Dove (!) (Jeff Bridges), who is now working for the Boston police. While there is a basic honesty and decency to Dove, Gaerity is too mad and too bad even for the IRA. There are no politics to the film, of course, and it revolves around a series of set-piece bomb moments (the 'which-wire-do-I-cut' drama endlessly replayed). The film does not pretend to say much about the political motivations of the characters. The opening sequence (the most interesting aspect of the film visually) creates well the real cinematic genesis of Gaerity. The gothic outlines of an elemental structure, perched on the edge of cliffs overlooking storm-tossed seas, is revealed, illuminated by lightning and battered by heavy rain. This, as it turns out, is not the castle of some Franken-stein monster or the court of Count Dracula. Implausibly enough, it turns out to be a prison in Northern Ireland and the opening shots establish a jail-break sequence that is grisly and monstrously clever in its execution. The generic con-ventions are clear enough about the cultural genesis of this monster. However, the Irish dimension (specifically the IRA 'back story') is alluded to throughout the film. In its sympathetic portrayal of Dove's uncle and retired Irish cop, Max (Lloyd Bridges), the film is careful to locate a sympathetic 'civic' Irishness, simi-lar to Harrison Ford's Tom O'Meara in *The Devil's Own*, in opposition to the mad bomber. However, in the crudest manner possible (short of the simian stereotype) the film confirms the dominant representation of political violence in Ireland. Tommy Lee Jones hams it up as the mad bomber to great effect, cre-ating a cartoon villain of outrageous ingenuity and callousness. The Irish plot is used merely to establish how Gaerity achieved such expertise in explosives but beyond this there is little in the film to explain why the violence was hap-pening in Northern Ireland in the first place. Given the irrelevance of character motivation to what is basically a revenge plot wrapped around a series of tense set-pieces it is a wonder that an Irish back story was employed at all.

The psycho IRA stereotype is also at the centre of Phillip Noyce's *Patriot Games* (1992). While in London on holiday with his wife and daughter, CIA analyst Jack Ryan (Harrison Ford) wanders into an IRA assassination attempt

The ultimate psychopathic republican: Tommy Lee Jones in *Blown Away*

and in foiling the gang he kills one of them. The dead man's brother, Sean Miller (Sean Bean), leads a renegade faction of the IRA in a revenge mission against Ryan and his family. Miller's fanaticism, like Gaerity's, is such that even the IRA must take its distance. Paddy O'Neil (Richard Harris) is a Sinn Féin representative Ryan meets in the course of his investigations. O'Neil is given a few lines of political justification for the 'legitimate' republican movement while clearly distancing that movement from Miller's wayward fanaticism. Although Ryan is shown to be sceptical the insertion of this brief scene is interesting and, as we shall see, suggestive. However, if the film had aspirations to anything more politically significant, these are lost as it settles into a basic thriller narrative ending up with a spectacular chase and fight sequence that is more energetic than cerebral. There are three points worth noting, however. First, in its central investigative sequences, the film is a paean to American technology and know-how, as Ryan enlists the latest satellite technology to track down and eliminate a terrorist training camp located in the Sahara desert. Second, the spectre of international terrorism is raised when this same technology reveals that the renegade IRA unit is part of this international conspiracy. Any cultural or political specificity is neatly removed and the real nature of the threat comes into closer focus – a kind of generalised anti-American fanaticism. Third, the assassination attempt that Ryan thwarted in London involved a member of the British royal family and this same aristocrat of the British establishment is a guest at Ryan's house when Miller launches his final attack. This close association of American and British interests is actually quite rare in genre cinema, outside the CIA/MI5 axis of the James Bond films, because of the more democratic and classless nature of American cinema. Linked to the Irish dimension of the story, it seems that the Irish-American CIA man Jack Ryan, played by the Irish-American Harrison Ford and based on the books of Irish-American Tom Clancy, is suggesting a new political alignment to the Irish-America inhabited by Paddy O'Neil.

On the other hand, though, the small but significant scenes with O'Neil suggest something else as well. There is a tradition in American cinema of 'paranoia thrillers', which also require the plot device of a renegade unit that is out of control. In a film like Sydney Pollack's *Three Days of the Condor* (1975) or Harrison Ford's second outing as Jack Ryan, *Clear and Present Danger* (1994), again directed by Phillip Noyce, this renegade element is in the CIA itself. The ideological thrust of such films is to suggest that the basic institutions are fine and that these mavericks will always fail because of the presence of moral figures like Joe Turner (Robert Redford) in *Condor* or Jack Ryan in the Clancy adaptations. If this basically conservative ideology is applied to the Paddy O'Neil sequence in *Patriot Games*, it becomes a kind of backhanded compliment to the 'legitimate' republican movement. Despite the presence of Miller's splinter group, or, as in the paranoia films, because of the presence of the group as a negative indicator, the movement is basically moral and respectable and is engaged in a noble cause. This might be to stretch the genre conventions just a little but it is worth registering it here because something similar is to be found in the films of Irish directors which also deal with political violence.

... Irish Stories

The emergence of Irish cinema coincides, as we noted, with the beginnings of the peace process back in 1993. It is hardly surprising that Irish film-makers should begin to look at aspects of Northern Ireland themselves. The greater involvement of Irish creative talent has meant that many of these films are more interesting and more complex than the American films. However, responding to the commercial imperatives that film production operates within, none of these have been political films, at least in the sense understood in the more combative cinema of the 1970s. Rather, the Irish films have attempted to adapt various genre conventions to the politics with generally mixed results.

Hollywood films are driven either by character (preferably involving big-name stars) or action, often involving an array of stunts and special effects. In most cases, there is a clear-cut division of labour between these two elements in establishing narrative momentum. Thus, some films are largely driven by, and some kinds of film stars largely associated with, one or other of these basic elements. Jim Sheridan's *In the Name of the Father* (1993) is character-driven, involving two high-profile stars in Daniel Day-Lewis and Emma Thompson and an array of accomplished Irish and British character actors, headed by an impressive performance from Pete Postlethwaite as Guiseppe Conlon. In adhering to this basic requirement, something has to give and in this case, it is strict documentary realism and an engagement with the politics of the situation.

Sheridan has chosen to emphasise the central father–son relationship between Guiseppe and Gerry Conlon (Day-Lewis), wrongfully convicted and imprisoned for the Guildford bombing of 1974. The film's concentration is on how their joint ordeal rescues their strained relationship, a basic reworking of father/son oedipal tensions consistent with the type of oedipal universe that underpins so much recent Irish cinema (see Chapter Eight). It also taps into a kind of 'men-without-women' prison drama genre. Gerry Conlon's imprisonment, therefore, is presented as a form of personal and spiritual redemption – a journey from petty criminal non-conformist to embracing the law of the father. The character of Guiseppe is central here.

Guiseppe's ill health and frailty is contrasted with his own inner strength and spiritual vitality. He is the centre of a film which constructs a moral rather than a political universe and in the earlier scenes Gerry's unstructured adolescent rebellion is shown to be a pathetic, self-defeating act of defiance. He is presented with three alternatives to his own dysfunctional and anti-social actions. He can bow down to the corrupt authority of the British, the first 'law of the father' which attempts to reign him in. Although his rejection of this option is never in doubt, in the moral universe which the film constructs, this is essentially a moral rather than a political choice. In the character of the British policeman Dixon (Corin Redgrave), Gerry confronts his first father figure on a journey towards moral redemption. In prison, he meets his second, in IRA leader Joe McAndrew (Don Baker), under whose influence he falls for a while. For Gerry, this is a question of virility – McAndrew's single-minded attachment to physical violence and his capacity to fight back offers a clear-cut alternative to his own father's seeming impotence in the face of adversity.

Gerry's eventual rejection of McAndrew leads him back to his own father. The moral strength of Guiseppe's pacifist resistance to injustice is finally recognised by the prodigal son. There is no moral ambiguity in Gerry's acquiescence to his father's will. The overtly religious theme is emphasised by Guiseppe's devout Catholicism (mocked earlier in the film by Gerry) and when he dies in prison at the point of Gerry's redemption, the Christian theme is complete. Indeed, Gerry's spiritual journey from the iconoclastic 1970s to the moral 1990s is marked on the soundtrack by the musical journey from Jimi Hendrix to Bono. In all the sound and fury over the film's lack of documentary realism, the fact that it is one of the most overtly Christian films to emerge in popular cinema in recent years has largely been missed.

In the Name of the Father emerges as a moral rather than a political film largely because of the narrative structure and visual style employed by Jim Sheridan. The relative underuse made here of Emma Thompson in the role of campaigning solicitor, Gareth Peirce, is significant. One could imagine a different telling of the Guildford Four story which made greater use of the investigation plot, one in which the uncovering of injustice, conspiracy and cover-up would require at least some direct encounter with the political forces which have shaped the situation in the first place. This plot device has been a staple of popular cinema over the years, using either a campaigning journalist, attorney or cop as the nemesis of injustice and corruption. The political possibilities of the device are exemplified in the French *policier*, though it has a strong pedigree in classic Hollywood cinema as well. It is Costa-Gavras' favoured narrative structure, especially in his American films like *Missing* (1981) and *The Music Box* (1989). It is most effectively employed for political purposes in his 1972 study of CIA involvement in South America, *State of Siege*. However, despite the undoubtedly key role played by the campaigners in breaking open the case, Sheridan eschews such an approach and the Thompson character is used largely as a device which allows Conlon to tell his own story, through her, to the audience. Certainly, she gets two rousing set pieces in the

Northern Irish politics as oedipal melodrama: Pete Postlethwaite and Daniel Day-Lewis in *In the Name of the Father*

film – her accidental discovery of suppressed evidence corroborating Conlon's alibi and her emotional outburst when producing this at the appeal hearing. In other regards though, the investigation plot is very much secondary to the central father–son relationship.

Visually too, Sheridan closes down the epic scale of the film after the opening scenes of street riots in Belfast. Driven by Hendrix on the soundtrack and shot with real verve and style, these scenes are myth-making cinema of a high order. After that, the film is shot largely in a shot-reverse-shot claustrophobic style, the highly stylised opening replaced by a series of head-to-head encounters between father and son in prison. Sheridan's great strength, of course, is his ability to coax convincing performances from his cast. Six Oscar nominations and two wins (Day-Lewis again and Brenda Fricker for *My Left Foot*) is a remarkable achievement in his first three films, and is testament to his years of apprenticeship in the Dublin theatre. The problem, though, is that his cinema is often very stage-bound and static. The first encounter between Gerry and Guiseppe is particularly stagey: for the benefit of the audience it relies on that old theatrical device of having one character remind the other in detail of some incident in the past which he must well remember – 'And then you said … And then you did … Remember, Da?'

These prison scenes work well enough for the oedipal tensions in the relationship and for establishing the moral universe in which these are played out. However, the resulting emphasis on character limits the political potential of the film and renders it unsatisfyingly poised between oedipal melodrama and political thriller. On the other hand, though, if the politics of the situation are subsumed under the moral universe which the film constructs, they are not entirely contained within it. There are leakages and interesting contradictions.

To understand these better, it is important to remember that *In the Name of the Father* exists in relation not only to the real world of Irish politics, but also to other cinematic representations and, indeed, to the much older traditions of representation that we looked at above. We have also noted that John Hill has carefully delineated the way in which dominant cinematic portrayals of violence work against an understanding of Irish politics and society and especially of the nature of political violence in Ireland (Hill, 1988). It could be argued that despite the creative input from Ireland, Sheridan's film, in the portrayal of IRA man McAndrew, prolongs the disabling myth that violence in Ireland is basically irrational, flowing from an innate tendency or character flaw in the national psyche.

In the film, there is no doubt that the portrayal of McAndrew, the IRA leader, is a chilling one, effectively realised by Don Baker in another acting performance that is a credit to the director. In the pivotal scene which marks Gerry Conlon's final turning-away from violence, McAndrew viciously attacks a prison officer using an ingeniously improvised blowtorch. Since the film has slowly built up audience empathy with the officer, the cold-blooded nature of this assault hits home. Audience revulsion is mirrored in Gerry's actions in going to his aid and Gerry's subsequent distancing himself from the IRA leader again reinforces the moral position that the film constructs for the audience. The fact that this attack takes place during a prison screening of Coppola's *The Godfather* (1972) is suggestive, to say the least. As we have noted, part of British government strategy over the years has been to deny that violence in Northern Ireland is politically motivated. Indeed, government ministers have consistently used terms like 'gangsterism' or more pertinently, 'Godfathers of terrorism' in condemning the IRA. The structure of this scene would seem to reinforce this attitude.

And yet, the reference to *The Godfather* suggests another reading. In *The Godfather II* (1974) Michael Corleone is in Cuba to conclude a deal with the Miami crime bosses that would carve up the island between them. At a military roadblock, he witnesses a futile act of bravery by one of Fidel Castro's young insurgents and immediately decides against the deal. These are not people he can do 'business' with, precisely because they are not gangsters. They are motivated by politics rather than the greed and self-interest that he understands. This is the situation that Harry Shand finds himself in *The Long Good Friday*, as we have seen. There is something of the same aura about McAndrew in his confrontation with a prison full of hardened criminals, seething with anti-Irish prejudice. One word in the ear of the toughest prisoner, pointing out the power of the IRA to reach his family, and the prison is his. This is not a man that mere criminals can do business with (i.e. intimidate).

McAndrew's political acumen is well established later when he effectively organises the disparate prisoners into collective action to protest at prison conditions. Thus, the film's rejection of him is not on the grounds of his criminality or gangsterism, as some critics have suggested is the implication of the reference to *The Godfather*. Rather it is a rejection of his chilling and uncompromising politics. The political motivation of the IRA is at least acknowledged in the film, a considerable departure from dominant cinematic representations.

There is one final political reference in the film which is worth mentioning. At the beginning of his incarceration, when Gerry must deal with the anti-Irish sentiment among the English prisoners, he is able to make common cause with the black West Indian inmates, who suffer similar racial abuse. There is a clear reference here to a kind of post-colonial solidarity among peripheral and marginalised cultures, like that canvassed by some of the anti-revisionist theorists discussed in Chapter Four. However, like the film's treatment of the IRA, this political notion slips out in an unguarded moment in the film's otherwise controlling moral vision. Sheridan is undoubtedly a director who has politics – this was evident years ago in his work in Dublin's avant-garde theatre – but he is not a political film-maker and *In the Name of the Father* is not a political film.

It would be churlish, however, to deny the emotional power of *In the Name of the Father* or to decry the considerable craft which went into its making. It undoubtedly succeeds in bringing the enormity of the injustice to popular cinema audiences. But its engagement with dominant narrative forms is a problem in terms of making a film about politics. This is not a new issue, of course, and in many ways it continues to have relevance for contemporary representations of violence in Ireland. The critical issue, therefore, is not the extent to which it takes licence with the facts of the real case but how its aesthetic strategies force a particular melodramatic and humanist perspective on complex historical and social debates.

Hill returned to these issues himself in discussing Ken Loach's *Hidden Agenda* (1990) in the context of this wider debate (Hill, 1991). The problem is to what extent the dominant narrative forms of cinema can be utilised for radical political messages. Loach's film deals with the 'shoot-to-kill' policy allegedly sanctioned by the security forces in Northern Ireland in the 1980s and the failure of the subsequent inquiry (the Stalker Inquiry) to satisfactorily resolve the issue. It mobilises a political thriller format and, for Hill, herein lies the problem. The fundamental issue is whether thrillers make good politics and Hill instances the problems raised by the thriller form itself. 'Hollywood's narrative conventions characteristically encourage explanations of social realities in individual and psychological terms rather than economic and political ones ... (and) also inevitably attach a greater significance to interpersonal relations than social, economic and political structures' (Hill, 1991, p. 38). The result, as far as *Hidden Agenda* is concerned, is that the deeper political issues are rendered as rather implausible conspiracies (in narrative terms) involving criminally inclined individuals – political villainy and personal unpleasantness are thus conflated. Hill ends up canvassing, not the revolutionary avant-garde cinema of the 1960s and 1970s, but a form of 'Third Cinema' that will be discussed in more detail in Chapter Five. As we shall see, though, neither the funding nor the distribution environment is sympathetic to even this kind of cinema today. Those film-makers anxious to deal with political issues (whether Northern Ireland or not) are driven back, time and again, to a reliance on adapting popular forms for their purposes. Jim Sheridan and his production company Hell's Kitchen have now made a number of such attempts. If Loach had attempted to mobilise the thriller format, Sheridan and his collaborators have favoured a more melodramatic form.

Some Mother's Son (1996) and *The Boxer* (1997)

Writing about what he saw as the shortcomings of television drama which dealt with the 'troubles' in Northern Ireland, radical journalist Eamon McCann noted that 'since television drama must by its nature personalise issues, the standard theme, upon which variations are played, is of personal relationships being ripped apart by the sectarian divide' (McCann, 1988, p. 18). This inevitably led to a preponderance of 'Romeo and Juliet' scenarios that never came close to dealing meaningfully with the politics of the situation. What was needed, McCann argued, was an approach that looked more deeply *into* aspects of the situation, rather than an approach that looked *across* the conflicting divide. He suggested that such a drama could and should be made about the conflicting pressures and emotions which the mother of a dying hunger-striker must have had to endure (ibid.). In 1988, the idea seemed far-fetched, given that broadcasters and film-funders were hardly likely to touch such an emotive and controversial topic. It is a measure of how much the climate has changed since the peace process began in 1993 that Terry George, who co-wrote *In the Name of the Father* with Jim Sheridan, could produce just such a drama eight years later.

He wrote and directed *Some Mother's Son*, based on the 1981 hunger strikes, which follows the dilemma facing two mothers as they face up to the imminent deaths of their hunger-striking sons. Film drama, no less than television, depends on personalising issues and the dramatic device that George employs is a variation on the theme of 'relationships ripped apart'. Like *In the Name of the Father*, the film approaches the controversial politics of the subject matter obliquely. If the previous film erected a father/son oedipal drama as the hook on which to hang the narrative, here George constructs a maternal melodrama through which he attempts to explore the complexities of the hunger strike. Helen Mirren plays Kathleen, the politically naive mother of Gerald Quigley (Aidan Gillen), an IRA prisoner who shares a cell with Bobby Sands (John Lynch) and follows him on to the hunger strike in protest at the government's criminalisation policy. Kathleen's experience is contrasted with that of the more politically aware Annie Higgins, whose son Frank (David O'Hara) is also on hunger strike and whose family has a long history of active involvement in republican politics.

Although the film shows how these two women from very different backgrounds eventually come to share an understanding born of their shared anguish, the film also shows the contrasting responses of the mothers. As George himself says of the basic scenario,

> The women in the film are fair representations of a type of woman, a type of mother that I was familiar with in the nationalist community. They just represent two strands of women, mothers whose families are involved politically and support the various strands of the republican movement as opposed to women who, because of the negative aspects of politics in Northern Ireland, have no interest and have a deep aversion to politics and try to keep their family away from it ... (McSwiney, 1996, p. 11)

The scenario is important for a number of reasons. As McCann has indicated, the need to personalise is at the centre of drama and conflict is at the centre of personalised issues. The contrast allows the film to engage the dilemma facing the mothers from different, though internal, positions raising the conflict within each of the mothers to a political level. If the impact of republican politics on women is an issue, then the film shows that these women are not mere passive observers but are centrally involved and that the conflict has an impact on them in different ways. As John Hill has noted, the film belongs to a longstanding tradition that goes back to Sean O'Casey of contrasting the humanity and common sense of women to the unyielding and destructive fanaticism of men (Hill, 1996, p. 44). Yet, this is vitiated in two ways. First, through its opening coda showing the election victory of Margaret Thatcher and in the many references to her through her representatives in Northern Ireland, the fanaticism and unyielding attitude is clearly linked also to one particularly powerful woman, albeit, one who remains off screen for the rest of the film. As George himself asserts, 'Basically, the hunger strike was about winning and losing. Thatcher had to win. … She became the iron lady on the basis of that one battle' (McSwiney, 1996, p. 17). Second, in the character of Annie Higgins, the film clearly demonstrates a different female engagement with male intransigence, one in which the political principle at stake is more important than the humanitarian issue of her son's life.

On the other hand, Kathleen is the centre of the drama, as Hill rightly notes, and the film's emotional power rests on its ability to tap into the universal pathos that the tragic mother inspires. It is this pathos, more than anything else, which ratchets up the emotion to an almost unbearable level and this is even more pronounced by the fact that the film is remarkably restrained in its treatment of the actual physical debilitation of the hunger strikers themselves. It is, in other words, a canny attempt at making mass entertainment out of a complex political situation and it works remarkably well despite the thin line it has to negotiate. Inevitably, the film loses focus on the actual politics themselves. As Hill concludes '… it is arguably too much a film of remembrance and pathos, one which has avoided making the past fully resonate for the present by rather too readily side-stepping the difficult challenges presented by the current political situation' (Hill, 1996, p. 45). George, though, plausibly argues that the story of the hunger strikes does have a contemporary relevance. In the end, as the film so graphically shows, the final showdown between government and the hunger strikers revolved around a formulation of words, much as each stage of the peace process has been similarly dogged by the interpretation of words.

> The end of this film is both analogous to and almost a mirror image of what's happening at the moment … the attempts to resolve the hunger strikes fell down over the interpretation of certain words … We need to fight out this battle of ideas and beliefs in the arts: in films, theatre, books, literature, debate and take it off the street … (McSwiney, 1996, p. 17

In a sense, then, it is the words – the high emotional melodrama of words – that drives *Some Mother's Son*. Just as the film-makers in *In the Name of the Father* could not replicate the sheer emotional intensity of the news pictures of Gerry Conlon's statement on his release from prison, so in this film, they cannot replicate the visual impact that the images of the actual hunger strike had on an international audience. In many ways the film is rather coy about the iconography of the hunger strikes and the film, competent and efficient though it is at conveying the emotion, is visually dull and conventional.

George collaborated with Jim Sheridan again on *The Boxer* and, interestingly, here the visualisation, directed by Sheridan this time, is much richer and more expressive. *The Boxer* is another melodramatic approach to the politics of Northern Ireland, personalised in the story of Danny Flynn (Daniel Day-Lewis) who, after spending fourteen years in prison, attempts to restart his life by taking up boxing, which was his adolescent passion. This passion was shared, though, with his love for Maggie (Emily Watson), daughter of IRA leader Joe Hamill (Brian Cox). Maggie is married to Danny's best friend of their teenage years, who is now himself in prison. Needless to say, Danny attempts to restart his relationship with Maggie as well, very much a taboo in the sharply defined morality of republican Belfast. This peculiarly narrow set of relationships is as unlikely as it is excessive and points up the other approach to melodrama that the film taps into – overwrought and intense relationships among family and friends within a claustrophobic community. And yet, the fact that Danny and Maggie are forbidden by the strict codes of republican sexual morality from consummating their love means that their relationship is peculiarly cold and unemotional. It is a relationship that is patrolled and constantly under surveillance by neighbours, the IRA, Maggie's son and even the protagonists themselves in their emotional reserve (in this regard it echoes the themes of Orla Walsh's short film *The Visit* [1992], discussed in Chapter Seven).

What is most interesting about *The Boxer*, therefore, is its manipulation of topography and space to create the resulting claustrophobia. The film visualises a Belfast of the imagination that has neither sweep nor realistic geography and yet does so in an intensely cinematic manner. A helicopter constantly hovers over the action and much of the film's action scenes are filmed using helicopter or crane shots, giving the impression that in the constricted space of the city the only freedom is upwards. Space is manipulated in the IRA's secret meeting places in the houses and clubs, hidden entrances and exits open up from behind furniture or false walls. The whole city seems to consist of one block of flats in which everyone lives and fights and conspires and one square in which all the action takes place. Journeys outward are through barriers that give way from republican to loyalist areas within a few yards and a sign welcomes the visitor to loyalist East Belfast like some kind of Irish 'Checkpoint Charlie'. Such is the claustrophobic intimacy of the city that Danny and Maggie are spotted almost as soon as they cross this checkpoint and only Danny's association with boxing – that which can unite the warring sides – saves them from an untimely end. When Ike's body is dumped in open ground, it is visible to everyone in the close community and one gets the feeling that it might be too to the citizens of 'East Belfast' just beyond 'Checkpoint Charlie'. Such is the smallness of this world that it is also no surprise that Ike should know the murdered RUC officer and that he had a wife and two children. Sheridan pays so little attention to the actual sectarian geography of Belfast that the world he creates is almost beyond rational criticism. In a melodrama singularly lacking in emotion (one, indeed, in which the inability to express emotion is a theme) the excess that melodrama depends on comes through the *mise en scène* and cinematography. Thus, while the film's geography of the imagination is impressive cinematically and highly enjoyable in a perverse sense, it is ludicrous in terms of realism. In many ways this sums up the film's whole grasp of the reality of the politics of the North.

The film almost acknowledges this too. In the scene where Danny fights for the first time at the inaugural programme of the reopened gym, his old trainer Ike (Ken Stott) reads out the names of former boxers, Catholic and Protestant, members of Danny's club, who died in the Troubles. He welcomes back the Protestant parents of one of these dead boxers and asks for a round of applause. The hardline IRA man, Harry (Gerard McSorley) mutters, 'Sentimental shite!' – and of course it is. There is a sense here in which Sheridan is trying to have it both ways, subscribing to the attractive aspects of this sentimentality and yet taking his distance from it. This sentimentality (really, wishful thinking) is repeated in an even more excessive manner later on. The film's manipulation of space logically ends up with half the IRA in the same room as half the city's loyalist paramilitaries, both there to cheer on Danny in his big professional debut. This reimagined geography also logically means that when IRA leader Joe Hamill walks into the hall, he is immediately recognised by all the Catholics, who cheer and by all the Protestants who boo and hiss. As the whole audience sing out 'Danny Boy' in unison, there are two striking cut-aways from the crowd to show two faces in close up. One is painted in the green, white and orange of republicanism and the other in the red, white and blue of loyalism and both are singing the song heartily (even reverentially).

We do not get the advantage of Harry's earthy judgment on this scene but sentimentality is not the word to describe it. This is a scene of such crass impossibility that it almost defies belief. In many ways it is as removed from reality as the geography of the city is and maybe it is logical within the particularly confined world that the film constructs. It is, however, a scene straight out of the optimist's book of wishful thinking and reflects the level at which the film deals with the politics of Northern Ireland. Again, though, the film undermines its own belief in the scene when the evening ends up in a full-scale riot following Harry's unsanctioned bomb attack on the RUC's 'community relations officer'.

Harry's renegade IRA man is a familiar character by now. He is opposed to all compromise and in the lineage of James Cagney in *Shake Hands with the Devil* and Sean Bean in *Patriot Games*, Gerard McSorley plays him with cold-blooded relish. Also in the tradition of both *Patriot Games* and *Blown Away*, the character of Harry is contrasted to the more sympathetic and more flexible IRA leader, Joe Hamill, reconfirming the post-ceasefire politics of the film that the only way forward is through compromise and accommodation. However, given the incredible lack of emotion in the central love relationship between Johnny and Maggie, albeit explained by the particular sexual politics that operate around prisoners' wives in the republican heartland of Belfast, the film fails as melodrama. Its flight from realism leaves its treatment of politics stranded close to the absurd, without making this pay off in any illuminating way. In this regard, despite its more conventional style, *Some Mother's Son* emerges as the more convincing film.

Finally, it is worth mentioning a number of other films that emerged from within Northern Ireland in one way or another and which have attempted to offer a different perspective on the violence. Thaddeus O'Sullivan's *Nothing Personal* (1995) was written by Daniel Mornin from his own novel and Marc Evans' *Resurrection Man* (1998) was scripted by Eoin MacNamee, also from his own novel of the same name. Both deal with loyalist paramilitary violence and are noteworthy for this fact alone. Two factors in particular are relevant here. First, there has been a paucity of film material which has dealt with the unionists in Northern Ireland in any capacity at all. The majority of screen representations are either about nationalist culture in the south or about republican, as opposed to loyalist, paramilitaries in the north. In one sense this has had a detrimental effect on the unionist political position, which has been largely underrepresented, thus confirming the siege mentality of the unionist community that comes from its sense of isolation. On the other hand, the unrelieved concentration on the IRA has given the impression that the violence in the North has been entirely the fault of republicans, and the loyalist community, by dint of its being ignored, has largely escaped scrutiny. Second, in his analysis of screen representations of the violence in Northern Ireland, John Hill had to deal with the films that had been made and his critique, therefore, operated only as far as representations of republican violence were concerned. Indeed, Hill noted the absence of screen representations of Protestants as a problem as far back as 1987 (Hill, 1988, p. 191, note 68) and more recently, Brian McIlroy has explored this absence through a pro-unionist critique of many of the same films discussed by Hill (McIlroy, 1998). How relevant, then, are Hill's conclusions to representations of loyalist violence as they have emerged in recent years?

The first significant film to deal with Protestant culture in the North is Thaddeus O'Sullivan's earlier *December Bride* (1990), which we discuss in Chapter Ten (and see also a more detailed analysis in McLoone, 1999). What distinguishes this film is its reworking of landscape in Ireland and its great strength is that it does so visually. The same careful concern with visualisation is obvious in *Nothing Personal*, though this time, the world reimagined is an urban setting of streets, alleyways and dingy clubs, the backstreet Belfast of 1975. But the film demonstrates the same kind of visual flair in its rendition of 'streetscape' as O'Sullivan brought to the landscapes of *December Bride*. In many ways, O'Sullivan plays with the geography of Belfast in a way that is similar to Sheridan in *The Boxer*, but with the greater control the film exudes there is more credibility about this Belfast of the imagination that he creates. The city here becomes a warren of indistinguishable streets dominated by the outside shell of a gasometer and barricaded off to keep sectarian factions apart. The constriction suggests a confined set which is then opened up cinematically through a system of backlights, floods and shadows. The whole 'set' is suffused in a ghostly blue light, sometimes further enhanced by mist drifting across the background. In other words, this is a highly stylised version of Belfast (actually shot around the streets of Ringsend in Dublin) and, incredibly, is both highly theatrical and cinematic at the same time.

Against this rich visual background, O'Sullivan plays out a complicated set of plots and subplots that look at the effects of violence across three generations of interrelated characters. The main plot is centred on a gang of loyalist gunmen, barely under the control of their more politically motivated commander Leonard (Michael Gambon). Leonard attempts to work out a ceasefire with his IRA counterpart Cecil (Gerard McSorley again) and to set 'civilised' ground rules for conducting their conflict. The young hotheads on either side are unimpressed by these peace moves and seethe and posture in the background. On the loyalist side, Leonard's main lieutenant is the attractive and charismatic Kenny (James Frain) whose own lieutenant is the clearly disturbed Ginger (Ian Hart). Ginger just hates Catholics and takes great pleasure in killing and mutilating them. As played by Hart, he is a twitchy, uncontrollable psychopath and though he is allowed one speech in which to articulate a crude loyalist politic, he is clearly in the same lineage as so many republican psychopaths and renegades down the years. The IRA does not have a monopoly on dangerous renegades.

The message of the film is the standard humanist moral about the ultimate futility and corruption of violence. This message is carried by the children in the film, who are at the edges of the adult violence, the girls appalled and disgusted by it, the boys enviously looking in from the outside. However, the future lies with them. This is most clearly articulated in the subplot involving Tommy (Rúaidhrí Conroy). He begins the evening in rapt hero-worship of Kenny, but, after a night 'on the town' with him and Ginger, is so disgusted and disturbed that we can safely assume that he has been turned away from violence for life. (Interestingly, there is a clear implication that Kenny invites Tommy along hoping for precisely that outcome.)

In an earlier scene, Tommy gets an insight into the negative effect that violence has on relationships and the family. He walks a young girl, Gloria, home from the drinking club and as she gives him a goodnight kiss, she feels the gun Kenny has given him stuck into the back of his belt. She removes it, puts it on the ground and invites Tommy to choose between the gun and another goodnight kiss. When Tommy chooses the gun, she walks away. Tommy still has a learning curve to negotiate, one that the extreme violence of Ginger later in the evening will provide. This association of women with love as opposed to the violence of the men is paralleled on the Catholic side by Kathleen's similar response to the teenage Michael. In the opening sequences of the film we find out that Kenny's commitment to violence has alienated his wife, Ann, and, to hammer home the point about the nurturing and loving nature of the female, Ann happens also to be a nurse.

Through all the mayhem of one mad night of violence, Kathleen's father Liam (John Lynch) wanders from disaster to disaster, being taken care of after one beating by Kenny's estranged wife and finally being picked up by Ginger and Kenny and badly beaten again. In one more of the film's many plot contrivances, Kenny and Liam turn out to be old friends from a time before the Troubles when Protestant and Catholic kids could play together. This precipitates Kenny's final break with the uncontrollable Ginger that ends in Kathleen's death and that of Kenny and Ginger. It is an ending of melodramatic excess that mirrors the torturous complex of subplots that drive the film's humanist message.

We are used now to the device of contrasting the 'good terrorist' with the renegade and here the film lays out a variation on the theme. Ironically, it turns out to be a version of the Frankenstein myth. The older commanders on both sides – Leonard and Cecil – are shown to be reasonable men driven by their convictions but clearly also still in touch with their humanity. Leonard thinks that Ginger is a 'nauseating wee shite' and he remarks to Kenny, 'Don't you think things are bad enough without men behaving like beasts?' The problem is that the older men like him have unleashed the beasts like Ginger and are rapidly losing control of them. There are no politics in the film as such. It is a group of loyalists at the centre of the narrative but all that this means is that the iconography behind them is different. In the end, the film merely confirms the impression that the violence is a fault of the people themselves and that the fatal flaw of the Irish is also a fatal flaw of the loyalists. The role that the British might play in the turmoil is never broached. Despite its impressively atmospheric cinematography, *Nothing Personal* says little that is new about Northern Ireland and does this by employing yet again many of the traditional tropes of cinema's treatment of Northern Ireland.

In *Resurrection Man*, the characters of Ginger and Kenny are combined to chilling effect in Stuart Townsend's portrayal of Victor Kelly, a 'Shankill butcher' psychopath. Victor is as handsome and as charismatic as Kenny and likes to mutilate his Catholic victims with colder and more calculating pleasure than does Ginger. The only explanation offered for his almost vampiric love of Fenian blood is his 'mammy's boy' oedipal problem with his ineffectual

Catholic father. Ashamed of his Catholic taint, Victor must prove his Protestant credentials in ever increasing extremes. However, given that this irrational pleasure for Catholic blood is a response to his own Catholic father, then each atrocity he commits is both an act of symbolic patricide and a demonstration of self-loathing. Beyond that, the film says nothing about the politics of Northern Ireland and perhaps it does not set out to do so. What we get is a portrait of a man and a society deeply immersed in unmotivated violence and almost incomprehensible evil.

At the beginning of the film there is a brief scene from Victor's childhood. He is in the projection box at a cinema with his father who is talking to the projectionist, an old friend, about some tragedy involving a fifteen-year-old Catholic girl who died giving birth. Victor watches the film from the projection box – a scene involving James Cagney in *The Public Enemy* (1931). This reference to Cagney's psychopathic persona is hardly unusual but it establishes one of Victor's role models and links the film to a long cinematic tradition. As Victor succeeds in the world of loyalist paramilitaries so he, like Cagney's gangster, begins to enjoy the power and wealth that comes with it. He is, however, used and manipulated by an equally squalid and sinister operator, McClure (Sean McGinley), who seems to lack any conviction other than a sexual perversity that mirrors his admiration for the Nazis. This, in other words, is a view from the extremes of human depravity, shot in a cold and claustrophobic manner that perfectly catches its despairing nihilism. In the world of genre cinema, such a cold-blooded psychopath is usually pursued by a cop or a journalist who provides a kind of moral centre to the film. In *Resurrection Man* this role is taken by drunken journalist Ryan (James Nesbitt), who is shown to be as complicit as anyone else in this bleak world. He is slowly sucked into the violence and ends up as compromised as Victor and as vulnerable to McClure's machinations. Ryan's own marriage foundered when he beat up his wife after one of his binges. There are no redeeming characters in this bleak universe.

In all these films, then, there is little progress in the representation of Northern Ireland and no advance on a dominant tendency just because the central characters are loyalists. Indeed, the opposite is the case. Because they are loyalists, it is difficult for either film to offer even the excuse of a political idealism that has gone wrong, so often the theme of IRA films. Loyalist idealism is seemingly resistant to representation and both films collapse into psychopathology in their exploration and depiction of the violence. In many ways they confirm a dominant mode of representing loyalism – a fascism singularly prone to human depravity and signally deficient in even the pretence of political idealism. This might satisfy the expectations of republican and nationalist prejudices as well but the enduring mood of these films is that of a whole society which has fallen below the civilised standards of rational behaviour. It

The ultimate psychopathic loyalist: Stuart Townsend in *Resurrection Man*

is the return of a series of age-old representations that are bedecked in contemporary garb and produced with at least a modicum of local input. They are,
however, ultimately as debilitating as any set of images that have emanated from
foreign productions and are all the more disappointing for this.

The drunken journalist is the catalyst in David Caffrey's *Divorcing Jack*
(1998) and the bleak pessimism of a society beyond morality is the setting for
Colm Villa's *Sunset Heights* (1997). Both these films exist in an uneasy relationship to the late 1990s zeitgeist established by Danny Boyle's *Trainspotting*
(1996): *Divorcing Jack* in trying to tap into it and *Sunset Heights* in studiously
opposing it. Caffrey's film is written by Colin Bateman, based on his novel of
the same name. The film attempts to capture both the anarchic humour and
energy of the novel and at the same time the blackly humorous world of
Trainspotting, where a serious topic is treated with an irreverent and challenging black humour. *Divorcing Jack* almost succeeds in this but the complexities
of Northern Ireland and the tragedies that its political instability has engendered are simply not amenable to this brand of irreverent humour. The film
is aware of the problem to some extent (there is a blackly humorous joke in
the film that highlights the difficulty of knowing when to joke and knowing
when to laugh). In many ways, the film is just not irreverent enough and falls
into a kind of limbo that is halfway towards being the kind of scabrous comedy it set out to be. *Sunset Heights*, on the other hand, is a very bleak and
pessimistic film indeed that lacks any (intentional) humour. Set in some kind

of post-apocalyptic near future it is a strange mixture of moral degeneration and pagan ritual. Visually, it offers some interestingly different iconography and settings and evokes an almost pagan atmosphere of ghostly apparitions and Halloween spookiness. In doing so, however, it then ends up promoting a familiar image of a Northern Ireland caught in a cycle of aimless violence of its own making, devoid of political or historical context.

Perhaps these are the true reflections of peace process Northern Ireland. As the political situation grows more hopeful and the ceasefires continue to hold then culture in general and film in particular can begin to deal with the suppressed horror of the recent past. These bleak visions could only come out of a situation that is seen to be improving. Thus the cinema of the peace process is bleak in direct proportion to the optimism that is in the air. The fact of the peace process has allowed commercial cinema, and the state-funded partnerships that operate from within commercial cinema's universal embrace, to open up a space where the legacy of thirty years of violence in Northern Ireland can be represented. However, the cinema that has so far emerged, with minor exceptions in the case of a number of films, has largely played on the existing traditions of representing violence, offering only a variety of generic conventions from the thriller, the melodrama and the horror film to recycle the myth of atavism. In most cases, it is not just that the films are determinedly apolitical, more that they are studiously anti-political. Their humanist message (that violence is corrupting and self-defeating) is banal in its common-sense obviousness and their exploration of political context is non-existent. In the end, this cinema's relationship to the present is that it reminds us of the past and so underpins the necessity for continuing the search for peace. That this is the extent of its political sophistication is disappointing and only reinforces the feeling that cinema in general today, including Europe's state-subsidised national cinemas, has lost its ability or its potential for radical political and social analysis (a point which is elaborated on in Chapter Five).

Chapter 4
Modernisation and Cultural Ferment

In a special supplement on Irish cinema in the journal *Cinéaste*, film-maker Bob Quinn observes rather acidly, 'Now that this country has finally shed its antediluvian religious beliefs, its national identity, its sense of personal and communal responsibility, its ethical inhibitions, its political sovereignty, even its own currency, all those things that retarded it for so long, the future glows with promise' (Quinn, 1999, p. 73). In his heavily ironic style, Quinn indicates rather well the scale of change that has taken place in Ireland since the 1960s. Economic growth and a process of modernisation were originally stimulated in 1959 by a change of direction from the protectionist policies of the previous four decades. Although progress was slow and spasmodic until the late 1980s, in the 1990s, Ireland consistently produced the highest rates of economic growth in the European Union and moved into an era of affluence and prosperity that has brought its standard of living into line with European norms (Sweeney, 1998, p. 3). Inevitably, such rapid economic growth has wrought profound changes on the social and political structure of contemporary Ireland, at the same time engendering what in effect has been a considerable cultural ferment in which the fundamental principles of Irish identity are debated. This anxiety over definitions of Irishness has a double focus.

On one hand, it looks inwards to Ireland itself and, as Quinn indicates, is concerned with the relationship of contemporary Ireland to its own past – a past built on its nationalist identity and the long political and cultural struggle for independence. The focus here is on the relationship between tradition and modernity, the one handed down by Ireland's nationalist past, the other resulting from its newly gained position within the global culture of capitalism. The other focus, therefore, is inevitably on Ireland's relationship to the outside world, especially to the centres of both economic and cultural power in the USA and Britain. 'Ireland', Quinn observes with some exasperation, 'is now a backlot of New York, Los Angeles and London' (Quinn, 1999, p. 73). As a film-maker, Quinn is primarily concerned with the cinematic aspect of this relationship. His polemic is derived from the perception that contemporary film-making in Ireland, benefiting from a more industrial infrastructure than was available in the 1970s and 1980s, and responding to the demands of the country's recently won position within the global marketplace, has become increasingly commercial in its orientation and less concerned with addressing specifically Irish audiences through Irish themes.

Bob Quinn is one of Ireland's leading indigenous film-makers, with a remarkable body of challenging work that stretches back to the early 1970s. He is also one of the country's most acerbic commentators and has been a consistent critic of many aspects of Ireland's economic development. Much of his polemic is carefully and astutely directed against the worst excesses of commercialisation and consumerism. (In 1998, for example, he resigned from the Board of RTÉ, the national broadcaster, in protest at the amount of advertising broadcast during children's programming.) In his own films, however, he has been equally trenchant and polemical about the banalities and absurdities of traditional Ireland. He has, himself, delivered a few well-aimed blows against the hypocrisies of Catholic Ireland as well as the romantic rural sense of identity it once sustained (*The Bishop's Story* [1994] released in earlier versions as *Budawanny* [1987] and *Poitín* [1978]). He has explored the nature of Irish ethnic identity with great wit and some considerable mischief, undermining the more purist versions of Irishness implicit in much of Irish cultural nationalism (*Atlantean* [1984]; *Navigatio* [1999]).

Quinn and his films, in other words, exist in an intensely contradictory relationship to both tradition and modernity and, as such, they reflect the complexity of cultural debate in Ireland generally. For Quinn, something is inevitably lost when something is gained. What has been lost may or may not be missed but what has been gained may well have brought with it as many problems as it has solved. Not everything, therefore, about 'tradition' is necessarily regressive ('ethical inhibitions', 'personal and communal responsibilities', 'political sovereignty' and 'sense of national identity') and not every aspect of 'modernity' is to be uncritically welcomed (individualism, consumerism, integration into global capitalism). The inventory of change and development needs to be monitored constantly, the impact on society carefully assessed. If the nation was imagined originally according to the principles of Irish-Ireland nationalism, it is being reimagined today in light of modernisation and the impact of global forces. A critical approach to the latter is as important as a critique of the former. The resulting debate about culture and identity touches all aspects of Irish creative and critical endeavour and has been further energised in recent years by the success in the international arena of Irish culture of all kinds – literature, drama, dance and especially popular music. What is perhaps new is that Irish cinema, one result of the modernising process, has now begun to contribute to this cultural ferment, a remarkable achievement given that, for most of the last hundred years, it was a very poor relation indeed compared to Irish achievements in the other arts.

That this has changed in the 1990s is due in no small measure to the pioneering group of film-makers in the 1970s and early 1980s, like Bob Quinn, who, as they struggled in a relative cinematic vacuum to get their own films made, also lobbied long and hard for the establishment of an infrastructure that would allow a film culture in Ireland to emerge. In this regard as well, Quinn's ironic response to contemporary Ireland is significant. If film-making in Ireland exists in relation to other aspects of Irish culture, it, nonetheless, has a special relationship to the cinema globally and to Hollywood cinema in particular. As Irish film-making began to develop it was bound to respond, consciously or not, to the pre-existing representations of the Irish that had emerged originally as a result of the Irish diaspora, especially in the case of Hollywood. In other words, as the lobbyists of the 1970s and early 1980s argued, film is both an industry and an expression of national culture, however this might be defined. Ireland needed not just the economic infrastructure that would allow a film industry to emerge but also the critical and educational infrastructure that would ensure that film *production* happened in a wider film *culture*.

The first sustained film-making in Ireland since the 1910s began tentatively in the 1970s as part of wider cultural changes wrought by the modernisation process. The changes initiated by the new policies of the 1950s were in essence consistent for the next forty years. The results, however, were mixed. In retrospect, we can see that this period falls into three distinct phases, each having significant impact on the social and cultural climate in Ireland in general and is reflected in the growth and content of Irish cinema in particular. The first period from 1958 to 1978 is characterised by a then unprecedented growth in the economy and the beginnings of a wholesale reimagining of Ireland and Irishness that reflected the optimism and innovation of the times. The second period, from 1978 to 1988, in contrast, is characterised by a prolonged economic recession and a particularly acrimonious period of social and political controversy. The third period, beginning in 1988, witnessed a spectacular economic recovery that coincided with an unprecedented run of success internationally for Irish culture of all kinds, including film-making. This economic success has given rise to the sobriquet the 'Celtic Tiger' to describe Ireland's increasingly vigorous and assertive presence on the world stage and needless to say has energised internal debate more completely than even the years of gloom had done.

Economic Performance 1958–2000

By the end of the 1950s Ireland was languishing far behind every other stable democracy in Europe in terms of economic growth and prosperity. In fact, it could proudly boast the worst economic record in Europe in the twentieth century (Ó'Gráda, 1997, p. 27). A mood of deep pessimism hung over the country and emigration, as we have seen, reached crisis proportions. As one commentator characterised the situation, while the rest of Europe boomed and progressed, Ireland economically, politically, and in every other way 'was dozing on the sideline' (Ó'Gráda, 1997, p. 25). Something radical needed to be done. A hard-hitting analysis of the failures of the Irish economy, *Economic Development*, was published in 1958, the work of the Secretary of the Department of Finance, T. K. Whittaker. In the following year, de Valera resigned as Taoiseach (Prime Minister) and was replaced by Sean Lemass. The *First Programme for Economic Expansion* that followed ushered in a new era in which many of Whittaker's policy options were embraced with remarkable results. The 'Lemass Era' lasted until 1966 and changed the Irish economy profoundly. As Cormac Ó'Gráda puts it, these years 'established some patterns that would prove enduring: a commitment to outward-looking policies, a less restrictive fiscal stance, a willingness to experiment, an economic growth that would make Ireland a largely urban society and would erode the importance of the agricultural sector and the farming lobby' (Ó'Gráda, 1997, p. 30).

The new strategy was based on the abandonment of protectionist economic policies (the 'Sinn Féin' policies first articulated at the end of the nineteenth century) and the embracing of free trade and foreign investment. The results were impressive during the 1960s and early 1970s. By the end of the 1960s, nearly four hundred foreign firms had begun operations in Ireland, boosting exports, employment and income levels. Between 1960 and 1973, economic growth averaged 4.4 per cent per year and, in 1966, the first growth in population since the Famine was recorded, reflecting that the greater optimism and prosperity had finally stopped the 'mass expulsion' of emigration. Belatedly, Ireland had joined in the post-war boom in Europe and began to make up the ground lost during the years of stagnation (Ó'Gráda, 1997, pp. 74–9; Sweeney, 1998, pp. 32–9).

Immense problems still remained, of course. There continued to be large pockets of both urban and rural deprivation and inevitably the modernisation programme had a rather heavy impact on these areas to the considerable detriment of traditional modes and practices. The steady drift from the land only exacerbated the problems in the city. Dublin in particular suffered from an acute housing shortage in the 1960s and this was thrown into sharp relief by the rampant property speculation that characterised the times. This urban and housing chaos forms the context for Cathal Black's first feature film *Pigs* (1984). There were, throughout this period, intermittent campaigns against censorship, against compulsory Irish and other aspects of the education system, in favour of changing the laws on contraception and the ban on divorce and in support of a more developed and caring welfare state. The first flush of film-making in the 1970s tackled many of these issues as cinema in Ireland finally developed a critical social agenda. As in many other parts of the developed West in these years, a revitalised women's movement conducted the agitation on a lot of these issues. Indeed, one of the characteristics of the politics of the modernisation era is that issues around women's rights and legislative control of women's bodies became increasingly central to the ideological struggle over the new Ireland. This reached its crisis point in the 1980s and is the subject matter of some of the best feminist films to emerge in later years.

The biggest political problem facing the Republic of Ireland from 1968 onwards, however, was the spillover from political turmoil and violence in Northern Ireland and this was to have a profound impact on the nature of political and cultural debate. A basic contradiction was set in train. Despite the South's nationalist credentials and aspirations towards a united Ireland, its economic policy was geared to a European future and an accommodation with the 'traditional enemy' in Britain. The political turmoil in Northern Ireland came to be seen increasingly as an embarrassment to the modernising impulses in the South. If the first revisionist impulses in Irish political culture came as a result of the abandonment of Sinn Féin economics and the internationalisation of the economy, then the conflict in Northern Ireland added considerably to the country's reassessment and rethinking of its nationalist heritage. The conflicting demands of international and national perspectives have characterised Irish culture ever since. The resulting debate has hung heavily over all aspects of politics and cultural production in the South and has been a key theme in much of Irish cinema.

And yet, despite the problems that remained and the new issues that were thrown up, this first period of modernisation is marked by a sense of change and optimism. Ireland voted overwhelmingly to join the EEC in 1973 and the impetus of this kept the economy moving forward until the late 1970s.

However, the project of modernising the economy ran into severe difficulties between 1977 and 1987. Growth slowed down considerably in the mid-1970s as successive oil-price increases resulted in a world recession. This was compounded in 1977 when an incoming Fianna Fáil administration introduced a series of economic policies that Ó'Gráda has described as extravagant and irresponsible (Ó'Gráda, 1997, p. 30). Wild electioneering promises and short-term election fixes replaced the policy of medium- and long-term planning that had been inaugurated by the Whittaker strategy of 1958. In a situation in which Ireland still had a relatively underdeveloped welfare state and an inadequate income tax regime the results for public finances were disastrous.

Another period of prolonged economic gloom followed, with high levels of inflation and unemployment and a consequent return to mass emigration. Between 1979 and 1985 private consumption barely rose and unemployment rose from 7.8 per cent to 18.2 per cent. The depth of the recession, as always in Ireland, can best be illustrated by looking at the emigration rates. While the figures for the 1970s show a net inflow to Ireland of 104,000 those for the 1980s show a net outflow of 208,000 (Sweeney, 1998, p. 33). It is hardly surprising that many commentators during the 1980s felt that the modernisation project had failed and that the country had slipped back into the depressing past that so many had felt was left behind in the dark 1950s. Again, the social and cultural implications of this new period of economic stagnation were significant. The inadequacies of the tax regime gave rise to militant trade union activity and a widening antagonism between rural and urban Ireland. Bolstered by the Pope's visit of September 1979, the forces of Catholic traditionalism and social reaction launched a determined campaign to push back the liberal reforms ushered in during the previous two decades of modernisation and to stem the tide of secularisation. This was, however, matched by an equally determined liberal and progressive alliance intent on consolidating and pushing forward the modernisation gains already achieved. The halting pace of the modernisation process, coupled with frustration and exasperation about the continuing crisis in Northern Ireland, also witnessed a consolidation of renewed nationalist sentiment and the beginnings of a more vigorous challenge to the liberal modernisers (in academic and intellectual circles, if not in popular consciousness). The period, therefore, is also characterised by a particularly acrimonious set of political, social and religious controversies and the sedate pace of internal reassessment turned increasingly into a bitter ideological struggle.

From 1988 on, however, the Irish economy has boomed to such an extent that the economic growth of the 1960s now looks sluggish and unimpressive. Growth in the ten years to 1998 averaged 5 per cent per year. The pace of this growth quickened as the 1990s developed, reaching an astonishing 10 per cent in 1995 and averaging 7.5 per cent in the four years to the end of 1997 (Sweeney, 1998, p. 1). The 1999 figures from the Economic and Social Research Institute (ESRI) estimate that growth in 1998 and 1999 was 8.1 per cent and 7.25 per cent respectively (ESRI, 1999, p. 1). This has far surpassed that of all other countries in the European Union and has been consistently higher than both the US economy and the so-called 'Tiger' economies of Asia. The ESRI forecast is that the Irish economy will continue to grow at a faster rate than most of its European partners for the first decade of the new century, slowing down to the European average by 2010. This forecast confirms the growing international consensus that Ireland's economic growth is more than a passing aberration or merely a long-delayed 'catch-up' spurt. It has been real, sustained and deeply grounded and is likely to continue for some time to come.

The surging economy has reduced unemployment substantially and the ESRI forecast for 2000 is that it will have fallen to 4.9 per cent, the lowest figure for many decades and well below the EU average. Significant in the growth of employment is the number of women entering the paid labour force on a full-time as opposed to a part-time basis and the high level of skilled and experienced emigrants who began to stream home again in the 1990s (Barrett and Trace, 1998). Living standards have increased significantly since the 1980s and it is estimated that in Ireland they have now overtaken those in the UK and by 2005 will have approximated the slightly higher European levels (Sweeney, 1998, p. 3; ESRI, 1999). Income tax rates have fallen during the 1990s but the public finances have continued to grow, the country boasting a healthy balance of payments surplus each year of the 1990s.

The strategy of encouraging foreign investment, introduced in the gloom of the 1950s, continues to play an important part in the success of the economy. However, it is the nature of new (especially American) investment which safeguarded the Irish economy from both the economic recessions of the early 1990s and the hiccups of 1996–7 brought about by the downturn in the Asian economies. The main new investors have been in areas that maintained consumer demand throughout the world, despite local downturns – chemicals and pharmaceuticals, computers and soft drinks. Throughout the 1990s, in other words, Ireland boomed even when the rest of Europe and the USA did not (Sweeney, 1998, p. 75). According to most economists (Ó'Gráda, 1997; Sweeney, 1998; Durkan, Fitz Gerald and Harmon, 1999; ESRI, 1999) a significant factor in the success of the Irish economy has been that the investment in education and the reforms introduced as part of the early modernisation programme in the 1960s at last began to pay dividends in the 1990s. Of specific importance here was the country's early investment in training for new technologies and the availability of a highly skilled and educated workforce has been a major factor in attracting the international computer industry to the country (Apple, Hewlett Packard, Bell, IBM, Intel, Compaq). There is a double bonus in this. Research has clearly established the gains to individuals of a good education in terms of higher earnings and thus greater spending power. This has helped to boost the domestic market for indigenous industries as well as for imported goods and plays an important role in social cohesion. There is also a measurable impact on what economists refer to as 'human capital' and a clear correlation between human capital and economic growth (Durkan, Fitz Gerald and Harmon, 1999, p. 119).

Another key component in this upsurge is the fact that native Irish industry has also developed and consolidated alongside the success of the foreign multinationals, increasing its share of the domestic market while both exports and export market shares have risen (Barry, 1999, p. 2). Both Irish industry and farming have benefited from European membership to such an extent that neither is today dependent on the British market to the same extent as previously and Irish economic performance is no longer linked to the sluggish British economy. Tourism has also boomed, growing by well over 100 per cent during the 1990s, second only to Turkey in a table of OECD countries. The number of overseas tourists to Ireland rose from 1.9 million in 1986 to 4.2 million by 1995 and this has increased by an estimated 10 per cent each year since that (Barrett, 1997, pp. 39–48). Ireland now finds itself in the position of selling itself abroad as both a dynamic and modern economy with a young, highly skilled and energetic population and as a thinly populated rural country with beautiful unspoilt scenery steeped in tradition and removed from the bustle of a busy world. This has interesting ideological implications for culture in Ireland in general and raises in particular complex questions about the representation of landscape and rural life in Irish cinema.

During the 1990s, a remarkable consensus held sway in which government, business and the trade unions agreed national plans for economic development, employment, taxation and wages. These agreements attempted to establish a national consensus over social and economic policy while at the same time maintaining an environment of enterprise that would allow industry and business to prosper. The results have been spectacularly successful and with the economy approaching a situation of full employment in the early 2000s, further national agreements will have to deal with the likelihood of a labour shortage as well as grappling with the problem of those sections of society so far excluded from the burgeoning wealth (Sweeney, 1998, pp. 155–82; ESRI, 1999).

The kind of national politics that this consensus implies has continued to sideline a traditional left/right split in Ireland, so that the politics of nationalism has given way to the politics of 'national development'. Modernisation and affluence, of course, have their down sides. Ireland, like most developed countries at the beginning of the new century, now has a measurable 'underclass', a lumpenproletariat of the inner cities that is riven with poverty, drugs and crime. Not everyone has benefited from the new wealth. As the next phase of economic planning was being discussed in 2000, the problems facing single parents and their children, Ireland's substantial travelling community and those in low-paid employment were identified in particular as medium-term issues that needed to be addressed (Mac Laughlin, 1997).

Already by the year 2000, there is a sizeable non-Irish immigrant population in Ireland, again, in the main, highly skilled and educated (Barrett and Trace, 1998). Many of these are 'black Europeans' – European citizens from the multicultural heartlands of the EU – but in a country like Ireland (probably the 'whitest' country in Western Europe) the potential for racial tension is real. As the country becomes more attractive for both political and economic refugees, and as it faces up to the possibility that there will be a labour shortage in the early years of the new century, Ireland is having to come to terms with a problem that is also characteristic of its European partners – racism and race relations. At the end of the 1990s, incidents of racial abuse were being reported and accusations of racism in regard to the immigration service in Dublin only confirm that Ireland has to learn to deal with the negative aspects of new wealth and that, like its partners in Europe, the Irish are not immune to racial incitement and far-right scaremongering (Aniagolu, 1997; Cullen, 1997; Murphy, 1997). The corporatist consensus has meant that left political opposition to these problems has been minimal. Indeed, given the seriousness of all these issues, there is a sense in which Irish culture in general has so far failed to come to terms with the negative aspects of, or the challenges posed by, its newfound affluence. Rather, as Hugh Linehan has suggested, there seems to be an uncritical, self-satisfied complacency to much of the culture that has emerged in recent years (Linehan, 1999, p. 49). We will consider this argument in relation to the 'cinema of the Celtic Tiger' in Chapter Eight.

The Cultural Debate

Needless to say, the shift away from protectionist nationalism that has characterised Irish economic strategy for the last forty years has had an impact on other aspects of Irish social and cultural life. The narrow nationalist consensus of the period down to the 1960s, outlined in Chapter One, has been subjected to an almost continuous process of reassessment and re-evaluation so that few aspects of Irish life and culture have been left unaffected. This has amounted to a cultural ferment that has reaped dividends in all aspects of Irish cultural production, including latterly in Irish cinema, but which has also given rise to a sometimes heated, acrimonious and bitter debate. Just as the process of modernisation itself has gone through a series of different phases, so too has this debate.

What has become known as 'revisionism' in Irish culture actually began in the 1940s in the field of academic history, as the assumptions and traditions of nationalist historiography were subjected to a more rigorous analysis and critique. However, from the 1960s onwards, the shift to a policy of modernisation meant that this process of rethinking the past and adapting to present needs became increasingly more public. In the first phase of modernisation, arguably the single most important cultural development in this process was the inauguration of an Irish television service on 31 December 1961, originally Telefís Éireann but, since 1967, known as Radio Telefís Éireann (RTÉ). Television, in other words, was itself part of the modernisation process but went on to become the main channel for both mediating and defining the cultural ramifications of the drive for progress (McLoone and MacMahon, 1984). The implications for notions of Irish cultural identity can be gauged by considering the small but significant differences in the wording of the two pieces of broadcasting legislation that frame the beginning and the end of this first period of modernisation. In the Broadcasting Authority Act of 1960, Section 17 stipulates that in its programming the new Authority should bear in mind 'the national aim of restoring the Irish language and preserving and developing the national culture' (Fisher, 1978, p. 26). With its emphasis on the Irish language and its assumption about a single and fairly self-evident national culture, this provision offers nothing that would scandalise the Irish-Ireland cultural nationalism that had held sway in the period down to the 1960s. However, by the time the Broadcasting Authority (Amendment) Act was passed in 1976, the political culture of Ireland had shifted considerably. The new section on programming charged that the Authority should, among other things:

> (a) be responsive to the interests and concerns of the whole community, be mindful of the need for understanding and peace within the whole island of Ireland, ensure that the programmes reflect the varied elements which make up the culture of the people of the whole island of Ireland, and have special regard for the elements which distinguish that culture and in particular for the Irish language …

> (c) have regard to the need for the formation of public awareness and understanding of the values and traditions of countries other than the State, including in particular those of such countries which are members of the European Economic Community. (Fisher, 1978, p. 43)

The changes here are profound and mark a shift away from the old nationalist consensus to a new orthodoxy built around a liberal, European sense of identity. It embraces a more pluralist definition of Irishness that downgrades the importance of the Irish language. It also represents an attitude to the outside world that is in marked contrast to the hostility, suspicion and xenophobia redolent of Irish-Ireland cultural nationalism. Significantly, the formulation here also reflects the impact of the deteriorating situation in Northern Ireland and the linkage of cultural diversity and pluralism with peace in the new wording reflects an ideological worldview that continues to be the orthodox opinion of 'official' Ireland today. The phrase 'the whole island of Ireland' reflects a tacit acceptance of the different state of Northern Ireland, an acceptance endorsed eventually by the overwhelming majority of the Irish people in the referenda of 1998 following the signing of the Good Friday agreement.

The new broadcasting legislation was drawn up under the auspices of the minister of the time, Dr Conor Cruise O'Brien, whose writings as an historian and political polemicist had already earned him the sobriquet as Ireland's leading revisionist – a staunch opponent of nationalism in general and of militant republicanism in particular. His history of contemporary Ireland, *States of Ireland* (O'Brien, 1972), was a polemical contribution to the tradition of historical revisionism that had been characteristic of Irish historiography as it developed in academia from the 1940s on. His elevation, therefore, to ministerial power and the new regime of broadcasting he proposed (including a more restrictive policy in regard to interviews with members of paramilitary groups and parties which supported paramilitary activities) marked the consolidation of the new elite in Irish society. This was a largely urban, liberal middle class committed to an open economy, the free flow of culture and the abandonment of the cherished ideals of Irish-Ireland nationalism. O'Brien's proposals for broadcasting proved to be controversial, however, and mobilised a broad constituency in opposition. The controversies of these years established the pattern of much public and academic debate that was to follow – a debate between the modernisers on one hand ('revisionists') and a loose coalition of different nationalist opinion on the other ('anti-revisionists'). Both of these camps represent diverse political and cultural positions (both, for example, have decidedly right-wing and left-wing tendencies within them) and, at best, the terms operate as journalese shorthand (and, at worst, as polemical abuse).

This phase of cultural debate in Ireland was considerably energised by Cruise O'Brien's extraordinary proposal in 1973 in regard to a second national television channel. He responded to pressure for an expansion of Irish broadcasting by proposing that a second channel be established to relay British television to all parts of the country ('open broadcasting', as he called it). Both a practical and an ideological imperative motivated him. By that time nearly 50 per cent of the country was already receiving British television anyway in either 'overflow' signals from Northern Ireland (the border areas and along the east coast) or from cable networks (especially Dublin). The proposal aimed at extending the privilege to the 'single channel' areas of the south and the west, which would have been a popular move in electoral terms. He further argued that the proposal, with the agreement of the British authorities, would allow for the extension of existing RTÉ services to the whole of Northern Ireland, thus satisfying the cultural identity needs of the large nationalist population there that had no access to Irish broadcasting at that time. However, he also felt that the exposure of the whole country to the best of British television would speed up the integration of Ireland into a common Anglo-European culture and so finally end the insularity and isolation of Irish-Ireland culture. At the same time he hoped that this would destroy the residue of traditional nationalist (or anti-British) sentiment within the country that gave tacit support to militant republicanism in Northern Ireland. The whole process would help to maintain and extend a sense of mutual understanding between the two traditional enemies, Ireland and Britain, and between their traditional adherents in Northern

Ireland, nationalists and unionists. O'Brien argued at the time, '... as Irishmen grow more acquainted with one another's cultural background, it is inevitable that they will find that much of their shared heritage is shared also with people in Britain' (quoted in O Caóllaí, 1974, p. 3).

O'Brien's proposals, and the opposition that they gave rise to, cemented his position as Ireland's most uncompromising anti-nationalist intellectual. As his amendments to the broadcasting legislation indicated, he was motivated by a rejection of the violence of militant republicanism in Northern Ireland as much as he was by an intellectual distaste for the narrow definitions of Irishness proposed by Irish-Ireland nationalism. In this he represented, perhaps in its extreme form, what Liam O'Dowd has described as 'an anti-nationalist intelligentsia' which dominated Irish cultural and social debate throughout the 1960s and 1970s. 'As the Northern conflict has persisted ... the Southern intelligentsia began to change orientation to national identity,' he argues. Whereas in the 1960s, questions of national identity and sovereignty were set aside in favour of other national goals, such as economic development and the establishment of a welfare state, in the 1970s and 1980s, O'Dowd argues, there was a concerted attack on nationalism itself. The clear implication here is that the liberal modernisers were prepared to throw the baby out with the bathwater to the detriment of Ireland's sense of national identity, a consistent theme in the polemics of much revisionist writing, as we shall see (O'Dowd, 1992, p. 35). O'Brien's proposals for the second television channel were a perfect illustration of this.

The Irish language lobby group, Conradh na Gaeilge, and the broadcasting branches of the trade unions led a successful campaign against the proposal and the second channel was established by RTÉ as an alternative to its main general channel. One result of this campaign was that it embedded the notion of cultural imperialism into public discourse in Ireland. A series of pamphlets published by Conradh na Gaeilge in the mid-1970s established the political parameters of this new nationalist counter-attack (Jones, 1974; O Caóllaí, 1974; O Caóllaí, 1975a: O Caóllaí, 1975b; Schiller, 1978; O Caóllaí, 1979). These pamphlets argue that the Irish are the products of centuries of domination and exist in a neo-colonial relationship with Britain. In a larger sense, the imperialist aims of the past are re-presented in contemporary Ireland as 'modernisation' and demand the assimilation of Ireland into an Anglo-American cultural hegemony, even if America was now the hugely dominant element in this. For O Caóllaí in particular, the liberal modernisers epitomised by Cruise O'Brien represented nothing less than a vanguard for the recolonisation of the Irish and the destruction of those cultural elements that make the Irish distinctive. Rather than bow down to the market forces of international capitalism, he argued that if Irish culture were to grow 'we need to throw off the traces of colonisation, to take a more objective view of the distinctive Irish elements in our own culture, to scale down the influence of the Anglo-American cultural elements and to widen our horizons beyond the Anglo-American cocoon' (O Caóllaí, 1975b, p. 2). The minister's proposal to rebroadcast British television through an Irish network 'can serve only to copper-fasten our neo-colonial relationship with Britain' (O Caóllaí, 1975b, p. 4).

It is important here to emphasise the shift in thinking that that this anti-revisionist, pro-nationalist opinion represented. Conradh na Gaeilge was particularly concerned with the place of the Irish language in the newly modernised culture of Ireland and, in O Caóllaí's arguments in particular, we can detect much of what had been articulated eighty years earlier by Douglas Hyde. However, the justification for defending and promoting the Irish language is now premised on arguments from the political left, that resistance to an 'Anglo-American cocoon' is to resist, in Schiller's phrase, 'new forms of cultural domination' and the exigencies of international capitalism. We can detect here, as well, the beginnings of a discourse about neo- and post-coloniality that was to become a key element in the cultural debate of the 1980s and 1990s.

If the cultural imperialism thesis was mobilised by nationalist opinion in an attempt to reinstate some of the arguments of cultural nationalism, it is well to recall the rather paradoxical role that foreign popular culture actually played (indeed continues to play) in the lives of ordinary people. We have already noted that between the 1920s and the 1960s, the Irish enthusiastically embraced American cinema, music and dance. At the height of the nationalist consensus they did so against the considerable opposition of 'official' Ireland (McLoone, 2000). As Rockett has argued in relation to American cinema, 'Despite ... the severity of Irish film censorship ... especially from the 1920s to the 1950s, it is probably true that Hollywood cinema provided an attractive and perhaps liberating alternative to official ideologies' (Rockett, 1991, p. 20). Rockett also points out that this relationship between Hollywood and a stifling national culture was not confined to Ireland. It was a global phenomenon and might just as well be applied to most to of the countries of Europe. In this regard, Geoffrey Nowell-Smith has argued that, compared with Hollywood, British films appeared to be 'restrictive and stifling, subservient to middle-class artistic models and middle- and upper-class values' (quoted in Rockett, 1991, p. 20; McLoone, 1994, pp. 150–51). American popular culture projected a classless, democratic impulse that made it attractive not only to the diverse ethnic cultures that made up the American audience but also to diverse ethnic audiences across the globe (Webster, 1989). Indeed, as has been argued in Chapter Two, the sturdy democratic traditions and egalitarianism of the Irish-Americans did much to define the ideological world of early Hollywood genre cinema.

Recent research into popular music has also shown that the success of American music – from jazz and blues to rock and roll and mainstream pop – has also emerged from the melting pot of many diverse musical influences, the traditions of Irish music and balladry being an important element (McWhiney, 1988, pp. 105–45; King, 1991; O'Connor, 1991; McLaughlin and McLoone, 2000). The appeal of American popular culture, therefore, cannot be put down simply to the economic muscle of the American industry, though this is undoubtedly a factor. In trying to come to terms with the dominance of American popular culture it is important to take into consideration the genuine pleasures and aspirations that this culture offers in contrast to the often narrow and restrictive ways in which 'national' culture and identity have been constructed. In addition, as we shall see, American culture (including the dominant Hollywood form) interacts with other cultures in ways that are actually dictated by the characteristics of the receiving or indigenous culture and does not itself remain unchanged by the encounter. This represents a considerable conundrum for the idea of a national cinema (or indeed a national culture) and this became a key element in the continuing debate about Irish identity in the 1980s and 1990s.

As Ireland entered the 1980s, public discourse was dominated by a series of tragedies, scandals and controversies that polarised public opinion and seemed to exacerbate the tensions between tradition and modernity. The economy slipped inexorably into recession and unemployment and emigration (especially of the educated young) began to rise to levels not experienced since the 1950s. Escalating violence in Northern Ireland, this time in the wake of the IRA hunger strikes of 1980–81, impinged on the political culture of the South to a greater extent than it had since the earlier phase of turmoil in 1969–73. This only exacerbated an already fractious climate riven by the conservative backlash often attributed to the effects of the Pope's visit to Ireland in 1979. On the surface, the forces of liberalisation seemed to suffer a double defeat in 1983 and 1986, when the Catholic lobby won two referenda, one on abortion (inscribing into the constitution the rights of 'the unborn') and the other on divorce (which maintained the constitutional ban on divorce legislation). Two tragedies in particular focused public debate on questions crucial to the status of women in Ireland (implicit already in the fractious abortion debate) and on church/state relationships in general.

In January 1984, only months after the abortion controversy, the bodies of a schoolgirl and her new-born baby were found in a field beside a grotto of the Virgin Mary in the small Midlands village of Granard. Apparently she had managed to hide her pregnancy from family and friends as well as social and religious authorities and had died of exposure after giving birth in complete isolation. The resulting wave of revulsion throughout the country raised again the level of acrimony between Catholic traditionalists and the progressive lobby in Ireland, including in this case most of the media in Ireland. In April of the same year, the body of a new-born baby was found on a beach at Cahirciveen in Kerry. When the gardai (Irish police) interviewed a young single mother, Joanne Hayes, they extracted a confession that the baby was hers and that she had killed and disposed of the body with the help of various members of her family. Later, Hayes withdrew the confession and gave the location on the family farm of the body of another baby which was hers and which had died in childbirth. Blood tests revealed that the baby on the beach was not related to either Hayes or the baby on the farm. The charges were dropped and the family lodged complaints against the gardai. A public inquiry was set up to investigate how the gardai had extracted from an obviously distressed young woman a confession to a crime which forensics proved she could not possibly have committed. The resulting tribunal, however, became a public inquisition, not into the behaviour of the gardai as its terms of reference stipulated, but of Joanne Hayes herself, her sexual history and lifestyle. Increasingly bizarre theories to explain the parentage of the baby on the beach were entered by counsel on behalf of the gardai in an attempt to exonerate them from accusations of insensitivity and of having browbeaten the original confession from the distressed mother. To many people, it seemed that patriarchal Ireland was subjecting the women of Ireland to a public inquisition akin to medieval witch trials (McCafferty, 1985).

The whole climate in rural Ireland, already traumatised by the Granard and the 'Kerry babies' tragedies, slipped into the surreal or the downright absurd when, throughout 1985, the media reported incidences across the country in which people claimed to have seen religious statues of the Virgin Mary move, bleed or shed tears. It seemed to urban Ireland that rural Ireland, weighed down by a revitalised Catholic fundamentalism, was slipping inexorably into superstition and a kind of pre-modern religious hysteria. Rural and urban Ireland, now increasingly seen to represent respectively tradition and modernity, had rarely seemed so antagonistic or so far apart (the whole tragic background to this unhappy phase of modern Ireland provides the context for Margo Harkin's extraordinary film *Hush-a-Bye Baby* [1989], discussed in Chapter Six).

This perception of a pre-modern Ireland, together with the deepening economic recession and escalating national debt, seemed to some commentators to confirm that the modernisation project had failed. Ireland was compared to a Third World country, totally dependent on Anglo-American capitalism and its attendant culture, heavily in debt, riven by religious fundamentalism, struggling with poverty, unemployment and emigration and politically unstable. These observations formed the basis of a conference held in Dublin in 1991 called, without a sense of irony, 'Is Ireland a Third World Country?' The papers read at the conference and published the following year indicate that many of

Trauma and hysteria in the 1980s: Emer McCourt in *Hush-a-Bye Baby*

the contributors were reluctant to accept the premise outright, though they were concerned to explore issues relating to colonialism in the Third World for their relevance to Ireland (Caherty et al., 1992). In the contribution most clearly aligned with the logic behind the conference title, Carol Coulter highlights the intellectual tradition that this renewed nationalist discourse had began to mine (Coulter, 1992, p. 6). She quotes from Edward Said's pamphlet published for Field Day, the theatre and publishing group based in Derry. Said implicitly links the Irish experience with that of Third World colonialism and, its main purpose, links the poetry of Yeats to the great tradition of decolonialising literature that includes Neruda, Vallejo, Césaire, Faiz and Darwish (Said, 1988, p. 8). Thus the cultural politics of 'post-coloniality', which derive so much of their impetus from Said's pioneering *Orientalism* (Said, 1978), were applied to Ireland in an attempt to open up the dominant narratives of tradition and modernity and to reinscribe a sense of Irish 'difference', of Irish nationalism, to a country that seemed to be faltering in its embrace of an international or transnational sense of identity.

The faltering nature of modernisation in the 1980s forms the context for much of the work of Luke Gibbons, the commentator who has launched the most concerted and most complex attack on revisionism. In an essay published in 1988, he argues: 'The idea that modernization is helping Ireland to "catch up" with its advanced industrial neighbours is no longer tenable.' He notes two

major events in 1979 that mark the transitional conflict in Ireland between tradition and modernity. In March of that year, nearly one million PAYE workers
marched throughout the country in protest at a punitive tax regime that,
despite the secondary importance of agriculture to the economy, still favoured
farmers at the expense of industrial workers. In September, one million people
gathered in Phoenix Park in Dublin to attend Mass celebrated by the Pope. Gibbons argues that it was this gathering, rather than the PAYE march, which was
the portent of things to come. 'The Phoenix Park', he muses, 'was an appropriate setting for confessional Ireland to emerge from the ashes' (Gibbons, 1988b,
p. 218). Gibbons himself later acknowledged the problem inherent in taking
such an historical long-term view on the evidence of just a few years (Gibbons,
1996, p. xii) but the depths of his scepticism then certainly reflects the general
pessimism of the 1980s. His scepticism, at least on these matters, was to prove
unfounded.

In fact, the 1980s began with a second PAYE march in January of 1980 in
which 750,000 people marched to protest at the iniquities of the tax regime and
ended symbolically with the election of Mary Robinson to the Presidency in
November 1990. (This was a remarkable achievement in itself, given her already
high public profile as a socialist/feminist and a human rights lawyer who first
came to attention campaigning against the most oppressive Catholic aspects of
de Valera's constitution.) The 1980s proved, no doubt, to be a difficult and contradictory decade for progress in Ireland but, book-ended as it was by these
suggestive events, the portents were always there that the modernisation
process would get back on track. The decline of the Catholic church's influence,
already evident in the 1980s (Inglis, 1987), was precipitated in the 1990s by a
series of abuse and sex scandals. The successful, if narrow, victory of the liberal
lobby in a rerun of the divorce referendum in 1996 and a small but significant
adjustment to the rigidity of the abortion amendment in 1992 (Eijsbouts, 1999,
pp. 1–8) began to roll back what proved to be temporary and largely pyrrhic
victories by the forces of Catholic conservatism. The surge in the economy during the 1990s saw the Irish 'catch-up' almost completed. As the new century
began even that most intractable of problems, Northern Ireland, seemed close
to a solution with the implementation of the Good Friday agreement, an
accommodation that offered more optimism than at any time in the previous
thirty years.

The basic absurdity of the Third World analogy is a point taken up by econ-
omist Liam Kennedy. In a riposte to the 'Third World' conference, laced with
considerable indignation and exasperation, he challenged the basic premise of
the conference title. Using a range of economic indicators he compared Ireland's position at independence in 1922 with a number of other post-colonial
countries on the eve of their independence and argued that Ireland was in every

way, and by a substantial margin, indisputably part of the First World. Of course it was a peripheral part of Europe but it was not any worse off than a whole host of other European countries at the time. With rapid economic growth in the 1990s, the notion that Ireland was a Third World country appeared positively nonsensical and trivialised the suffering of those countries struggling with starvation, fractious and genocidal civil wars or grossly underdeveloped economic and social infrastructures (Kennedy, 1992/3, pp. 107–21).

There is another way of rationalising the religious and ideological extremes of the 1980s, other than seeing it as evidence of a failing modernity and a confirmation of Ireland's Third World status. In one of the earliest of the independent films made at the end of the 1970s, Tommy McArdle's *The Kinkisha* (1978), there is an interesting allusion to the tradition/modernity opposition. Margaret (Barbara McNamara) is a young woman who becomes pregnant when she has sex with Gerry (John McArdle) after a dance in the local community hall. The sex scene in a barn is ambivalent, where the line between seduction and rape is blurred. There is a deliberate downplaying here of notions of romantic love. Rather, there is an emphasis on the desperation of sex in a closely controlled social and religious environment – frustration and acquiescence rather than mature adult emotion. Because of the resulting pregnancy Gerry and Margaret must get married and move in with his domineering mother. When the child is born it refuses to settle and its constant crying adds further friction to the already strained relationships in the home. Margaret is revealed as an inadequate mother. However, the cause of the child's anxiety is put down to a curse, rather than these strained relationships within the home. The kinkisha of the title is a child born at Whitsun and folk tradition in that part of rural Ireland holds that such a child will either kill or be killed. The solution is to crush a robin to death in the child's hand to remove the 'curse' and, under pressure from Gerry's mother, Margaret sets out to perform this traditional ritual.

There is one extraordinary shot in the film that epitomises its overall critique of rural Catholic Ireland and captures the mood of quiet desperation that inhabits the characters. In a flashback sequence Margaret recalls the visit of the parish priest to the maternity hospital just after she has given birth. She discusses the superstition of the kinkisha with him but it is obvious that the real problem is the fact that the child has been conceived as a result of pre-marital sex. The priest is 'liberal' enough to suggest that if performing the superstitious ritual will expiate Margaret's guilt (and help her to reach an accommodation with her overbearing mother-in-law) then it cannot do much harm. He pauses in his conversation with Margaret to look around the maternity ward. A slow, silent point-of-view pan around the other women with their babies suggests the priest's great distance from, his stràngeness to, the world of women's sexuality and reproduction. While the scene reinforces the general air of desperation that afflicts the whole film, the suggestion in this shot is that the priest himself is aware of his own inadequacy. His celibate ignorance of an arena in which the church commands so much control is a powerful and telling moment and his acquiescence to a pre-Christian tradition is born of his own sense of desperate irrelevance.

Gerry's mother, Gran (Catherine Gibson), represents the domestic pressure on Margaret that parallels the social pressure of Catholic Ireland. Indeed, if the real transgressor in the story is Gerry, through his seduction/rape of Margaret, Gran ensures that it is again the woman who is to blame. It is Margaret who must go out, capture the robin and perform the ritual. As we have discussed in Chapter One, Tom Inglis' view is that the mother's role in post-Famine Catholic Ireland was to patrol the sexuality of her son, ensuring the 'voluntary celibacy' that was a requirement of the rural economy. She is the voice in the home of the priest in the community. If the son has erred, it cannot be his fault but that of the woman who transgressed her role as sexual guardian. However, what is interesting is that Gran resorts to the myth of the kinkisha for Margaret's penance rather than to the priest's confessional. The priest's hold on Gran is itself subject to an older, deeper rural tradition and this is another aspect of his irrelevance and social impotence.

On the other hand, Margaret emerges from her ordeal a stronger and more confident person and there is a clear implication that she can now assert herself more completely in relation to both Gerry and Gran. Her own desires and needs, in particular, can be more clearly articulated. Even if the dark and sombre atmosphere of Gran's house does not hold out much in the way of optimism, there is certainly, by the end of the film, a feeling that Margaret is up to the task of forging her own identity against the oppressive presence of Gran and the wheedling inadequacy of her immature son. Her acting-out of a superstitious ritual releases her from the stifling conformity of rural Ireland – she emerges from tradition into modernity by enacting an even older tradition. In this sense, *The Kinkisha* is a transitional film, capturing that moment in a time of change when, as Brandon French has argued, society displays an odd mixture of progressive and reactionary elements. 'When stable patterns break down, both old and new alternatives compete for ascendancy' (French, 1978, p. xxiii). This formulation can explain much of the acrimonious climate that was to follow in the 1980s especially in relation to women, sexuality and the traditions of rural Ireland. Thus, far from marking the failure of the modernisation drive, it confirms the moment when modernisation had begun to have a real impact on rural Ireland. Settled and secure patterns had begun to break down (symbolised in *The Kinkisha* by the strained inadequacy of the priest) and conflicting alternatives (here the myth of the kinkisha but in the wider community even a spate of visitations and moving statues) vied for ascendancy.

In light of the changed economic and social realities of Ireland in the 1990s, Gibbons has recast the crudity of the Third World analogy in a more subtle way and at the same time offers an altogether different perspective on rural Ireland and its traditions. 'Ireland', he declares, 'is a First World country, but with a Third World memory' (Gibbons, 1996, p. 3). This important qualification to the crudity of some other formulations echoes the distinction made by Paul Willemen between a 'Third Cinema' and a 'Third World cinema' (Willemen, 1989, pp. 1–29) and which will be discussed in Chapter Five in relation to the themes and formal strategies of Irish cinema in the 1970s and 1980s. For Gibbons, this 'Third World memory' is the result of Ireland's history of colonial domination and suppression. What is characteristic, therefore, about Irish cultural traditions, especially those of rural Ireland, is that they manifest both the pain suffered and the resistance offered to the traumas of colonial oppression. Rather than being seen as a conservative bulwark against progress and enlightenment they contain a radical and transformative potential which is too often ignored or traduced by liberal modernisers. His major disagreement with revisionist historians and cultural commentators is that they are prone to downgrade the importance of, or even to deny, the violent disruptions visited by colonialism on Irish culture (and this would include the Famine and decades of enforced emigration). But it is the memory of these disruptions, and the cultural response to them, that marks out Irish traditions as potentially radical and which define Ireland's 'particular' or 'peculiar' difference.

It is in this area that Ireland has an affinity to other cultures that have experienced such disruption (Third World colonial cultures, the native Americans and Afro-Americans, Mexico) rather than to the modern states of Europe to which it has become linked. Irish culture experienced modernity 'before its time' – modernity here defined in terms of shock, disruption and fragmentation – and resistance to this is found in the transgressive nature of the folk traditions and oral culture of rural Ireland – a kind of pre-modern play of signifiers which mirrored the hurt and the disruption. It is to these traditions, and contemporary cultures on the periphery which have shared similar experiences, that a radical and critical contemporary culture should look for inspiration, rather than to the Anglo-American global culture of modernity. It is just such an alliance of formerly colonised peoples that is hinted at in *In the Name of the Father* when Gerry Conlon befriends the black prisoners who share with him the opprobrium and racism of their white fellow prisoners (see Chapter Three). This 'radical memory' also explains the otherwise perverse avant-garde tradition of Joyce and Beckett. Both writers emerged from a culture that was relatively undeveloped to embrace the European metropolitan centre but in doing so, they nonetheless carried with them the 'nightmare of Irish history'. Thus the memory of colonial disruption and fragmentation found its expression in their modernist aesthetic. The Irish avant-garde, therefore, was motivated by the memory of Irish rural tradition, not by the rejection of it, a considerable revision itself of dominant Joycean scholarship (Gibbons, 1996, p. 6).

To some extent, this view is shared by Pat Murphy in her extraordinary recasting of the story of Nora Barnacle, James Joyce's long-time companion and later his wife, in her return to feature film-making with *Nora* (2000). Nora's earthy, non-metropolitan sexuality and passion are what attract and inspire Joyce. Thus, the epitome of modernist transgression in literature, *Ulysses*, and that novel's proto-feminist heroine, Molly Bloom, are premised on the radical and transforming Irish 'peasant', Nora Barnacle, rather than on some modernist, bourgeois figure from the Europe of Joyce's exile.

Gibbons thus reconfigures the dominant narrative of modernisation. The romantic nationalism of the Irish-Ireland movement and the authoritarian hegemony of the Catholic church are aspects of modernity, not their antithesis and revisionist attacks on these are 'akin to tilting at windmills of their own making' (Gibbons, 1996, p. 4). The price paid for this version of modernity was the stifling conservatism of de Valera's Ireland and the abandonment of centuries of resistant and radical popular traditions. This argument, then, refers back to the cultural imperialism debates of the 1970s. What Gibbons is arguing is that Ireland is faced with a choice in how it aligns itself. Will it become a peripheral, if self-satisfied, part of European capitalist modernity, culturally indistinct within a global culture dominated by America or can it plug into this radical memory again and reclaim its distinctiveness. Terry Eagleton characterises the dominant impulse in Irish modernity in similar ways. 'For some liberal revisionists, it would seem that Ireland will have assumed its distinctive place among the nations when it ends up looking exactly like Switzerland' (Eagleton, 1998, p. 312) (though there is surely here a back-handed acknowledgment of the success of Irish modernisation). Only by acknowledging the colonial dimension to its fractured history and aligning itself to other colonial histories and experiences can it achieve a distinctive presence on the global stage. It is at this point that Quinn, Gibbons, Eagleton and the Field Day group (that the latter two have contributed to) meet in their respective fears that Ireland's economic success has been at the expense of its national identity.

The solution offered by Gibbons is to reinstate nationalism as the driving dynamic in Irish culture but a nationalism now extricated from the essentialism of Irish-Ireland nationalism and the sectarian dimensions of de Valera's Catholic nationalism (Victorian and petty bourgeois nationalism). There is a sense, however, in which Gibbons' retrieval of nationalism from revisionism has a double focus (as, indeed does the Field Day project that both he and Said have contributed to). In other words, as well as trying to reconnect with the more radical and more secular strains of Irish tradition which lie outside the parameters of romantic nationalism, he, like Said and other contributors to Field Day, is concerned, nonetheless, to rescue the anti-colonialist impulse of romantic nationalism from the abuse which revisionism has visited on it. Thus, despite Yeats' romanticism, his commitment to an idealised peasantry and a benign aristocracy throughout his life and the authoritarian quasi-fascism of his old age, Said can still describe him as 'Ireland's national poet' and rescue him for a 'decolonising' project (Said, 1988). Another Field Day contributor, Terry Eagleton, makes the case for Maud Gonne as both radical feminist and secular republican despite the anti-Semitism of her ideology and the nakedly sectarian anti-Britishness and disdain for popular culture that were features of her Daughters of Erin organisation (Eagleton, 1995, pp. 294–6). In similar vein, Gibbons rescues Thomas MacDonagh (one of the executed leaders of the 1916 Rising) from revisionist accusations of racism in regard to his notions of the 'racial purity' of Gaelic identity. At the same time he attempts to map out an alternative internationalist and secular strand within Irish nationalism by reclaiming Frederick Ryan and John Eglinton for nationalism, despite the fact that both were condemned in their day by Irish-Ireland nationalists and have been acclaimed since by some revisionists for their implacable anti-nationalist sentiment (Gibbons, 1991, pp. 561–8).

Another area in which the revisionist/anti-revisionist debate has been central is in the debate about the relationship between nationalism and feminism. In fact feminism and gender politics, like class politics, have been fractured in Ireland by this debate – the fault-line that runs through Irish political culture in general. The politics of feminism, like class politics and gender politics more generally, presume an imagining that poses a challenge to the totalising tendencies of nationalism. In turn, though, nationalism itself poses a challenge to the cross-national imaginings of gender and class. Much feminist debate about nationalism has concentrated on the record of Irish nationalism as it has performed in practice in the politics of post-independence Ireland. It is hardly surprising, given the way in which Catholic nationalism in the South has had an impact on issues central to women, that the bulk of feminist opinion in the South has been negative to nationalism in general. However, the impact of Northern Ireland has, arguably, been just as important in fracturing the women's movement in Ireland. As we have seen, one way out of this impasse by a broadly nationalist constituency is to draw a distinction between nationalism as some kind of 'pure' form of resistance (usually rendered as nationalism 'per se') and the nationalism that carried Ireland to its successful revolution (variously called Catholic nationalism, bourgeois or Victorian nationalism,

Irish-Ireland nationalism or republicanism). Thus, in arguing her case for the importance of nationalism to feminism in Ireland, Carol Coulter takes her distance from what she calls 'the narrow, bigoted and prim ideology created in the 1920s and 1930s by "Official Ireland"'. She continues that the Irish state created an official ideology that was 'repressive, stultifying and anti-intellectual' but, in doing so, it 'negated its own historical roots'. These historical roots include 'a more diverse and diversified movement, seeking emancipation on a much wider front' (Coulter, 1998, p. 163). These historical roots, in other words, constitute the radical 'baby' in the oppressive 'bathwater', so to speak.

The difficulty here, though, is in deciding exactly when the 'moment' of this nationalism '*per se*' was (or is) or when the baby was conceived and born before it was plunged into the murky bathwater of 'prim repressive official ideology'. When was Irish nationalism a more 'diverse and diversified' movement?

Coulter's assertion that the ideology of Catholic nationalism was created in the 1920s and 1930s is contentious. As we have argued in Chapter One, the official nationalism of Ireland in the 1920s and 1930s was the logical outcome of the whole consensus that coalesced around the Catholic church from the Famine on. It is implicit in all the cultural societies and campaigns that underpinned political nationalism as it triumphed in the shape of Sinn Féin in the election of 1918 and underpinned militant republicanism as it triumphed in the IRA of the War of Independence. Rather than being a result of the state 'negating its historical roots' the oppressive nationalism of the 1920s was a result of its dogmatic adherence to its historical roots. This oppression goes much further back than the post-independence period. Nationalism is a totalising discourse but, of course, all discourse is riven with contradiction. There is no doubt, then, that around the edges of the Irish-Ireland consensus there were to be found more radical or more secular voices, like those accessed in the Field Day project. There were contradictions, in other words, and none more so than the labour voice of James Connolly. The debate in Irish socialism has been whether or not Connolly did the right thing by moving more centrally into nationalism in 1916. It is hard to argue, however, that the fate of class politics in Ireland would have fared any better had he ignored the Easter Rising. The popular upsurge in support for Sinn Féin would have happened anyway following the British response to the Rising. The point is that the radical secular politics that could have sustained a more diverse and diversified movement were marginalised and silenced, not by the oppressive forces of imperialism but by nationalism itself. To adopt a metaphor from Raymond Williams (Williams, 1985, pp. 9–13) it is a matter of historical perspective and, once on the escalator of history, how far back do we need to go to locate this 'nationalism *per se*'?

Sarah Edge has followed Coulter in the project of finding the common ground between nationalism and feminism. However, in distancing herself from a form of 'republican feminism' she argues that 'I wish to disengage nationalism, and its struggle for identity, from republicanism so that a much broader understanding of what Irish national identity might mean for women in Northern Ireland can be freely and openly considered without fear of intimidation or dismissal as "extremist".' Here again, then, is another form of nationalism '*per se*' – this time one which is not tainted by the republicanism that has so dominated nationalism in Northern Ireland for the last thirty years or so. Where, then, is the site of this nationalism when it is disengaged from the movement that has given it clearest expression, at least as far back as the 1918 election? If not mainstream SDLP politics then the escalator must begin to move again. What can a 'much broader sense of Irish national identity for women in Northern Ireland' mean? Broad enough to accommodate those women who view themselves as British? How would this much broader sense of Irish national identity relate to women living in the Irish Republic? Can this much broader sense of Irish national identity exist within present constitutional arrangements or does it require a centralised unitary state? Edge also notes that in its 'traditional patriarchal form, Irish nationalism has no space for feminism …' but where is it possible to find a nationalism that is not 'traditional' and is not 'patriarchal'? The answer is surely not in history but in a new imagining. This would have to be a sense of 'difference' that can accommodate the internationalist thrust of feminism and socialism so that it was neither patriarchal nor class exclusive; a sense of 'difference' that also accommodates different sexual preferences, and above all, a sense of difference that can accommodate other senses of difference(s). A 'nationalism' that can do all this is not nationalism at all, at least not in the sense of an 'imagined political community, imagined as inherently limited and sovereign' (Anderson, 1983, p. 14). Once you delimit nationalism to accommodate a plurality of such 'difference' you remove the rock on which nationalism was built.

This is surely what feminist scholarship has accomplished over the last ten to fifteen years. Women's histories have constituted a large part of what Tom Dunne has called the 'new histories – "beyond revisionism"' (Dunne, 1992). And in the same mode, Clíona Murphy makes the observation that 'The controversy regarding revisionism in Irish history is ironic considering the narrowness of the history that has been at the centre of the dispute – nationalist history' (Murphy, 1992, p. 21). She locates the present mushrooming of women's history within an international context, beginning with the project of excavating women 'hidden from history'. However, this project then had to respond to the challenge that it concentrated on 'elite women' and left the largely male narratives unaffected. In Ireland, the concern was that the only women who had received attention from historians were a handful of nationalist women. Murphy continues,

Increased attention has been devoted to other women who were politically active in suffrage movements, labour movements and various political, agricultural, educational and philanthropical organizations. There has also been a concerted effort to look at more 'hidden' women like prostitutes, workhouse inmates, domestic servants, peasant women and nuns. (ibid, 22)

In addition, there has been a new concern to discuss gender history in general. The picture that emerges from this scholarship is of a plurality of historical experiences that throw dominant patriarchal history into crisis. As Tom Dunne also argues, new women's history is not the only departure in historical revisionism. As significant, though even less favoured by the historiographical establishment, has been local history and other 'narratives of ordinary life' (Dunne, 1992, pp. 11–12).

Nationalism, then, is a form of cultural identity with an historical narrative adequate to its 'limited' imagining but it is not the only one. It is not possible to have a 'national identity' without having to take on board the historical baggage of nationalism itself (including its patriarchal ideology). It is possible to have a cultural identity that, removed from the 'inherently limited' imagining of nationalism, can be endlessly broad to accommodate differences of all kinds. It is, however, this 'postmodern promiscuousness' that is rejected by nationalist opinion in Ireland. As Seamus Deane has argued in this regard,

> ... while I would accept the need for a recognition of diversity, I don't at the same time say that because things are diverse, because things are so infinitely complex or apparently infinitely complex, there can be no supervening position, that you can't have a political belief or a religious belief. (Deane, 1992, p. 32)

In a sense, then, Deane identifies what is at the crux of this debate. It is not just a matter of endless academic speculation about the past. Ultimately it is about a political belief in the present. It is about developing a framework of analysis that will allow for the development of a political practice and a cultural practice that is adequate to contemporary Ireland. In the end, the debate between revisionism and the anti-revisionism, for all the complexities of their respective readings of the past, is a debate about political activity in the present and about the future imaginings of Ireland, North and South.

Such then has been the nature of the debate that has reverberated throughout Irish academic and critical thought and which has provided the background to the emerging cinema. As the 1990s progressed, the debate has had to accommodate the new affluence of the Republic of Ireland and its status now as one of the richest countries in Europe. It has had to come to terms, as well, with political developments in Northern Ireland and the new spirit of compromise implicit in the Good Friday agreement. This has meant that claims of its status as a neo-colonial country have given way to a more subtle discussion of the heritage of its colonial past, its post-colonial present and the appropriateness of nationalism as its guiding political philosophy. Certainly, some of the combatants have called for an intellectual ceasefire and the beginnings of a process of dialogue with their erstwhile opponents (Dunne, 1992; Graham, 1994; Eagleton, 1998). The two-and-a-half-stage dialectic proposed by Eagleton (nationalism vs. revisionism leading to a slightly amended nationalism), however, will no doubt bring a poor response from leading revisionist critics (Eagleton, 1998, pp. 310–11).

The point, though, is that this has been a debate conducted largely within academia and its impact has been felt mostly in Irish historiography and cultural criticism. Every so often it has emerged from its professional academic world to engage with popular consciousness over particularly contentious issues (successive Northern Ireland crises, the television debate, the scandals of the 1980s, the debate over Neil Jordan's *Michael Collins* or fears of growing racism in Ireland as the economy has improved). It has not, however, been felt in the field of economics, politics or the daily lived experience of ordinary people. The revisionist 'turn' has proceeded apace over the last forty years despite some temporary setbacks. The success of the economy in the South and the overwhelming endorsement of the Good Friday agreement throughout Ireland, including the dropping of the South's territorial claim to Northern Ireland, will be seen by the revisionists as confirmation that nationalism in Ireland is dead. What is more likely, though, is that the process of reimagining Irish national identity to accommodate the kinds of difference outlined above has reconfigured nationalism. It has been reconfigured as well by the exigencies of everyday existence and the daily grind of politics (including the involvement of Sinn Féin in the North as a central political force in this process) so as to be unrecognisable as nationalism in its classical sense. (This is certainly the opinion of those on the republican side and among certain sections of the left who are opposed to the Good Friday agreement.) While the debate has been lively in academic terms, there is, nonetheless, a strange paralysis on the left in Ireland in terms of daily lived experience and economic and social struggles. This is especially so in terms of coping with the problems thrown up by economic success in the South and the peace process in the North. Perhaps as well, it is reflected in aspects of the cinema that has emerged in recent years and we will pursue this point in more detail in Chapters Seven, Eight and Nine.

As we shall see, however, the cultural impact of this debate has been significant in the formulation of a notion of national culture in general and for the idea of a national cinema in particular. We will look at the cinema debate in more detail in the next chapter.

Chapter 5
The Emergence of a Film Culture

The spirit of liberalisation and the sense of renewal that characterised the first flush of modernisation also touched the cinema. In the 1960s, the harsh censorship regime began to collapse into absurdity, given the coming of television and rapidly changing public opinion. Cinema censorship was relaxed considerably in 1964 with the introduction of an age certificate system (Rockett, 1991), thus reversing the tendency towards infantilising Irish imagination identified in Chapter One. The censorship of publications was liberalised in 1967 when a limitation of twelve years was imposed on prohibition orders. At one fell swoop, over 5,000 previously banned titles were released (Fanning, 1983, p. 200). A new concern with the cultural life of the nation manifested itself in an increase in government funding under the Arts Act of 1973 and an important breakthrough was the fact that a newly expanded Arts Council recognised film as a legitimate area for support.

Film production had been slow to develop, however, though Rockett instances the influential documentary tradition that had established itself in the post-war period, many of whose practitioners worked on government-sponsored information and propaganda films (Rockett, 1988, pp. 71–94). As we have already noted, two influential and important documentaries had been made in 1959 and 1961, the Irish language films, *Mise Eire* and *Saoirse?*. Fiction film developed only very slowly and again Rockett notes a series of unco-ordinated strands that brought this about by the mid-1970s (Rockett, 1988, p. 128). An increasing number of Irish students from art colleges in both Britain and Ireland began to make short films (including Joe Comerford, Thaddeus O'Sullivan and Pat Murphy). Some of the documentarists from an older generation moved into fiction film-making and former RTÉ personnel began to make their own films independently (Bob Quinn, Tommy McArdle). The new affluence and the commercial basis of Irish television gave rise to an advertising sector that provided valuable training for individuals who later graduated to film-making. The most significant development was the introduction in 1977 of the Arts Council's Film Script Award, which at last provided some measure of state funding for independent indigenous film-making. In these years, though, it was largely British sources which provided funding – the early films of Joe Comerford, Pat

The 1970s New Wave: Joe Comerford, Cathal Black and Bob Quinn on location in
Down the Corner

Murphy and Thaddeus O'Sullivan were part-funded by the BFI and in the early
1980s, Channel Four in Britain became a major sponsor of Irish film-makers.
Thus, the volume and quality of independent films, especially short films,
increased as the 1970s progressed, and these are discussed in Chapter Six.

Tentative steps towards establishing a wider film culture were also taken in
the 1970s. Again, the Arts Council provided funding for the consolidation and
expansion of the film society network throughout the country. It also provided
funding for the Irish Film Theatre in Dublin and for an adventurous screening
policy at the Project Arts Centre. In 1978, the Arts Council also took an interest
in the activities of the National Film Institute of Ireland, originally set up in the
1940s as a educational film distributor but which occasionally ran 'film appreci-
ation' courses as well. The Institute was expanded with the appointment in 1980
of an education officer with responsibility for developing film and general
media studies and a director was appointed in 1983. In 1984, the revitalised
organisation, now renamed the Irish Film Institute, mounted 'The Green on
the Screen Festival' of Irish and Irish-themed films (eighty feature films and
eighty shorts spanning the history of the cinema and drawing on films made
in Ireland, Britain, Europe and America). This was envisaged mainly as a
launching pad for the campaign to establish a film archive but was indicative
of the key role the Institute was to play in the campaign for the Irish Film Centre

which eventually opened in Dublin in 1992. The Dublin Film Festival began in 1985, following the success of the previous year's 'Green on the Screen Festival'. In 1987 the Foyle Film Festival was launched in Derry, committed to a critical engagement with cinema in which lectures, seminars and workshops played a key role along side the film screenings. The Cork Film Festival was relaunched in 1986 with a renewed commitment to Irish cinema in addition to its traditional interest in international short film-making. Finally, the Galway Film Fleadh began in 1989 and when the reconstituted Film Board was decentralised to Galway from 1993 the city became an alternative focus to the established film activity centred in Dublin. By the early 1990s the country had two film magazines, *Film Ireland*, based in Dublin and published by the film-makers' co-operative FilmBase, and *Film West*, published by the Galway Film Centre, the west's main training, educational and advice facility for independent production.

In terms of film production, by the late 1970s, the small but growing band of indigenous film-makers formed the Association of Independent Producers to lobby for more concerted government action to help film production. This lobbying achieved a considerable victory in 1980 when the government finally established a Film Board specifically to fund indigenous production. The first film funded under this mechanism was Neil Jordan's *Angel* (1982), launching the career of the most successful of contemporary Irish film-makers. The Board operated with a small budget in film-making terms, about IR£0.5 million per year, but did manage to part-fund ten feature films, twenty short fiction films and documentaries for television, as well as fifteen experimental shorts. In addition, it provided loans and development grants to approximately sixty other projects. The general level of activity was increasing and the infrastructural framework was beginning to take shape. Unfortunately for indigenous film, the economic climate was deteriorating and this was to weaken severely the nascent industry.

In fact, during the prolonged economic recession of the 1980s, film culture in Ireland was subject to contradictory experiences. In 1984, two indigenous films, both supported by the Film Board, were shown out of competition at Cannes, Pat Murphy's *Anne Devlin* and Cathal Black's *Pigs*. In addition, Pat O'Connor, who had made the BAFTA award-winning film *The Ballroom of Romance* for the BBC and RTÉ in 1982, was in competition with *Cal*, based on Bernard McLaverty's novel and produced by David Puttnam, winning the best actress award for Helen Mirren's performance. Thus, as indigenous film-making was slowly growing, Ireland was also beginning to attract the attention of British (and later American) film-makers. However, the balance of payment problems and the escalating national debt resulted in severe cutbacks in government spending and the Film Board was suspended in 1987, casting the independent sector into gloom. Despite the fact that the Film Board funding amounted to only IR£0.5 million per year, it had managed to create a level of film activity that built on the small-scale independent film-making of the 1970s and promised eventually to stimulate a 'critical mass' that could be called a proper industry. With the suspension of the Film Board the essential plank for supporting indigenous film-making was removed and feature film production ground to a halt.

Ironically, at the same time that it suspended the Film Board, the government also introduced corporate and individual tax incentives designed to encourage international film activity in Ireland. Rockett saw in this a clear sign of the government's commitment to a more commercial film-making regime and the reinstatement of the values of 'industry' over 'culture' in approaching the whole question of film in Ireland (Rockett, 1994, pp. 129–30). These incentives did have an impact and the level of international interest in Ireland increased over the next five years. However, as a package, it ditched the indigenous aspect in favour of the commercial, and the independent sector had to wait until the changes of 1993 to see the implementation of a full package of support for both kinds of film activity.

A short-lived but vibrant animation industry flourished between 1987 and 1992 and the slowly evolving European production funds under the MEDIA rubric began to have an impact. In these years as well, there was an exponential growth in the number of short films being made, mostly by students in the two main film schools, at Dun Laoghaire School of Arts and the Dublin Institute of Technology at its Rathmines campus. A funding scheme for short films was also established between RTÉ and the co-operative support group Film-Base. The volume and increasing technical competence of these shorts at least confirmed that a new generation of film-makers was emerging, even if their prospects of making feature films in Ireland looked grim (short film-making is discussed in more detail in Chapter Seven). Significantly, the British and American industries' interest in Irish themes stimulated a steady flow of foreign-financed films, produced both in and out of Ireland (John Huston's last film, *The Dead,* in 1987 or the largely British-financed *Hear My Song* [1991] and *Hidden Agenda* in 1990). The most important of these was Jim Sheridan's *My Left Foot* (1989), which went on to win acting Oscars for Daniel Day-Lewis and Brenda Fricker in 1990 and to rack up impressive commercial returns, especially in the USA. The success of *My Left Foot* was seen at the time as vindication of the government's strategy of favouring the commercial sector but, as many observers argued, there is a price to pay for this type of financing. While Sheridan's film is by no means the worst offender, the fact remains that such financing inevitably involves compromises in the style and theme of the films. The danger is that, to attract financial support, such films propose a view of

Ireland that is already familiar to international funders and which funders in turn believe audiences are likely to recognise and identify with. Ultimately, they offer conservative images of Ireland that do not challenge existing cinematic traditions. The film community might have been prepared to accept this, if such increased activity had a genuine 'trickle down' effect on training and infrastructure in general and if it were part of a wider package designed to encourage the indigenous sector as well. But without the kind of support offered by the Film Board the exploratory and culturally specific cinema pioneered by the first wave of indigenous directors would simply not get made (Rockett, 1999, p. 24).

The change of government at the end of 1992 initiated what Rockett has called the most 'concentrated period of change ever for Irish film culture' (Rockett, 1996, p. 150). The new coalition government of Fianna Fáil and Labour established a Ministry of Arts, Culture and the Gaeltacht and appointed Labour's Michael D. Higgins to the post. Higgins was an academic, a radical supporter of the arts in general and a strong supporter of the film community in particular. Under his guidance the cabinet accepted new proposals to reorientate the tax concessions so that they had a more specific 'trickle down' brief (especially in the area of training), increasing the amount that could be written off as tax, and the introduction of a Business Expansion Scheme to encourage smaller-scale individual investment in film production. In addition, it agreed also to reactivate the Film Board to kick-start indigenous production again. The total package included the removal of a cap on RTÉ's advertising revenue, introduced by the previous government in pursuit of a policy to increase the commercial media base in Ireland, and a commitment that by 1999, RTÉ would commission 25 per cent of its programming from the independent sector. The new Irish Film Centre had opened in September 1992, providing another important part of infrastructural development, and the new initiatives were announced the morning after an all-night 'Oscar' party held at the Centre, which witnessed the consolidation of Irish film's global presence in the wins for Neil Jordan (script) and Michelle Burke (Hair and Make-up) (Rockett, 1996, p. 150). In 1998, a Screen Commission was established, financed through the Film Board, to promote Ireland as a location for foreign film-making. Each element of the total infrastructure was now in place – the Film Board for indigenous production, the Screen Commission for location promotion, the Film Institute for educational and archival activity and Screen Training Ireland to co-ordinate all aspects of training.

For the first time, then, there was a total film strategy that catered for the commercial development of Ireland as a base for film-making and at the same time provided for indigenous film-making and the nourishment of young film talent. This, as Higgins himself described it, was an integration of 'indigenous energy and the commercial space that tax incentive creates' (Higgins, 1995).

The results were impressive in terms of increasing the general level of film activity. At one end, the tax incentive attracted non-Irish themed films like Mel Gibson's *Braveheart* (1995) and Spielberg's *Saving Private Ryan* (1998), with considerable spin-offs for the economy in general. Rockett quotes statistics from the Irish Business and Employers Confederation (IBEC) which suggest that in 1997 alone, 104 film productions of all kinds were made in Ireland with a total expenditure of £123 million. Of this, £88 million was spent in Ireland itself, creating 1,892 jobs directly in the film industry and 2,296 indirectly in service and ancillary areas (Rockett, 1999, p. 25). The number of indigenous films increased from only three in 1992 to twenty by 1997 (ibid.) and to over fifty by 1999 (Linehan, 1999, p. 49). Many of the more interesting of these are discussed in Chapters Eight and Nine. Despite a change of government in 1997, the policy that Higgins initiated in 1993 has been continued, and following a new report commissioned in 1999, the budget of December that year confirmed that the package would remain in place for a further seven years.

Northern Ireland

It is useful, at this stage, to consider briefly the situation for film-making in Northern Ireland. As John Hill has reminded us, film-making in Northern Ireland does have a modest history going back to the 1930s. Singer and actor Richard Hayward produced a series of low-budget musicals (*The Luck of the Irish* [1935], *The Early Bird* [1936], *Irish and Proud of It* [1936] and *Devil's Rock* [1938]) all relatively light and inconsequential 'quota-quickies' that nonetheless proved popular with Northern Ireland audiences keen to see their local environment up on the big screen. Belfast-born director Brian Desmond Hurst was also a key early influence in both American and British film-making, making, among other films on an Irish theme, the controversial *Ourselves Alone* (1936), which dealt with the War of Independence and was banned in Northern Ireland by the Home Secretary in the old Stormont government (Hill, 1999c, p. 4). However, it was not until the 1980s that film-making in Northern Ireland was again visible in any meaningful way. The independent documentary work of John T. Davis, the workshop productions of the Belfast and Derry Film and Video workshops (funded by Channel Four), the radical video work of Belfast's Northern Visions and a number of independent productions funded largely by British television sources (including Pat Murphy and John Davies' *Maeve* [1981] and John Davies' *Acceptable Levels* [1983]) showed both the desire and achievement of film-makers in the North.

What was needed was a single source funding body, like the South's Film Board, and to this end, the NI Independent Film, Video and Photography Association (IFVPA) produced a report, *Fast Forward*, in 1988, calling for the establishment of a media council. This report rallied support and gave rise to a lot of anger and debate about the lack of public funding for all aspects of audio-visual culture in Northern Ireland (McLoone, 1988). The result was the establishment of the Northern Ireland Film Council (NIFC) as a lobby group and support body to indigenous film-makers. The NIFC followed a route similar to that in the South when it went into partnership with BBC NI in establishing a scheme for the production of fictional shorts, Northern Lights, in 1994. This was added to in 1997 when it went into partnership with UTV, Belfast City Council and British Screen to establish the Première scheme, again for fictional shorts. The big breakthrough came when British Lottery money was made available in 1995 and European money in 1997. The council changed its name to the Northern Ireland Film Commission when it was given the responsibilities of a Screen Commission to promote Northern Ireland as a location. The new Commission also moved into feature film production and developed a more concerted strategy for training. By the end of 1999, ten feature films had been made in Northern Ireland in just two years, including many films that also received funding from the Film Board in the South. The kind of partnerships envisaged in the 1980s have now begun to take shape in the North as well as the South, and optimism has replaced the angry pessimism of the past.

The slow and sometimes painful emergence of a film culture in Ireland took almost twenty years to secure, the result of a long campaign fought by film-makers, film writers, academics, film institutions and resource centres around the country. For most of this time, government was inclined to see film in terms of an industry only and film activity mainly in terms of job-creation and the economic spin-offs. It took longer for the cultural arguments to have an impact, despite the fact that the long years of campaigning took place against an increasingly heated debate about Irish culture and identity both North and South. To what extent then, given this debate, can we talk about such a film culture in terms of a *national* film culture?

National Culture, National Cinema

If the theoretical debate discussed in the previous chapter has direct implications for both cultural criticism and cultural production in Ireland, it is especially true in regard to the notion of a national culture or the definition of a national cinema. Crucial to the debate is the opposition between essentialism and hybridity. The application of post-colonial theory has focused these questions on the moment of encounter between the centre and the periphery, between the particular and the universal, and suggests a more complex relationship than that offered by Irish-Ireland nationalism or that implied in the cultural imperialism thesis. In his lecture of 1892 on 'The Necessity for De-Anglicising Ireland', Douglas Hyde used an interesting analogy to illustrate what he saw as the sorry condition of Irish culture if it did not reclaim its Gaelic past. 'We will become, what, I fear, we are largely at present, a nation of imitators, the Japanese of Western Europe, lost to the power of native initiative and alive only to second-hand assimilation' (Hyde, 1892/1986, p. 169). A century later, Roland Robertson arrived at a quite different conclusion about the nature of that 'nation of imitators', the Japanese:

> Japan's crystallization of a form of 'universal particularism' since its first encounter with China has resulted in its acquiring paradigmatic, global significance. … Specifically, its paradigmatic status is inherent in its very long and successful history of selective incorporation and syncretization of ideas from other cultures in such a way as to particularize the universal and, so to say, return the product of that process to the world as a uniquely Japanese contribution to the universal. (Robertson, 1992, p. 102)

In these two assessments of Japan, we can see two versions of the encounter between indigenous and foreign culture. For Hyde, what is at stake is the essential purity of the indigenous culture, which is severely compromised by outside influences. It invites a protectionist response to such influences, built on an uncomplicated and uninterrogated imagining of a pure national culture. For Robertson, on the other hand, the meeting of cultures is a site of creative contact and tension where both are ultimately changed. The success of Japan was that it then offered the products of this encounter back to the outside as a particularly Japanese entity. The point here, as we have already seen, is that the encounter is a complex dialectic rather than one-sided relationship. It is in this regard that post-colonial theory (and some postmodernist theory) offers a way through the considerable conundrums posed by the encounter between the local and the global in popular culture, between indigenous culture and its encounter with American popular culture in general and Hollywood cinema in particular.

Even if we accept that Hollywood has had a liberating influence on those cultures defined in terms of a narrow and restrictive national culture (the kind of culture which Hyde and his legacy achieved in Ireland) and even if we accept that it offers audiences everywhere real pleasures, there is still a problem in relation to its almost total global dominance. No other film culture can compete with Hollywood in economic terms and its worldwide control of production, distribution and exhibition goes largely unchallenged. The fear, as the cultural imperialist thesis has long contended, is that national cultures, in this case national cinemas, will be destroyed and that Hollywood will be the only cinematic culture available throughout the globe. This, in Michael D. Higgins' phrase, would mark the triumph of the last great colonisation – the colonisation of the imagination (Higgins, 1995). The choice, then, seems stark

– 'the choice between a self-defeating essentialism and a self-abusing domination' (McLoone, 1994, p. 153).

A totally protectionist response, however, is neither possible nor desirable. It
is not possible because no other film industry in the world (perhaps with the
exception of Indian cinema) has the potential to be self-sufficient. There are
two aspects to this. On one hand, the production costs of film are such that it
has become increasingly more difficult for non-American cinema to be self-sufficient in terms of financing. Despite state support, most Irish cinema is still
required to seek funding outside its own resources, either in Britain, America
or Europe, and, as we have discussed, the danger in this is that the co-production arrangements can have an impact on the creative aspects of the film. If a
truly 'national' cinema requires that the total funding arrangements are 'native'
to ensure native control over all creative decisions then there is little 'national'
cinema to be found anywhere in the world, other than in Hollywood. On the
other hand, it is now rare for a non-Hollywood film to recoup its production
costs from its home audience alone, so that at the production stage the mar-
ketability of the film across many territories and national audiences becomes a
key factor in creative decisions. There is, in the Irish case, the added problem
that until relatively recently, it has had no cinematic tradition of its own to draw
upon. Thus, there is no disabling native tradition to restrict its aesthetic
approach and, as it has developed, Irish cinema has had the potential, at least,
to explore its own aesthetic identity. On the other hand, though, it has had
nothing to respond to as either a negative or a positive precedent – no '*cinéma
du papa*', as Truffaut argued in the case of the French New Wave (although the
Hollywood tradition represented by John Ford has operated as a kind of *cinéma
du Pappy* in this regard).

A protectionist and essentialist response is not desirable either. The legacy of
Irish-Ireland essentialism and protectionism is still too strong in Irish memory
and the lingerings of its worst excesses still too obvious to contemplate going
down that road again. The only kind of 'radical memory' that makes much
sense to younger generations in contemporary Ireland is rejection of the fun-
damentals of this ideology as it manifests itself to them in the clinging relics of
its hegemony. This explains, as we shall see, why the sites of this hegemony still
feature so strongly in contemporary cinema – sexual repression, women's
issues, educational abuse and generational conflict. The combination of protectionism and purity is also a dangerously right-wing ideology. As an editorial
in *Sight and Sound* noted, when the leader of the French National Front, Jean-
Marie Le Pen, argues that 'the Trojan Horse of globalisation' is bringing in an
American cinema that is 'degenerate, depraved and negative' (*Sight and Sound*,
1996) then it is time to focus on a response to Hollywood that is more positively disposed to diversity.

Robertson's formulation of Japanese 'hybridity' indicates the kind of thinking that has become more influential as the debate about globalisation has proceeded. At the point of encounter both the universal and the particular are changed. The implication here is that the particular – national culture – is already deeply affected by other such encounters and is, anyway, not amenable to a purist definition. Equally, no matter how economically powerful the universal or metropolitan culture is, it does not encounter in the receiving culture an 'empty bottle' waiting to be filled. It must contend with the 'particularity' of this culture and is moulded in some respects by the encounter. This interface is analogous to that space identified by Kenneth Frampton as 'critical regionalism', an 'arrière-garde' which 'has the capacity to cultivate a resistant, identity-giving culture while at the same time having discreet recourse to universal technique' (Frampton, 1985, p. 20). This involves a mediation of 'the impact of universal civilization with elements derived *indirectly* from the peculiarities of a particular place' (Frampton, 1985, p. 21, original emphasis). In the Irish context this might indeed involve something like a connection to a 'radical memory', as Gibbons has suggested. However, the fear of collapsing into a kind of historicist nostalgia is real (and the essentially regressive ideologies of *Into the West* [1992] and *The Secret of Roan Inish* [1995] are in no way vitiated by the fact that they both mobilise aspects of Irish mythical tradition). Thus the 'critical' dimension of this strategy is dependent upon 'maintaining a high level of critical self-consciousness' and the avoidance of 'simple-minded attempts to revive the hypothetical forms of a lost vernacular' (ibid.). To that extent, it could be argued that, in retrospect, the best of national cinema in Europe since Hollywood established its global hegemony (Italian Neo-realism, the French New Wave, New German Cinema) has, in fact, been a form of 'critical regionalism' (McLoone, 1994, pp. 169–71).

Post-colonial theory has offered a complementary analysis of the contested space between indigenous and metropolitan cultures. In its first phase of analysis, it offered a teleological narrative of the effects of imperialism and colonialism – from colonisation through resurgence to nationalism, liberation and the nation-state (Graham, 1994, p. 30). This was itself then reworked from within post-colonial theory by the observation, discussed in Chapter One, that the concept of the nation was an imposition from imperialism itself, a reflection of colonialism's 'categorical imperative' to name and essentialise the cultures under its hegemony. This process involved a qualitative judgment which also posited the subject culture as inferior, thus justifying imperial domination in the first place. Nationalism, then, is re-presented as an ideology that is totalising, restrictive and oppressive. For Graham it is the Subaltern Studies Group in India, the main exponents of this revision of post-colonial theory, which has launched the most direct challenge to the primacy of nationalism.

This approach has been adopted by many Irish cultural critics to describe the eventual success of an oppressive Irish-Ireland nationalism, including, ironically, many of the writers associated with the Field Day project. As Graham points out, the attraction of the liberating narrative in early post-colonial theory is such that 'the post-colonial nation remains an entity continually reverted to, even in those who explicitly recognise the ideology of nationalism to be a replaying of imperialist structures' (Graham, 1994, p. 31) and he particularly discusses Field Day and Seamus Deane in this regard.

The way out of the impasse is to recognise the complexity of the relationship between coloniser and colonised and to explore the 'liminal spaces' of this encounter. This requires rethinking concepts of irony, hybridity, mimicry and transculturation. It requires at the same time being sensitive to the history of colonial oppression as well as to the narrowness of the essentialist nationalism that resulted. Above all it requires being conscious of the 'fractured range of complex cross-colonial affiliations which have existed within the British–Irish cultural axis' (Graham, 1994, p. 41). The space identified here seems to fit admirably the experience of Irish culture in the 1990s. The best Irish cinema in the last twenty years has operated within this complex and the success of various forms of Irish music (U2, Sinéad O'Connor, The Cranberries, Van Morrison, The Corrs) or the *Riverdance* phenomenon raise interesting questions about Ireland's particular relationship to both its own traditions and to universal culture (O'Toole, 1997, pp. 143–56; McLaughlin and McLoone, 2000).

Irish cinema, then, inhabits a complex cultural space. Internally, it grows out of a contested sense of Irishness itself, contested both in terms of its British/unionist 'other' and, as we have seen, in terms of an increasingly expansive revisionist debate. Externally, it exists also in close contact with the former colonial power Britain, which gives rise to many unresolved post-colonial and nationalist questions. Yet it has also taken its place within a modern Europe committed to greater integration and co-operation and with its own unresolved issues about a sense of common European identity. Finally, it is linked to American culture in a close kinship that grows out of the diaspora and yet, like most cultures on the globe, is subject to the economic and ideological muscle of American popular culture. The themes and issues of Irish cinema are one response to living in this concatenation of pressures and influences.

We have noted as well that the increasing volume of production over the last ten years or so is the result of three levels of financing and budgeting, an outcome anticipated in the package introduced by Michael D. Higgins in 1993 (Higgins, 1995). Each of these has its own implications for film content, its commercial viability and its visibility to audiences, both at home and abroad. This suggests another way in which we could begin to analyse the nature of Irish cinema as it has developed as a film practice. In a way, there is an analogy here with the debate about a 'Third Cinema' (as opposed to the cinema of the 'Third World'). In the 1960s and 1970s, radical political film-makers from Latin America tried to define what a political cinema should be. The initial theoretical concerns were laid out by the Argentinian film-makers Fernando Solanas and Octavio Getino in an essay 'Towards a Third Cinema', which was to be hugely influential to oppositional film-makers the world over (Solanas and Getino, 1969/1976). Their argument was that political, oppositional cinema, represented by post-revolutionary Cuban cinema or by their own *La Hora de los Hornos* (1968) was a 'Third Cinema', not because it spoke to the so-called 'Third World' only (though this was the context out of which it grew) but because it marked a clear aesthetic and political difference to what they saw as two dominant modes of film-making. 'First Cinema' was big-budget, mainstream Hollywood feature film-making, 'destined to satisfy only the ideological and economic interests of the *owners of the film industry* (ibid., p. 44; original emphasis). 'Second Cinema' was a more modestly budgeted 'auteur' cinema, independent to some extent from the economics and aesthetics of the Hollywood model, but nonetheless caught up in the ideology and politics of the establishment – 'at best the "progressive" wing of Establishment cinema' (ibid., p. 45).

'Third Cinema', therefore, was a revolutionary form of oppositional film-making, anti-imperialist and decolonialising in its politics, artisanal and collective in its working methods and geared towards raising political questions in its audience, rather than merely offering ideology marketed as entertainment. In his later discussion of the concept of Third Cinema, Paul Willemen notes how Solanas revised his original formulation to take account of the fact that the Third Cinema idea was being adopted throughout both the 'First' and the 'Third Worlds' to meet the needs of oppositional film-making in diverse social and economic contexts (Willemen, 1989, pp. 1–29). Solanas' reformulation is interesting from the perspective of Irish films and films about Ireland. The defining characteristic of the three cinemas is their relationship to dominant aesthetics, politics and ideologies. Thus the kind of intimate auteur cinema that in a production context might belong to the Second Cinema could and should be considered as First Cinema if its political effect is to reproduce unquestioningly the dominant representations of that cinema. As Solanas explains: 'So-called author cinema often belongs in the second cinema, but both good and bad authors may be found in the first and the third cinemas.' It is useful to quote his reformulation of Third Cinema in detail.

> … Third Cinema is the expression of a new culture and of social change …
> (it) gives an account of reality and history. It is also linked with national
> culture … It is the way the world is conceptualised and not the genre nor the
> explicitly political character of a film which makes it belong to Third Cinema

... Third Cinema is an open category, unfinished, incomplete ... (quoted in
Willemen, 1989, p. 11)

In all formulations of Third Cinema, there is an agreed assumption that this
cinema will promote a socialist consciousness, both stimulating debate and
finding a space within and without dominant culture where this can take place.
Its object was not to foreclose such debate through dogmatic assertion, rather,
to provide analyses and explorations that would be worked through by 'the
people' themselves. As such, the whole Third Cinema question reflects the
socio-historical moment of the 1960s and 1970s when there still seemed the
possibility of developing alternatives to consumerist capitalism. The context in
the 1990s has changed. Thus Michael Chanan notes that Third Cinema had
always responded to everyday exigencies and since those have changed so completely then, if it is to survive, Third Cinema needs to develop a 'new geography'.
The new terrain has been mapped out by post-colonial theorists who, recog-
nising the global nature of capitalism and its consumer culture, attempt to
identify the spaces within which the voices (and images) of the marginal and
the oppressed can find expression. 'The original Third Cinema was premised
on militant mass political movements of a kind which in many places no longer
exist and upon ideologies which have taken a decisive historical beating. ... The
survival of, Third Cinema depends on its origins within the margins and the
interstices' (Chanan, 1997, pp. 387–8).

This new geography implies the internationalising of the debate, locating the
liminal spaces where the local and the global, the particular and the universal,
interconnect. But this, itself, has interesting implications for how we might now
understand the relationship between specific national cinemas and the global
cinema of Hollywood. Even a few years ago, for example, it might have seemed
perverse to include a former imperial power like Britain in a discussion about
national cultures which are increasingly under threat. It might have appeared
even more incongruous to include a multinational conglomerate of former
imperial powers like Europe in such a debate. But today this is common. In a
rather amused comment on debates about national cinemas in Europe, Julio
García Espinosa, formerly head of ICAIC, the Cuban Film Institute, and one of
the early theorists of Third Cinema, has observed:

Almost a 100 years ago Latin America began calling out in the wilderness,
declaring its right to make films. The only thing to have happened is that after
a 100 years Western Europe also declared its right to make films. Today it
turns out that an English film is just as exotic as a film from Ecuador ... Today
we are witnessing the unexpected, as the problem of national culture ceases to
be a concern only of Third World countries. (Espinosa, 1993, pp. 12–16)

There might, indeed, be a certain amount of glee here at the historic irony of Europe's (and England's) predicament, though to be fair to Espinosa he is motivated more by shared experience and shared loss than he is by bitterness or rancour. As he argues, 'Yesterday, Latin America asked for Europe's solidarity. It still does, but it also offers solidarity to Europe' (Espinosa, 1993, p. 12). Behind Espinosa's argument lies the spectre of the USA and the seemingly total supremacy of Hollywood cinema on a global scale – First Cinema in its most universal sense. The consequent collapse of Europe's national cinemas is not only a great loss in itself but it raises doubts about the very idea of a national cinema in the first place. For if the formerly powerful nation-states of Europe can no longer sustain national film cultures, what hope is there for the Third World? Espinosa raises the possibility of transnational solutions to national problems – Ecuador within Latin America, England within Europe – but, perhaps not surprisingly, he misses some of the subtle ironies within the European (and British) situation.

For if Latin America has been 'calling out in the wilderness for a hundred years, declaring its right to make films', then within Europe so has a host of less visible and more peripheral nations and states, including, of course, Ireland. Indeed, the debate about national culture has been almost constant in Ireland since the 1840s, pre-dating the birth of cinema and covering every aspect of cultural production since. In this regard, then, Espinosa is mistaken to link, until relatively recently, the debate about national culture to only the Third World. In fact, this debate has flourished in the 'First World' (for example, in the Celtic periphery of Europe) but was generally regarded as a rather archaic relic of pre-modern times, an irrelevant sideshow to the onward march of modernity and progress.

A number of factors coincided to change this. First, in the political arena, the accelerating pace of European integration within the EU has given rise to wider debates about regional, national and supranational identities. We have noted, in this regard, that Ireland, much more so than its British neighbour, has linked its future to the European project. The considerable irony here is that a country that prides itself on its nationalist past has collapsed aspects of that identity into an international frame much more so than a former imperial nation that prides itself on having avoided the rancours of nationalism. Second, the sweeping changes in Eastern Europe at the end of the 1980s and the collapse of the Soviet Union in 1991 have rekindled a whole range of ethnic nationalisms and ethnic conflicts held in check by state communism. Finally, in the cultural sphere, the worldwide and the total market dominance of Hollywood and American television has given a renewed urgency to questions about cultural imperialism and fears about the survival of national cultures everywhere. The irony is that Ireland's own local difficulties (epitomised, for example in the television debates of the 1970s) are now being played out in a larger arena. (Even the tragedies of the violent conflict in Northern Ireland are mirrored on a larger scale in the ethnic wars of Eastern Europe.) Ireland's long and continuing preoccupation with questions of national culture are, therefore, peculiarly relevant to these wider cultural debates and Ireland's negotiation of core/periphery relationships is particularly instructive to current debates in Europe about the idea of a national cinema.

If we return, then, to the three levels of state support for film-making in Ireland we can make some observations about the kinds of film that have emerged in recent years. In big-budget USA productions, like Ron Howard's *Far and Away* (1992), artistic control has remained outside of Ireland itself (with implications for meaning and representation) but the level of studio and big-star involvement has meant that the films have received wide international exposure. In terms of the Third Cinema debate, these are clearly part of the First Cinema, tied unquestioningly to the consumerist thrust of commercial cinema and offering no challenge to existing representations. However, at this level, as well, non-Irish-themed films like *Braveheart* or *Saving Private Ryan* (which availed themselves of the tax incentives merely to take advantage of Irish locations) allowed for a spin-off to both the general economy and to the infrastructure of film-making. Higgins specifically wrote into the tax incentives scheme provisions about training requirements for Irish personnel and, as we noted, characterised this part of the strategy as exploiting the 'commercial space' for the benefit of 'indigenous energy' (Higgins, 1995). All of these films are undoubtedly First Cinema, according to definitions of the term, but Irish state policy has attempted to engage with them at a production level to create the opportunities for more specific and more relevant indigenous film-making. The 'liminal spaces and interstices' where the local meets the global are being explored.

In medium-budget films, often the result of co-production partnerships, the incentives and other state-support mechanisms have allowed a greater level of artistic control to remain in Ireland, despite the need to secure a large part of their budgets from outside. These films are subsequently more interesting and more complex as a rule (as is the case with the films of Neil Jordan, Thaddeus O'Sullivan or Jim Sheridan) and have made a critical impact that far outweighs their commercial achievements. It is not easy, in these cases, to read off reductively the artistic concessions that have been made as a result of foreign financial arrangements, though it is tempting nonetheless to do so. Thus in a film like Sheridan's *In the Name of the Father* (1993) there is an interesting question about the extent to which the displacement of a political story on to an oedipal father/son story is the result of the American backers or Sheridan's own way of inhabiting genre conventions. (The film is discussed in detail in Chapter Three.)

Ireland has also attracted the attentions of both American and British film-makers whose films, although more modestly budgeted than the blockbusters, have nonetheless retained artistic control to an extent that it is difficult to judge them as indigenous in any meaningful way. For example, despite the fact that both were financed largely outside of Ireland there is surely a distinction to be made between Neil Jordan's *The Crying Game* (1992) and John Sayles' *The Secret of Roan Inish* (1994). The source of the financial backing is not primar-ily the issue here. Rather, Sayles' film is extraneous to Ireland in a more crucial manner. It draws little on Irish creative talent other than in the employment of Irish actors. Jordan's film, on the other hand, is creatively dependent on the director's Irish sensibility and his obsession with exploring the interface between sexuality and violence in Ireland. This does not, of course, mean that Sayles fails some kind of 'purity' test – his film is about Ireland and was set and shot in Ireland and interacts in telling ways with Irish themes and iconography. However, as we shall see, its artistic genesis does have an impact on the kind of film that it is and this moulds the nature of this interaction.

In terms of the Third Cinema debate, we can see in these medium-budget films the porous nature of the three-way distinction alluded to by Solanas. The determinedly independent Sayles probably occupies a clear Second Cinema position in regard to his American theme films but in his commitment to col-lective political opposition (*The Return of the Secaucus Seven* [1979]; *Matewan* [1987]), in his exploration of American memory and myth (*Lone Star* [1996]) and in his concern to represent marginal, ethnic experiences (*Lone Star* again, *Hombres Armados* [1997]) he comes close to the Third Cinema category. How-ever, his Irish film, *The Secret of Roan Inish*, moves perilously close to the dominant ideology of First Cinema in the way in which it recycles some of the hoary old myths about Ireland and the Irish. So too does Kirk Jones' *Waking Ned* (1998). As we discussed in Chapter One, for a film that uses its landscape setting to register the familiar markers of Irishness that it trades on, it was not even shot in Ireland. This seems to confirm the shoddiness and inauthenticity of the whole project. But again, this is not the point. The film trades on a bla-tant recycling of outrageous clichés and on rehashing old myths about rural Ireland. Despite its modest budget, it is, in Solanas' typology, clearly 'First Cin-ema' in its relationship to the status quo.

However, in its treatment of age, and its bold decision to use two seventy-year-olds as the heroes, the film also offers at least some opposition to dominant Hollywood ideology. How the film is received, therefore, is a matter of the cul-tural context of consumption – who sees the film and in what context. For the Irish, it is an insult (Linehan, 1999, p. 46). For 'Help the Aged' groups it may well provide the kind of debates among audiences (in this case about ageism) that is characteristic of Third Cinema. It might, in other words, achieve some of the objectives outlined by Solanas in relation to moving individuals from passive spectators to active participants (though hardly in the socially and politically transforming manner which he envisaged).

Most of the medium-budget Irish film-makers are more clearly oppositional to the dominant modes of Hollywood representation than this and in the case of some film-makers (Jordan, for example) the degree to which their films exhibit both thematic and formal innovation moves their work closer to a Third Cinema perspective. The most significant films, and therefore the most 'Irish' films, are those that operate in a Third Cinema sense of exploring the complex realities of contemporary Ireland, challenging cinema audiences by challenging dominant and sedimented notions about Ireland and the Irish.

The value of adapting the Third Cinema debate to Ireland is not just that it is suggested by the three-tier funding strategy outlined by Michael D. Higgins but that it provides a pathway through the vexed question of what exactly constitutes an Irish film. In one regard, both *Far and Away* and *The Secret of Roan Inish* are Irish films and as representations of Irish themes they are quite rightly discussed as part of a study of 'film and Ireland'. They have also played their part in generating the necessary infrastructure in Ireland that can sustain indigenous film-makers. The critique offered here is not that they are, by dint of their production contexts, less 'Irish' than those, say, of Jordan or Sheridan (and, after all, Jordan's *Michael Collins* operated on a First Cinema budget) but that their representation of Ireland is extremely problematic. They interconnect with contemporary Ireland in regressive aesthetic, ideological and political ways. This may, indeed, be a result of their creative distance from Ireland and the Irish. The judgment here, however, is a critical, not an ethnic or an economic one, informed by aesthetic and political concerns about the films' relationship to dominant representations of Ireland and the socio-political complexities of contemporary Ireland.

The third category of funding for films produced wholly within Ireland itself, then, has tended to be that of low-budget films, which are very particular in their concerns and dominated by younger writer/directors determined to hold on to artistic control of both form and subject matter. This was particularly true of the earlier period of film-making in the 1970s and early 1980s but it is also the logic of the Film Board strategy since 1993, especially in regard to first-time directors. This is Ireland's 'third cinema' – and, as we shall see, in some cases as well Ireland's Third Cinema – relatively unknown outside the country and, with the exception of a few individual films, largely unseen in Irish cinemas either. Their main impact has been at festivals around the world and their main audience is picked up when the films have been screened on Irish or British television. They fall into two distinct periods. The first wave lasted up to 1987, when its demise was signalled by the suspension of the Film Board. The second

wave began in earnest after the 1993 initiatives and the re-establishing of the
Film Board in an economic and cultural climate that had changed considerably. The differences between the films of these two periods are pronounced
and form another internal point of debate. We will consider the implications
of this in Chapter Eight.

Taken together, then, these medium- and low-budget films represent an
emerging national cinema defined, not by an essentialist conception of Irishness, but by a desire to explore the contradictions and complexities of Irish
identity as it looks inwards and backwards at its own history and outwards and
forwards to its European future. The scope of the films' attempted revisioning
of Ireland can be gauged by looking more closely at some of the characteristic
issues and concerns that they share. We might schematise their recurring
themes thus:

- an interrogation of the rural mythology which underpinned cultural
  nationalism and is encapsulated in the use of landscape;
- a new concern to represent urban experience which was largely submerged
  and ignored by this rural mythology, especially the urban experience of the
  rapidly modernising contemporary Ireland;
- a consequent desire to reveal the social and political failures of independent
  Ireland and latterly to probe the failures and contradictions of the Irish
  'economic miracle';
- an interrogation of religion in Ireland, especially in relation to education,
  sexuality and gender;
- the question of women in Ireland, especially in relation to nationalism,
  Catholic teaching and imagery and the discourse around women's bodies
  engendered by the abortion debate in Ireland;
- an interrogation of Irish history and Irish tradition and the conflict between
  tradition and modernity (often rendered as a generational conflict);
- the question of Northern Ireland, political violence and the disputed
  notions of identity which form the crux of the conflict;
- a new concern to imagine the nation differently, sometimes in its European
  context and sometimes probing its 'special relationship' to the USA and
  American culture, especially through diasporic Irishness;
- a concern with film form itself, especially the desire to work through existing forms in the search for a new or more characteristic aesthetic.

Like all schemas, there is a danger that this one isolates recurring themes in a
way that the films themselves do not. These are intensely interrelated issues and
in truth, many Irish films cover a number of them at the same time, while a
complex film like Neil Jordan's *The Butcher Boy* (1997) touches on most of

A new concern to represent urban experience: Dublin in *Down the Corner*

them. The process of modernisation and the fall-out from the conflict in Northern Ireland has resulted in an intellectual and cultural ferment in Ireland where the very notion of what it is to be Irish is a key contemporary debate. New Irish cinema is a product of this larger cultural environment and has begun in various ways to contribute to the continuing debate. Finally, it is worth noting that Irish film-makers do not work to any agreed manifesto (other than, perhaps, a shared desire to tell Irish stories to Irish audiences in the first instance). There is a great deal of artistic and political variety in their work and even in a film culture so recently emerged, a clear generational divergence between the first wave of writer-directors of the 1970s and early 1980s and the younger film-makers of the 1990s.

Thus, Kevin Rockett has argued that the younger film-makers are more aesthetically and politically conservative than their immediate predecessors even if their films demonstrate a higher level of competence and skill (Rockett, 1996). This is essentially the same point that Bob Quinn has made, adding the observation that the most recent films exhibit all the characteristics of a culture that has effectively joined an Anglo-American sensibility uncritically (Quinn,

1999). Even in such a relatively short time span the context of film-making in Ireland has changed profoundly and it would be pointless trying to define too narrowly what this new cinema is or should aspire to be. The schema proposed here, therefore, is the result of *post hoc* critical activity and is not suggested as a programme or a prescription for a clearly defined movement.

We will look at the work of the 'first wave' directors in more detail in the next chapter.

Chapter 6
The First Wave: Indigenous Film in the 1970s and 1980s

The first period of independent film-making in Ireland lasted from the mid-1970s to 1987, when the first Film Board was shut down. In this period a group of both young and more experienced film-makers began to explore the contradictions of a changing society in a form of culture (the fiction film) in which there was little in the way of a national tradition or precedence. The films of this period, therefore, vary in the degree in which they adhere to a traditional cinematic narrative norm and in the way they attempt to explore the medium of film itself in innovative or experimental ways. Nonetheless, taken together they amount to an impressively adventurous group of films that augured well for a critically engaged indigenous cinema.

Rockett follows film critic Ciaran Carty in citing Bob Quinn's *Caoineadh Airt Uí Laoire (Lament for Art O'Leary* [1975]) as a key film in this early experimental process (Rockett, 1988, pp. 137–8). This was the film that announced the arrival of an indigenous Irish cinema and also the first independently produced film in the Irish language. It is also an extremely complex and ambitious film, demonstrating the kind of formal exploration that is rare today. The film tackles some of the key elements in Irish cultural nationalism, including the legacy of its colonial past, the cultural significance of the west of Ireland, the vexed question of the Irish language itself and Irish history and tradition in general. It is particularly concerned to explore the ways in which these impinge on contemporary Ireland.

The film is based on the Irish-language lament of the same name, written in the 1770s by O'Leary's widow after her husband was killed in a confrontation with an English landlord. The lament was passed on in Ireland's oral tradition, inevitably being added to and modified as it was filtered through the mediation of successive generations. In this way, the poem is an illustration of what Gibbons has called 'radical memory' and Bob Quinn's film (indeed much of Quinn's work) could operate as a template for the kind cinema which Gibbons has called for, informed by the radical traditions of pre-modern Irish culture (Gibbons, 1996). However, the lament itself is at the centre of a complex set of contemporary forms and representations that make up the film. A group of actors is rehearsing a play based on the poem. This play employs a series of filmed inserts, shot as a costumed fiction re-creating the events of the poem and featuring the same actors. Interwoven into this complex, the actors discuss their own filmic portrayals and argue historical interpretations with the play's director (played by English playwright John Arden, who is also the landowner, Morris, in the filmed version of the poem). The dramatic centre of the film is the confrontation between the main actor, Sean Ban Breathnach, and the director of the play, which mirrors the historical confrontation between Art O'Leary and Morris. Formally, then, we have a poem within a film, within a play, within a film that, from a contemporary perspective of reappraisal and reconsideration, refers back and forwards across two hundred years of history.

This complex structure involving an array of forms raises issues of cultural representation in general and presents history in particular, not as a given set of irrefutable facts, but as a question of representation itself, a matter of interpretation which is used to meet the ideological needs of the present. At the centre of the film is a debate over the courageous acts of violence represented by the historic Art O'Leary's confrontation with English authority and the significance that these have for the continuing tradition of militant nationalism in Northern Ireland. As the actors discuss their performances in the filmed sequences and debate the significance of the events they portray, we get a perfect illustration of that key objective of Third Cinema identified by Solanas and Getino – the opening up of debate or 'the participation of people who, until then, were considered spectators' (Solanas and Getino, 1969/1976, p. 61).

The film was funded by Sinn Féin, the Workers' Party, at a crucial point in that organisation's development away from radical nationalist politics to the more socialist views espoused by the party (Democratic Left) that it evolved into before it finally merged with the Irish Labour Party in the late 1990s. In many ways, the evolution of this branch of the republican movement mirrors the shift away from nationalist politics in the South in general. This, as we have seen, is characteristic of modernisation in the South and is in stark contrast to Sinn Féin in Northern Ireland, which continued to promote a politics of national liberation. It is, therefore, a key cinematic statement of a time of reappraisal, reassessment and transition. The film's renegotiation of key elements in Irish nationalism, no matter how tentative they look in retrospect, nonetheless pointed forward to a dominant theme in subsequent films. Still, in retrospect, Quinn's film can now be seen also as an early key statement of the anti-revisionist sentiment that would become more dominant in the years of stalled modernisation in the 1980s. It was an attempt, in other words, to reinsert, albeit in a more radical and a more secular sense, the nationalism that was in danger of being jettisoned in the rush towards modernity. Reappraisal, the film seems to say, should not mean collective amnesia. Quinn continued to contribute important, questioning films throughout the next three decades, creating in the process a formidably eccentric and challenging body of work which not only explores the myths that bound together the traditional discourses of cultural nationalism, but which also offers an acerbic critique of the 'modernity' which threw this into crisis in the first place.

Thus, *Poitín* (1978) offers a deliberately unromantic view of the west of Ireland which, in cultural nationalism, was the repository of those Gaelic, Catholic and rural values which were to be the basis of Ireland's anti-modernist and romantic utopia. Its study of the grim realities of rural life, including its endemic criminality, is neither Flaherty nor Ford and marked a key stage in the reimagining of Irish rural life. In his three-part television documentary, *Atlantean* (1983), Quinn scrutinises the whole Celtic mythology in Ireland in an ironic and absurdist manner by arguing the case for the Irish being descended from North African Arab seafarers. In *Budawanny* (1987), re-visited in a longer version as *The Bishop's Story* (1994), Quinn returns to the west of Ireland to explore the clash between the formal, organised structures of the Catholic church and a more pagan or elemental form of religion which the people themselves adhere to. The clash is precipitated by a priest who lives in the remote Clare Island parish with his housekeeper. When she becomes pregnant he seeks the indulgence of his parishioners to pursue his priestly duties regardless (and largely succeeds). 'You will soon have another reason to call me father,' he announces from the pulpit. It is only when one parishioner alerts the bishop that the priest is brought to heel. Again, the implication here is that the traditions of Irish rural life, moulded in the post-Famine era by a Catholic asceticism involving the suppression of sexuality, were a recent imposition on much older traditions that themselves were more ambiguous and more earthy about such matters. *Budawanny* proved prescient when a real scandal engulfed the church in 1993. The Bishop of Galway admitted that he had fathered a son by an American woman years before and had used church funds to provide maintenance ever since. This was one of the many scandals during the 1990s that further weakened church influence in Ireland and the fact that the bishop involved was generally regarded as one of the more enlightened and liberal members of the hierarchy was an irony not lost on many.

Quinn's work is witty and ironic, constantly undermining its own seriousness and pretensions with a built-in leavening of humour. His films exist in an ironic relationship with both tradition and modernity, on one hand castigating cultural nationalism's use, or abuse, of Gaelic Ireland while at the same time, being deeply suspicious of the modernity represented by Dublin (and Hollywood). His commitment to the Irish language flows from the same feeling, expressed by various commentators throughout the period, that the language is not just the repository of a long and radical tradition in Ireland but also the most effective bulwark against being subsumed into an Anglo-American cultural universe. Quinn's ambivalence to both cultural nationalism and modernity is emblematic of the whole contradictory interface between the particular and the universal discussed in Chapter Four. His films offer no final resolutions, indeed pretend to no definitive statements, but in their scepticism, irony and self-deflating humour, they offer important instances of the kind of conditional negotiation with tradition and modernity which is characteristic of the best indigenous films.

In its complex formal structure, its mixing of different modes of representation, *Caoineadh Airt Uí Laoire* also established what later emerged as another key element in indigenous Irish films of the 1970s and early 1980s – the interrogation of film language itself and an attempt to explore the relationship between politics and film. Joe Comerford is another director who has been responsible for inserting a new content into Irish culture as well as exploring this relationship. After a number of short films made in the 1970s, Comerford has since made three feature-length films of considerable importance: *Traveller* (1982), *Reefer and the Model* (1988) and *High Boot Benny* (1993). Comerford established his importance with his 1978 short film *Down the Corner*, which was financed by the British Film Institute. *Down the Corner* is set in the working-class Dublin estate of Ballyfermot and marks a considerable milestone in the cinematic project of giving voice and image to the urban working class. The opening sequences of urban industrial Dublin, scenes shot in a foundry, are a remarkable departure in cinematic imagery of Ireland, establishing the missing discourse of the city and industrial labour almost for the first time. The film was shot using a local, non-professional cast and taps into a tradition of working-class realism which, as we discussed in Chapter One, although common in Britain, was all to rare in Irish culture.

As with Bob Quinn's films, Comerford's work is always ambiguous and elliptical, but whereas Quinn's ambiguity is a result of his own deep irony, Comerford's results from the severity of his vision. He is most interested in the totally marginalised and dispossessed in society (an earlier short, *Withdrawal* [1974], dealt with heroin addicts) and these severe victims of modernity's inequalities give Comerford's cinema a cold bleakness. Indeed, his films are lowly (as opposed to highly) stylised, probing at the edges of society with an angst which eschews embellishment. His feature films, *Traveller* and *High Boot Benny* in particular are narratively disjointed and confusing, mirroring the dysfunctional confusion of the main characters.

Comerford's films are always deeply metaphorical, so that his marginalised characters and oblique narratives can be read as symbolic motifs of contemporary Ireland. Thus, the travellers in *Traveller* are the forgotten victims of progress, but also can be read as a metaphor for the dispossessed nationalist people of the North. The dysfunctional families in *Down the Corner, Reefer and the Model* and the perverse family grouping in *High Boot Benny* are all metaphors for the sickness of the nation itself. Comerford's bleak imagining of the nation is a result of what he sees as the unfulfilled idealism of Irish national-ist rhetoric. No other Southern film-maker has engaged with Northern Ireland and its continuing significance so completely as he has. No other film-maker has explored the gap between the high idealism of Irish nationalism and the sick and sorry state of contemporary Ireland in the way he has.

This is most evident in *High Boot Benny*. Comerford here creates his most emphatically bleak vision of Ireland (the film was shot in the Inishowen penin-sula of Donegal in mid-winter), which challenges visually the dominant romantic imagery of Irish landscape. Indeed it is difficult to enjoy this scenery for its own sake, for behind every rock, and just over every hill, one feels the presence of masked military or paramilitary gunmen engaged in a incoherent and inconclusive bloodbath (blood, entrapment and death permeate the film). This is a nightmarish border community of the imagination; Comerford's most complete vision of the dysfunctional nation which he sees is a result of the bleeding sore that is Northern Ireland. But in keeping with his own non-con-formist vision, the setting for *High Boot Benny* is one of high idealism at the margins of society. The action centres on an alternative school (motto: 'Inde-pendence in education is a dangerous aspiration') established in the ruins of a former British fort isolated from the scrutiny of both the British and Irish establishment. The attempt to forge an alternative community with a liberat-ing educational ethos is compromised by a series of events which bring the school to the attention of the British Army, the RUC, loyalist paramilitaries and the IRA – a potent mix of disruptive forces that inevitably brings tragedy and ruin to the whole experiment. The 'family' established here is an outcast one – the father figure is a failed priest with republican sympathies who unearths an informer in their midst and so initiates the events that lead to tragedy. The matron of the school is a southern Protestant whose idealism is driven by a 'plague on both your houses' mentality. The 'son' is Benny himself, an emo-tionally scarred teenage victim of the alienation of the northern violence who is prepared to follow Matron's lead into an idealism beyond the dogmas of both North and South. His tragedy is that he is not allowed to do so and is forced to take sides in the end.

In *Reefer and the Model*, Comerford offers a new imagining of the nation in the constructed family of similar outcasts and alienated individuals – the model herself, no exemplar of traditional values, is a pregnant ex-prostitute and drug addict, recently returned from London. Badger is gay, Spider is an IRA man from the North who is on the run and who has lost faith in the cause (at one point he admits to having only joined in the first place to attract the girls). Reefer is an eccentric mix of Walter Mitty, petty criminal, west-coast adventurer and fireside republican. There is, though, in Comerford's vision, a deep and genuine human sympathy for these marginalised and largely inarticulate characters. The idealism and the aspirations that motivate them may be vague and unarticulated – even contradictory and irrational when they are articulated – but the point is that these ideals are a response to the lack of idealism in conventional society. Their elliptical and imprecise nature requires an equally ambiguous cinematic form to allow them to emerge.

Comerford's challenging vision of Ireland's identity crisis, therefore, poses extreme problems for the audience. His adherence to a naturalistic aesthetic (his films, for example, feature many non-professional actors in main parts) and his narrative disjunctions are at odds with dominant realist forms, especially, of course, the high-octane narratives of Hollywood. To that extent, his film language is engaged in a debate with dominant forms anyway and his concerns remain doggedly those of Third Cinema.

However, what is remarkable about *Reefer and the Model* is that he builds into his visual style and narrative construction a stylistic inner dialogue about film-making itself. Thus, the film employs two styles – an austere, European art cinema aesthetic, which is his own preferred style, and a pastiche of the Hollywood chase movie. Both styles of course are rendered problematic in their encounter with Irish stereotypes and the west of Ireland scenery. In this clash of styles and traditions, everything is changed and the resultant vision is one of amusing, and bemusing, strangeness.

The most subversive aspect of *Reefer and the Model* is the scene in the pub on the Aran island ('The American Bar') in which Badger dances with, gently fondles and then kisses his male dance partner, an Irish soldier on leave, during the céilidh. In relation to this scene, Lance Pettitt has made a number of interesting observations (Pettitt, 1997, p. 261). 'Their participation in the céilidh', he argues, 'defies "mainland" codes, and their kiss is a moment of remarkable tenderness between two men that provides for a poignant screen moment.' The fact that this encounter takes place on Inis Mór, a Gaeltacht area of the Aran Islands, is significant. The locals actually tolerate the two men dancing together and Pettitt points out that it is an outsider, the soldier's sergeant, who takes offence. He performs the same role that the outraged parishioner does in *Budawanny/The Bishop's Story*, initiating a regressive reaction to an act of social transgression that the local population is inclined to ignore. In this way, the film again seems to confirm Luke Gibbons' notion of a 'radical memory' deeply embedded in the so-called reactionary traditions of rural Ireland. It is, as Pettitt argues, a representative of the state, the army sergeant, who attempts to suppress such overt homosexuality and initiates the violence that follows. The action takes place, though, in 'The American Bar'. What then is the significance of this? (A detail like this is not accidental in the highly allegorical world of the film.) Is the tolerant attitude to the gay couple the result of the 'natural' sexual tolerance of the Irish, suppressed by the forces of Catholic nationalism but, like Quinn's more tolerant religion, alive in the remotest and most Gaelic parts of the country? Alternatively, is it the result of the influence of liberal, global culture intimated by 'The American Bar'?

Even more interestingly, according to Pettitt's research the character of Badger at script stage was clearly identified as a northern Presbyterian, though in the film as made this is not so clear. Badger, therefore, is meant to signify a double transgression of Catholic nationalism – through his sexuality and his religion. This is, of course, suggestively subversive: '… showing a northern Presbyterian man coupling with a soldier from the Irish Republic suggests a vision of sexual and political daring' (Pettitt, 1997, p. 261). Given Ian Paisley's much-vaunted campaign to 'Save Ulster from Sodomy' it is tempting to gloat at Comerford's daring. But problems remain with the representation here. Gayness works allegorically only because its perversity is implied. It is used as a metaphor for the outcast; it does not probe the human dimension of, or ideological reasons for, being an outcast in the first place. Like the model's perverse image of women, Badger's homosexuality is both a sign of the film's concern with the marginalised and the despised in society, but also a challenge to the dominant ideologies of cultural nationalism and Irish Catholicism. However, like the representation of women in the film, the price paid for operating on so many metaphorical levels is that dominant representations are confirmed. Thus, to oppose the dominant image of Mother Ireland and her chaste daughter, the feisty colleen, the model is presented as a drug-addict ex-prostitute – a transcription from virgin to vamp. Pettitt himself discusses the regressive portrayal of seedy businessman Val (Gabriel Byrne) in Frank Deasy and Joe Lee's *The Courier* (1987), where gayness in this case becomes another metaphor for general anti-social criminality (Pettitt, 1997, pp. 256–9). The metaphor of sexual perversion has been used in cinema generally in a similar manner to indicate 'fascism' (i.e. political perversion) as, for example, in Donald Sutherland's character in Bertolucci's *1900* (1976). We will note another example of this tendency in our discussion of Jimmy Smallhorne's *2 By 4* (1997) in Chapter Nine. Gayness here (and by implication, Northern Protestantism) is, therefore, another trait of 'marginality' or 'perversion'. Although treated sympathetically within the film, it is nonetheless a metaphor that only works by accepting its regressive connotations. The scene in the bar helps to work against this regressive representation but only in the sense that this scene packs a power and an importance in itself that might be seen to overdetermine other aspects of the representation.

Like Quinn, Comerford has an intensely ambiguous relationship to both traditional nationalism and the cultural logic of modernity. If his films display an ingrained sympathy to a radical and secular nationalism beyond the confines of 'official' nationalism, then they do so in an entirely ambiguous manner. As in Quinn's films, we can detect in Comerford's work an anxiety about losing the radical aspirations that nationalism can embody. But it is hard not to conclude that his reimagining of the nation that includes the marginal, the outcasts and the oppressed would require such a fundamental shift in patriarchal nationalist thinking, republican as well as 'official', that it would be barely recognisable as such. His bleak vision operates in a much more existential way than Quinn's retrieval of the radical traditions of rural Ireland, giving little comfort in contemporary Ireland to either the adherents of a republican nationalist sensibility, the anti-nationalist consensus of liberal Ireland or to the 'young Turks' of Celtic Tiger Ireland. In this regard, David Butler's wryly hostile review of *High Boot Benny* is apposite: 'I can certainly see a German arthouse audience enjoying it, but the audiences who flocked to *The Commitments*? I wouldn't be so sure' (Butler, 1993/4, p. 32). That though is surely the strength of Comerford's vision as much as it is a weakness. His strategy is the cinema of opposition, rather than the cinema of 'occupation' – to challenge rather than to accept and work within First Cinema conventions. Certainly, he is so far removed from the aesthetic forms and political stereotypes of other cinematic portrayals of Ireland that he has been unrecognisable at home. This kind of exploration and challenge is to be cherished.

The question of Catholic repression is the subject matter of perhaps the most prescient of the early short films, Cathal Black's *Our Boys* (1981). Black's film is emblematic and important for a number of reasons. Its completion at all is a triumph of will over adversity. It took over three years to make, costing in total a mere £5,200, a paltry sum even in 1981. The film stock and the finance were cobbled together from a number of sources, including RTÉ, the Arts Council of Northern Ireland and the Film Board. The film was shot in periodic bursts of activity, as these became available. Actors and crew worked for minimal or no wages. It was a truly artisanal production in every sense. *Our Boys* garnered great praise when it was released in the autumn of 1981, eventually winning an award at the Melbourne Film Festival. And then, inexplicably, having helped to produce it, RTÉ declined to show the film for ten years, finally relenting in February 1991. Its representation of religious education in Ireland was deemed too controversial in the wake of the recent papal visit.

However, *Our Boys* has sustained its interest through the 1990s for this reason. The film is a remembrance of, and an exploration of, a Christian Brothers' education of the early 1960s, written autobiographically by Black himself in collaboration with Dermot Healy. As with many of the films of this period,

Our Boys employs a complex formal structure, mixing different filmic devices that work to extend the film's significance. At the core of the film is a fairly naturalistic fiction drama about a Christian Brothers school in Dublin at the turn of the 1950s/1960s. This drama involves two storylines: the physical abuse of a young boy by one of the brothers and the subsequent complaint from the parents and secondly the issues involved in closing down the school because of falling rolls and a changing social and educational environment. Interwoven into this fiction at certain key moments are two highly emotional interviews with former pupils of the brothers and a contemporary interview with a brother who assesses the educational legacy of their style of education. These are in the form of a direct address to camera shot in conventional documentary style.

The third filmic discourse involves the use of archive footage and in particular two sequences which hold a deep significance for contemporary Ireland. The first archive sequence opens the film, with footage of a St Patrick's Day parade in Dublin, probably in the early 1960s. Floats in the parade include references to space exploration and the novelty of television and the footage captures the atmosphere in Ireland as it slowly came out of its long, protectionist period of 'dozing on the sideline' to embrace modernisation and liberalisation. The second archive sequence is from the Eucharistic Congress, held in Dublin in 1932, showing the arrival of the papal nuncio in Dun Laoghaire. He is greeted by local and national politicians who approach, bow and kiss his ring, pledging their allegiance to the church. The footage continues with scenes shot at the open-air Mass in Phoenix Park, which was attended by over one million people.

This sequence serves a double purpose. Firstly, it gives a rather graphic illustration of how closely intertwined Irish civil authority and Catholic church authority were in the period after independence. This archive sequence, in other words, provides the context for the film's exploration of Catholic education, itself a unique synthesis of religion and nationalism, and provides an earlier reference point against which the changes of the 1960s might be measured.

The second function of the Eucharistic Congress footage is much more contemporary and arguably much more significant. In September 1979, as Cathal Black was struggling to put his film together, Pope John Paul II made his historic visit to Ireland. He too celebrated Mass in Phoenix Park in front of more than one million people and received a rapturous reception from the people of Ireland wherever he went. This visit, as we have discussed in Chapter Four, has often been cited by commentators as the impetus behind the re-emergence of fundamental Catholicism in the 1980s which fought, ultimately unsuccessfully, to roll back liberalisation and the evolving secular society. We have noted that for Luke Gibbons, writing in 1988, Phoenix Park was an appropriate setting for confessional Ireland to rise from the ashes (Gibbons, 1988b, p. 218). On the other hand at the time of the Pope's visit, it was common for liberal and left commentators in the country to repeat a remark often attributed to an RTÉ producer that it 'set the country back fifty years – for three days'. In retrospect, the truth lay somewhere between these two extremes.

In *Our Boys*, the contemporary parallels were there to be drawn and the archive footage of the Eucharistic Congress does just that. Indeed, these contemporary resonances, and its raising of the question of abuse, make *Our Boys* a peculiarly prescient film. The abuse scandals that rocked the church in the 1990s, involving all branches of organised religion – priests, brothers and nuns – were to culminate in an unprecedented apology on behalf of the church for any hurt and distress that it had caused in former years. What the archive footage raises, then, is the question of just how much Ireland had in fact changed by the time of the film's production. In 1979–1981, when he was cobbling together the budget for his film, Cathal Black was not to know the impact that the Pope's visit was to have. However, many of the issues that were to dominate such debate are all there in this remarkable short film: liberalisation versus conservatism; Catholicism versus secularism; modernity versus anti-modernity; progress versus tradition. These archive sequences, in other words, speak beyond their filmic setting to the wider debate about cultural identity in Ireland.

The documentary interviews in the film are powerful in themselves. The two former pupils describe in graphic language the sadism and sexual repression that went with a Christian Brothers' education and the brother interviewed sounds liberal but impresses only with his complacency. But, placed in the context of the film's fictional segments, these interviews prove devastating. The fictional sequences dramatise the brutality and humiliation that the brothers visit on their young charges and it is difficult not to be repelled by the sight of powerfully built, grown men physically abusing the young boys. The sequences that dramatise the lessons themselves, however, are among the finest achievements in this period of Irish cinema.

In a series of brilliantly realised vignettes, the film perfectly captures the bizarre mix of religion, nationalism, brutality and learning which went into a strict Catholic education. Simplified history and complex theology mixes with Irish-language teaching, patriotic singing and ritual humiliation. Such is the power of these sequences that it is to Cathal Black's credit that the film manages also to elicit some sympathy for the brothers in their social gatherings, in their dedication and genuine religiosity and finally in the sadness and regret with which they face their own uncertain future. This sympathy does not cancel out the anger of the film nor does it exonerate the church from the accusations that the film entails. Conversely, the degree of understanding about the brothers' dilemma makes this anger all the more real and heartfelt.

In his attempt to bring the warring revisionist and nationalist factions together, Terry Eagleton has addressed this question of Catholic education. Among a list of other compromises that he sees both sides in the dispute over Irish tradition and modernity making, he states:

> If the traditionalists would only admit that the Catholic Church in Ireland has blighted the lives and damaged the psyches of countless numbers of its adherents, the modernisers might be able to bring themselves to concede that without the Church's precious work over the centuries, millions of men and women in Ireland would have gone uneducated, unnursed and unconsoled. (Eagleton, 1998, pp. 309–10)

The later point is, of course, debatable. They would have been educated, nursed and consoled according to the dominant ethos of nineteenth-century British civil practice heavily influenced by Protestantism. The triumph of the Catholic church was that it demanded and gained complete and unequivocal control over the Irish population at the behest of a government now convinced that only the church could deliver the necessary 'civilising' education (Inglis, 1987). As a result, the church educated the population for its own narrow Catholic ends, regulating a particular sense of Irishness by controlling and circumscribing exactly what was taught and how. As *Our Boys* makes very clear, by the 1960s the type of education it provided was no longer adequate to the economic needs of a state it had been instrumental in moulding. At the end of the film, as the brothers leave the school for the last time, they wear the same resigned look on their faces that the priest does in *The Kinkisha*. Their era is over and they now look increasingly irrelevant to the changing environment.

Education in Ireland is still a major concern. The reforms of the 1960s, which *Our Boys* anticipates, were to mould a system more geared to the needs of industry, commerce and entrepreneurial achievement than that pilloried in the film. As we have seen, part of the success of the Irish economy in the 1990s is attributed to the success of this reorientation of the education system (Durkan, Fitz Gerald and Harmon, 1999). There is, inevitably, a down side, however. The pressure that this more goal-oriented education puts on young people, especially in terms of exam results, has caused a mini-genre in Irish film-making, the 'Leaving Certificate Summer Movie' (see Chapter Eight) and is effectively parodied in Graham Jones' low-budget comedy, *How to Cheat in the Leaving Certificate* (1997). There seems to be a long way to go yet, in other words, before the memory of Catholic education has faded sufficiently to allow for the kind of rapprochement envisaged in Eagleton's formula.

Women, Nationalism and Representation

The church/state conflicts of the 1980s, which *Our Boys* so powerfully presaged, were fought around issues central to women, as we discussed in Chapter Four. Two referenda in particular, in 1983 on abortion and in 1986 on divorce, raised the whole question of the influence of church teachings on the civil code. However, the issues involved were not merely those around threatened liberalisation, but they were central to the wider feminist debate over legislation and women's bodies. As we discussed in Chapter Four, the series of traumatic events in Ireland, in the early to mid-1980s, focused these issues firmly within feminist discourse. The tribunal in Tralee over what became known as the Kerry Babies affair and the tragic death of pregnant teenager Anne Lovett in 1984, in particular, traumatised political/sexual discourse in Ireland in the years during which the referenda were held. It is not surprising, then, that these issues played an important part in the general debate about identity in Ireland, and increasingly became central to the discourse about modernity. Equally, it is hardly surprising that these issues should also feature prominently in indigenous filmmaking in the 1980s.

The best of these feminist films were produced in, and to a large extent dealt with, the problems of Northern Ireland, bringing together the two discourses of gender and nationality in a productive tension. Pat Murphy and John Davies' *Maeve* (1981) and Murphy's *Anne Devlin* (1984) are concerned specifically with the place of women within the predominantly male discourse of nationalism. *Maeve*, in particular, probes these issues in a complex formal structure, deeply influenced by the counter-cinema strategies of the 1970s avant-garde. The film, though, which encapsulates the whole debate in Ireland about gender, nationality and modernity is Margo Harkin's *Hush-a-Bye Baby* (1989), produced by Derry Film and Video, a Channel Four-funded workshop. Taken together, these films constituted the outlines of an impressively challenging feminist cinema that also, like the radical film-making already discussed, was to find itself out of favour in the more commercial environment of the 1990s.

In *Maeve*, the emigrant Maeve Sweeney (Mary Jackson) returns from London to her Belfast home for a brief visit. During her stay, she attempts to come to terms with her family and the republican community of Belfast that she grew up in. The film follows her first few days back home against the background of memories of her childhood and early adult life, revealed in flashbacks that are largely unsignposted. The naturalistic narrative at the centre of the story is interrupted and fractured by these memories and by stylised set-piece debates about republicanism and feminism. Slowly we become aware of the emotional and intellectual ways in which her growing feminist politics have alienated her from the dominant nationalist politics of her family and community. The film operates almost as a visual essay exploring the relationship between feminism and nationalism as potentially opposing political discourses. There is one scene in particular which encapsulates the film's complex inter-weaving of themes. Maeve and her younger sister Roisin (Brid Brennan) are getting ready for a night out together. Both women have had a bath and as they dry themselves off they discuss and swap stories about life as a woman in Belfast, fractured as it is by sectarian conflict and violence from all sides. What is remarkable about the scene is the way in which it is composed and shot.

Roisin is in the background, wrapped in a towel and drying her hair. Maeve lies in the foreground reading a book. As the women discuss and argue about politics and women's issues, the scene unfolds in one long take, a characteris-tic shooting style of Pat Murphy. However, in the foreground Maeve lies in a reclining position, naked and facing the camera. There are three discourses going on at the same time which are characteristic of the film as a whole. First, there is a discourse about sisterhood itself. There is a warm and sisterly inti-macy in the scene, reminiscent of the later scene of female solidarity as the sisters drink some whiskey with their mother at a cold and blustery Giant's Causeway. Second, there is a discourse about women within the dominant ethos of republican Belfast that is conducted through the women's argu-ment/conversation and in counterpoint to this visualisation of sisterhood. In fact, the intimacy is retained despite the fact that Roisin remains intensely scep-tical of Maeve's feminist politics and what she sees as her intellectual distance from the realities of life in Belfast. The third discourse is more complex and is rendered in purely visual terms.

The long take, focusing on Maeve's naked body in the foreground, operates a parallel critique of a male regime of oppression to that contained in the women's conversation. Maeve is *naked* because she has just had a bath but in another sense she is *nude* because this is a cultural representation of that natural state (she adopts a classical 'reclining nude' position as she reads her book and responds to her sister's conversation). As the camera maintains its unwavering stare, it draws attention, not to Maeve's nakedness, but to the cultural tradition of female nudity. It lingers so long over the shot that it challenges the (male) audience to question why the scene is constructed in this way. In other words, in line with the strategies throughout the film, the mechanisms of represen-tation draw attention to themselves. The viewer is then forced to ask questions about how and why the female form is usually displayed in cinema. As John Berger has argued, the European art tradition of the nude is an expression, not of the naturalness of the unclothed form, but of male sexual voyeurism (Berger, 1972, pp. 45–64). The nude in painting is an object of the male look, a display for the male viewer, who retains a position of dominance and ownership. 'Nakedness reveals itself. Nudity is placed on display', as Berger puts it (Berger, 1972, p. 54). Sometimes, as in the topic 'Susannah and the Elders' (Berger reproduces two examples by Tintoretto), a spectator within the painting spies on the woman having a bath or a lover looks at the naked woman. Here, the woman looks at the spectator outside of the frame rather than at the 'spy' within. She is on display, in other words, for the viewer outside the canvas for whom the viewer within the canvas is a surrogate.

In cinematic terms, this tradition is maintained in the use of shower, bathing or lovemaking scenes to show the naked female form as a gratuitous display for male voyeuristic pleasure. This is so common in mainstream cinema today that it rarely elicits much comment any more. If it does it is more likely to be of a salacious kind. There is a famous washing scene in Louis Malle's *Atlantic City* (1980) which illustrates very well the cinematic tendencies that *Maeve* here critiques and which is reminiscent in its 'architecture of looking' to that which Berger describes. Sally (Susan Sarandon) works as a waitress in a fish restaurant and to kill the smell of fish, she rubs lemon juice into her skin each evening after work. As she performs this ritual one evening, conveniently before an open window, she is spied on from the apartment opposite by ageing petty criminal Lou (Burt Lancaster). She spots his voyeuristic spying but continues with the ritual, slowly rubbing the lemon juice on to her breasts. There is a complex set of discourses here, to be sure. The older man represents failed male power rather than active male sexuality and he now lives on fantasies of a bogus former grandeur. When Sally becomes aware of this sad old peeping tom, she doesn't pull the curtains. Rather, she seems to thrive on asserting her lack of shame and her active sexuality in the face of his declining masculinity. (Alternatively, she is particularly accommodating to his sad old fantasies by providing a perverse 'public service' display that in effect becomes the catalyst for Lou's one epic adventure of a lifetime.) There is also, as in the fading glamour of Atlantic City itself, an ineffable sadness in the scene that mirrors the longing and failures of the characters' lives.

The point, though, is that the scene works as much for the male viewer as it does for the diegetic protagonist. The woman is on display and the voyeurism of the male character is a counterpoint to that of the male viewer. His old and weary demeanour only reinforces the active and powerful male viewer. It is a scene, therefore, which works for the gratification of the male viewer as much as it does for the themes of the narrative. *Empire* magazine, which chose this as one of its '25 hottest sex scenes in the movies', captures well the combination of art and pornography that the scene entails. 'This scene combines allegedly non-sexual nudity with wistful longing, creating a classic erotic moment that reveals the romantic longings and underlying frailty of these characters. And it's really horny' (*Empire*, 1994b, p. 2). This cinematic trope is most spectacularly reproduced in *Titanic* when Rose asks Jack to sketch her 'like the French models' (i.e. in the nude). Jack organises her into the pose of the classic (and passive) reclining nude and Rose displays herself for Jack and through him to the audience.

In Jean-Luc Godard's *Numéro Deux* (1975) there is a scene similar in its impact to that in *Maeve* which perfectly illustrates the kind of political cinema that Pat Murphy draws on for inspiration. In Godard, the woman strips to the waist to wash herself slowly and meticulously in front of a bathroom mirror. The shot is also done in one long take drawing the viewer's attention to the natural act of daily ablutions as a meditation on cinematic nakedness/nudity. Godard's challenge to the audience is that here the woman is a seventy-year-old grandmother long past the age of sexual attraction for the male viewer. The tradition that *Maeve* draws on is this 1970s political avant-garde which set out to challenge and question film as a symbolic practice, especially cinema as a patriarchal symbolic code, and to interrogate the political and ideological implications of representation itself.

In *Maeve*, this ambitious politics is woven into an interrogation of Irish nationalism/republicanism as another patriarchal symbolic code. In many of Maeve's reminiscences of childhood her father, Martin (Mark Mulholland) tells her stories and legends and literally interprets the details of the landscape for her. Again, Murphy chooses to render this overbearing patriarchal discourse visually. Thus, on the first evening that Maeve is back home her mother, Eileen (Trudy Kelly) begins to tell her a story about a neighbour. Her father takes over the narration and the camera slowly pans around to catch him in close-up so that he is eventually talking directly to the camera. In this way the camera is 'hijacked' for a male voice. This is most effective because it provides a nice contrast to Martin's character as it is developed within the naturalistic contemporary story. Martin is a 'weak' male, shown to be ineffectual and often the butt of others' jokes and pranks, but even he has privileged access to the narrative codes that define the world for women.

Part of Maeve's memories are concerned with her relationship to former boyfriend Liam (John Keegan) and the naturalistic narrative also charts her alienation from him and his republican politics. The highly stylised intellectual arguments between them form another fracturing device on the naturalistic narrative and operate as a verbal counterpoint to the themes explored visually elsewhere in the film. Maeve's alienation from Liam is not just a matter of politics, though. As Murphy herself notes, Liam represents the successive generations of patriarchy. 'As Maeve moves beyond her father's sphere of influence, Liam represents a powerful figure in her life. She moves from resisting the way patriarchy requires her to be a daughter, to resisting the ways in which the next generation of patriarchy requires her to be a wife' (quoted in Johnston, 1981, p. 66).

Maeve herself, though, is denied the position within the narrative as the

Challenging male discourse: women's solidarity in *Maeve*

bearer of truth, as the privileged voice within competing discourses. Again this
is represented visually. As the bus that brings Maeve into Belfast from the air-
port disembarks, the camera holds on the passengers as they leave one by one.
Cinematic convention would have the camera wait to pick up Maeve as she disembarks into the frame, but she does not appear. In fact, the camera pans to
reveal that Maeve is already on the tarmac to the side of the bus, a disorientat-
ing play with the convention that effectively emphasises Maeve's decentred
position within the film. Hers is one discourse competing in a dialectical conflict with others. If the patriarchal discourse of nationalism is severely
challenged by feminism, then the internationalist thrust of Maeve's feminism
is challenged by the specificities of nationalism. The gap that this prises open
can only be filled by the audience itself. This, of course, has allowed the film to
be read in conflicting ways. Murphy herself noted the way in which republican
women in Belfast responded negatively to the film. Because it is neither a liberal film that eliminates the contradictions nor a classic propagandist tract like
Arthur McCaig's *The Patriot Game* (1978) it does not close down any position
– it raises rather than answers questions. 'The women who saw *Maeve* in Belfast
identified the lack of a republican woman's voice as a problem,' Murphy says
and although she argues that she had hoped that the character of Roisin would

fill that role, she still accepts that this is a valid criticism. This has not, of course, prevented the film from being read as both an endorsement of, and as a condemnation of, nationalism but it is to the film's credit that it opened up, rather than closed down such a debate.

In Murphy's second feature, *Anne Devlin* (1984), the problem is revisited in an historical context. Anne Devlin herself remains a marginal figure in Irish history. She was Robert Emmet's housekeeper during the failed rebellion of 1803 and died in old age, forgotten and in poverty. Murphy rescues her from the male history that effectively silenced her and her role in the rebellion. In fact, as the film makes clear, she 'played' at Emmet's housekeeper merely to give his house the outward appearance of respectable bourgeois normality when, in reality, it was a centre of conspiracy and rebellion. After the failure of the rebellion she was captured and tortured but remained one of the few conspirators who did not confess or turn witness against Emmet. The themes of the film are again rendered visually. The opening sequence is set a few years earlier during the 1798 rebellion. Anne (Brid Brennan) is among a group of women who dig up a dead body hastily buried in the battlefield to bring it back for a proper burial. As the cart approaches a roadblock, the women stop. In silent defiance of the soldiers, they stand up and confront them collectively. Eventually, the soldiers step aside and let the women pass. As in *Maeve*, it is the collective solidarity of women that is visually captured in this scene. However, as we shall see, it is the defiant silence of women that the film is ultimately concerned with.

When Anne arrives at Emmet's house for the first time, she enters his study. In a scene evocatively lit and framed, she opens the shutters to let in the light. On the desk are all the accoutrements of (male) rebellion – maps, charts, chemicals for making explosives and so on. She wanders around the desk, curiously lifting and examining items in turn. When Emmet enters the room, he closes the shutters and throws the desk into shadow. He takes the chart that Anne is holding, refusing to shed further light on the details of the conspiracy laid out in the privacy of his male domain. When he explains the role that Anne is to play in the rebellion, he assures her that she is not a servant but 'one of us'. His dismissal of her is, however, reinforced when Anne meets another of the conspirators on the stairs. His response to her presence is to ask for hot water and some clean towels.

Anne's collapse into silence in response to torture, imprisonment and a particularly nasty interrogation by the British authority figure, Major Sirr, is not a collapse into the passivity of silence associated with the marginalisation of women, as Gibbons has pointed out. Rather, it is a 'mode of resistance, an act of intransigence which places a formidable barrier in the path of those who would seek to exploit and dominate others' (Gibbons, 1996, p.116). Curiously, though, he argues that 'Anne's enemy is not men as such, but Major Sirr and the paternalistic colonial regime which he represents' (ibid.). Actually, the enemy is not 'men', as Gibbons puts it, but patriarchal discourse, which includes Sirr and Emmet. Anne's realisation may in no way blunt her enthusiasm for anti-colonial struggle as such but it severely qualifies this struggle as defined by Emmet. 'It was not for you we did it', she says to Emmet when they meet in the prison yard. The problem that both films raise is the central question that we considered in the cultural debate in Chapter Four – the role of nationalism in the imagining of identity and as a route towards political struggle, especially, in this case that of feminist politics.

Margo Harkin's *Hush-a-Bye Baby* (1989) provided an occasion for celebration when it was premièred in Derry in late 1989. These were the dark days for Irish film following the demise of the first Film Board two years earlier and it was difficult for indigenous film-makers to get feature projects off the ground. The film was funded by British television's Channel Four with input from RTÉ, but the quality of the film and the enthusiastic reception it received from both cinema and television audiences proved something of a boost for a flagging industry in the South. The film is a study of a double oppression that covers much of the same ground as Pat Murphy's films, though within a more accessible and conventional narrative.

Goretti Friel (Emer McCourt) is a Catholic teenager living in Derry's nationalist Creggan estate, and the first section of the film tracks her interaction with the community and the beginnings of a relationship with the strongly republican Ciaran (Michael Liebman). The picture that emerges is one of warmth and mutual self-support. There is humour and compassion in the community and a strong sense of pride that comes from a shared experience of belonging. However, this is a community that also feels itself under threat from the outside in the presence on the streets of the British Army. It is above all a nationalist community and both a sense of oppression and a culture of resistance are built into the daily routines of teenage living and loving. In one scene for example, Ciaran has just left Goretti at home and is walking away from her house towards the camera. The scene is carefully composed in lingering long shot, the camera holding him in frame as he walks along in the euphoria of young love. A British soldier steps abruptly into the frame to accost him and shatter his teenage reveries.

Goretti and Ciaran first meet in an Irish-language class and walk home together practising Irish phrases. These are as much rituals of resistance as they are rituals of courtship. The mood of the film begins to darken as a series of 'supergrass' arrests end with Ciaran being lifted in a dawn raid. Goretti then finds that she is pregnant from the night she and Ciaran had sex while babysitting for her sister. Another form of oppression sets in as Goretti feels the pressures that her traditional Catholic community exerts. This is a culture that values the sanctity of conception above the rights of the mother, which frowns upon pregnancy outside of the sanction of marriage. Without Ciaran to confide in she feels increasingly alone and isolated. It is at this point that the film's careful delineation of Goretti's community life in Derry begins to pay dividends.

In a crucial passage in the film Goretti spends some time in the Donegal Gaeltacht (the Irish-speaking area). She has gone there to improve her Irish but it also provides her with an opportunity to escape the pressures that urban Derry now brings. (We see her framed against the famous gable wall – 'You are now entering Free Derry' – and feel with her the terrible irony of its message.) However, Donegal provides no rural retreat. As is the case in many parts of rural Ireland the crossroads here is dominated by a statue of the Virgin Mary, that impossible duality that Catholic Ireland promotes as the ideal of Irish womanhood. The film also references the controversies of the 1980s in the south, the abortion referendum, the trial of Joanne Hayes and the tragedy of Ann Lovett. The culture which sustains the community in Derry is now beginning to oppress her on all sides. Just as resistance to the outside oppression in Derry is possible and indeed is part of the daily lives of the nationalist teenagers, so the film here offers a wonderfully witty moment of female solidarity and resistance to the ideologies of Catholic Ireland. Goretti finally confides in her friend, Dinky, and the next time the two pass the statue Dinky hisses contemptuously, 'Don't you fucking move!'

The film moves into the same territory as Pat Murphy's films when Goretti finally gets a chance to visit Ciaran in prison. Ciaran's reaction when she tells him the news is patriarchal and accusatory: 'Fuck it, Goretti. Am I not in enough shit as it is!' The issue here is the relationship between republican politics and women's issues and the clear implication is that Ciaran's male response supercedes any sympathetic female perspective. Is this, the film asks, the total relationship between the two forms of politics? *Hush-a-Bye Baby* reserves most of its anger for the attitude of the Catholic church to women but it clearly asks searching questions of both nationalist politics in general and republican politics in particular. It does so from a position of sympathy and support clearly delineated in the film's sympathetic portrayal of both the community in general and Ciaran in particular. As such, like *Maeve* in particular, it invites debate about the relationship between women's politics and nationalist politics. It is centrally involved with Goretti's predicament – the narrative does not follow Ciaran to prison – and so it asks its questions from within women's politics and women's culture. But it is a complex question and the interface between nationalism and feminism is a dialectical quagmire. Just like *Maeve*, and just like the final image of the film itself, *Hush-a-Bye Baby* is ambivalent and leaves the questions it raises to the audience to answer. In this regard, it follows in the lineage of Pat Murphy's films but does so within a broadly conventional narrative that interacts with its audience in real and meaningful ways.

These three feminist films marked a real achievement in the development of a recognisably oppositional and questioning cinema in Ireland. If Pat Murphy's films are more clearly located within the counter-cinema or avant-garde cinema traditions of the 1970s and 1980s, Margo Harkin's film rests within mainstream narrative. It was, after all, made to be shown in primetime television (which it was to excellent viewing figures and considerable public reaction [Harkin 1991; Kirkland, 1999]). The situation since, as far as women film-makers or an avowedly feminist cinema is concerned, is such that it raises many questions and worries about women in Irish film (Barton, 1999). Only three feature films out of a total of over fifty that have been made since *Hush-a-Bye Baby* over a decade ago have a feminist orientation: Trish McAdam's *Snakes and Ladders* (1996), Geraldine Creed's *The Sun, The Moon and The Stars* (1996) and Pat Murphy's *Nora* (2000). The latter, based on the life of James Joyce's partner, Nora Barnacle, is Murphy's first feature since *Anne Devlin* in 1984. Margo Harkin has not made another fiction feature since she finished *Hush-a-Bye Baby*, although she has been involved in documentary film-making with some success. Murphy's two earlier films were made at a time and within the supportive context of considerable avant-garde activity and debate and in addition *Anne Devlin* had the sympathetic support of the first Film Board. Margo Harkin had the institutional support of the Channel Four workshop agreement and her film grew out of the workshop's roots, sunk deep in the local Derry community. She was able to access the real-life stories of teenage pregnancy within the community and this deep research structured the script. Both film-makers, in other words, had a supportive infrastructure to work from. The more commercial orientation of Irish film-making in the 1990s has not been supportive of a challenging women's film practice and this is a cause of considerable regret and concern. We will look at this question in more detail when we consider short film-making in the next chapter.

Chapter 7
Short Films and Plural Visions

When the first Film Board was closed down in 1987, the result was a hiatus in indigenous feature film production in Ireland that was to last until 1993. It is ironic, then, that this period also saw an exponential growth in short film production. With the benefit of hindsight, we can now see that, as many economists have argued in relation to the economy in general, underneath the visible surface of film culture some of the conditions that would create a spectacular recovery were there, requiring only imaginative government policies to stimulate them. In addition, we can also see more clearly now that the influence of the indigenous film-makers in the 1970s and the early 1980s and the policies of the first Film Board had begun to build towards a 'critical mass' in indigenous production that was having a particular impact just under the visible surface. This only confirms the impression that closing the Board at that time was a particularly ill-judged decision. Given the minuscule amount of public spending it saved the feeling remains that an altogether more political agenda was at play. The films produced, with their harder critical edge, found little favour with the government of the day.

The main impetus for the rise in the production of short films came originally from the two colleges that offered film-making courses: Dun Laoghaire School of Art and Design and the College of Commerce, Rathmines, now part of the Dublin Institute of Technology. Indeed, these courses were to provide a refuge for many of the film-makers who had struggled through to relative success in the earlier period and then felt isolated and abandoned when the Film Board was shut down so peremptorily in 1987. Cathal Black is a case in point. His 1984 feature, *Pigs*, had been screened out of competition in Cannes and was favourably received by critics and audiences. He was not, however, to make another feature for twelve years until *Korea* (1996). He spent a lot of the intervening years teaching on the Rathmines course. As he reasoned later:

> It was something I had to do in order to survive. I found it frustrating because I had no time for my own projects but while you are teaching you are still working with the raw materials by reading scripts, shooting footage and so on. Teaching as well made me more patient, which I think comes out in *Korea*.

Perhaps there is a sensitivity in the film that I wouldn't have been able to call
up ten years ago. (Black, 1996, p. 20)

Certainly, *Korea* was an impressive return to feature film production, confirming Black as one of the best stylists in indigenous film-making in Ireland.
However, like so many of his contemporaries, he has suffered from the lack of
continuity in production over the years and it is a great pity that he hasn't been
able to make films on a more regular basis. Black was, of course, responsible for
one of the great achievements of short film-making in the early years, *Our Boys*
(1981), discussed in detail in Chapter Six. His influence on his students was,
therefore, likely to have been considerable and this, at least, ensured some level
of continuity during the years of stagnation. In a way, Black here articulates
what short film-making and teaching meant for film culture generally. The
short became a way in which the whole film community in Ireland kept in
touch with the 'raw materials' of film-making and its importance in this regard
should not be underestimated.

The short film was also the way in which indigenous film-making maintained some kind of public profile. The emergence of short films from the
colleges was confirmed in 1987 when two graduation films from Dun
Laoghaire, Liam O'Neill's *Frankie and Johnny* and Enda McCallion's *Madelaine*,
were shown at that year's Cork Film Festival and were later given a television
screening. The productions from the colleges came, of course, in a variety of
formats – low- and high-band video as well as 16mm film. The influence of
experienced and professional teaching was confirmed in their improving overall technical quality. However, even within the institutional environment of the
colleges, it was still a considerable struggle to get a film produced to a satisfac-
tory level of competence that would guarantee both festival and television
screenings (O'Neill, 1987, pp. 4–5). Even here, the film-makers were presented
with a funding problem if their ambitions to shoot on film outstripped the educational resources available.

FilmBase had been established in Dublin with Arts Council funding in 1986,
as its manifesto says, 'to provide a resource facility of equipment, information,
training and skills for an emerging but under-nourished low-budget film sector' (*FilmBase News*, 1989). It established its bi-monthly newsletter, *FilmBase
News* (now *Film Ireland*), the following year. To begin with, FilmBase established what it called 'training film' production but in partnership with RTÉ
from 1989 on, it has run a short film award competition in an attempt to provide the infrastructure for quality productions which are guaranteed at least a
television screening.

The same route was followed in Galway (and later in Cork) with the setting
up, again with Arts Council funding (and with the support of the local council

and local business), of a film resource centre, now the Galway Film Centre, the establishment of a film quarterly, *Film West*, and a script award again in association with RTÉ. When the Film Board was re-established in 1993 it wisely decided to build on these initiatives in short film production by instituting its own Short Cuts strategy. As Rod Stoneman, the Board's chief executive, pointed out in the 1994 annual report:

> Recognising the consolidated and continuing role of the FilmBase/RTÉ and Galway Film Centre/RTÉ shorts, the Board has begun to build on these existing schemes by adding a complementary level of short film production. *Short Cuts*, financed in partnership with the Independent Production Unit of RTÉ, is an attempt to help provide an extra stage of experience for directors (and producers, writers and crews) before embarking on a first feature. (Stoneman, 1995, p. 4)

This was an important principle to establish, since experience in the past had shown that new initiatives in film production often meant a reduction in existing arrangements so that there was no appreciable increase overall in the level of support. The Board also introduced animation, documentary and Irish-language schemes, so that finally there was a comprehensive range of support for short film-making across different genres.

In the 1990s, as we discussed briefly in Chapter Five, developments in the North also eased the funding crisis for film-makers. Although the Film Boards in the South during the 1980s and 1990s always supported film-makers from Northern Ireland, it was difficult for these to find support locally. For a number of years, the only source was the Cultural Traditions Group (CTG) of the Community Relations Council, which had a fund of about £200,000 per year for the production of films and videos which in some way explored the issue of cultural identity in Northern Ireland. The CTG operated its brief widely and many film-makers benefited from both development and production funding. However, there was a tendency for the broadcasters to use the CTG fund as an opportunity to cut down on their own investments accordingly so that the CTG funds were being used to fund programmes and films that the broadcasters would or should have funded as of right anyway. What was needed was a scheme specifically designed to provide support for film-making that was clearly an addition to, not an alternative to, existing arrangements. From 1994, the NIFC, with British lottery and European money and in partnership with the local broadcasters, was able to do this through the Northern Lights and Première schemes in association with BBC NI and UTV respectively.

The increase in the production of short films being made all over the island by the late 1990s is well illustrated by the Cork Film Festival programme of

1999. This festival has always had a particular commitment to the short film and is still one of the best events in Europe to gauge the state of the short film internationally. In 1997, the Festival introduced a 'Made in Cork' programme to showcase the latest in local film-making. By 1999, this had expanded to three programmes, showing thirteen locally made shorts, most in Beta format. Those that were on film received the additional funding required from either the RTÉ/FilmBase or RTÉ/Cork Film Centre schemes. In addition to this there were eight other programmes of Irish shorts, screening over forty films in all genres, including the latest batch of Première shorts from Northern Ireland and the latest Short Cuts from the Film Board and RTÉ. At the Galway Film Fleadh earlier in 1999, there were eight programmes of Irish shorts with a total of over eighty films on view and while Cork had some overlap, there were surprisingly few of the same films on offer at both festivals.

This prodigious output raises some interesting questions about the short film in general and about its cultural role in Ireland specifically. Indeed, the very way in which these films are programmed and viewed is particularly sugges-tive. As with a lot of festivals, to get through so much product the films in Cork were scheduled in feature-length slots (generally two hours but up to three hours in the case of Galway). This is entirely understandable for the festival director who wants to give as many films as possible a public screening and is no doubt appreciated by those connected to the films who want to see their work shown on the big screen to an audience. It is a bonus, too, for academic researchers or for (often foreign) programmers looking for interesting films for their own events and venues. However, it does highlight two problems. First, the short film no longer has a natural outlet of its own, given the reluctance of the commercial cinemas to include shorts with their normal programming. The only way to see them on the big screen now (with the occasional exception) is in these feature-length programmes at festivals. Even as far as television is con-cerned, unless the film is close to a 'television hour' (about fifty minutes) it is difficult to find slots that fit in with current scheduling strategies. Often on tele-vision, therefore, short films are packaged into television scheduling norms as well (which could mean three or more being shown together). This is one of the reasons, presumably, for the Film Board and RTÉ introducing the 'Real Time' scheme for films of approximately one-hour duration.

The second point follows from this. The exhibition and scheduling of short films seems to run counter to the very aesthetic of the short. They are now being made in such numbers that this problem has been exacerbated over the years. How, then, can we define what the short film is *aesthetically* and what is its relationship to the feature film or the television film whose ghostly slots it is being asked to fill? If it has an integrity and an identity of its own, then its short duration is part of what it is – its aesthetics are premised on its length. If the short film is not merely a small feature, then it must be qualitatively a different genre entirely. The obvious analogy here is with the relationship between the short story and the novel. Certainly, for marketing reasons and for reasons to do with economies of scale, short stories are published in collections that approximate the length of a novel. There are, however, two important differences here to the situation facing the short film. First, there still remains a wide range of outlets for the short story – in literary journals, popular magazines and (in Ireland at any rate) national newspapers. Second, even with the collection of short stories, the reader still controls the rate of consumption in a way that scheduling requirements of cinema and television do not allow for. Thus, there is a recognised integrity to the short story that survives the exigencies of the marketplace and which is not always apparent in relation to the short film. Given the premium on time in the genre, the short exhibits an economy of exposition, depending on large measure on visual clues for filling in narrative details or necessary 'back story' information. It is therefore above all else a visual form and at its best it works with an emphasis on the visual at the expense of dialogue. Perhaps in this way, the fictional short, no matter how 'slight' its subject matter, demands a greater degree of commitment from an audience more comfortable with the less restrictive narratives of the feature or the television hour. Thus, when viewed with a number of other shorts to fit a television schedule or a feature film schedule, it then loses part of its identity and the audience is less likely to appreciate its aesthetic quality as a *short film*.

One way of looking at short films in Ireland is to see their dependence on (largely) public funding and arrangements with broadcasting, educational and training bodies as constituting an 'institutional space' carved out from the cut and thrust of the commercial world of feature film-making and the tyranny of the television schedules. Such a space offers the potential for the films to try something different. This would require an approach to the short film that acknowledges the aesthetic characteristics of the form not as restriction but as possibility. The form, in other words, is granted a legitimacy of its own and its potential considerably enhanced when it is seen as rather more than merely a truncated version of what exists already, either in the cinema or on television. The constant attempt to fit the short film into the pattern of existing programming and scheduling strategies suggests that this uniqueness is not always appreciated. (One area where the screening of short films is now beginning to happen is on the World Wide Web. Advances in streaming technology and greater access to the Internet promises to give the short film a new lease of life. This might, indeed, reconfigure the whole relationship of the short film to distribution and exhibition but the technology and its use in short film promotion is still at a relatively undeveloped state.)

If the outlets are not there for short films, or only exist in a schedule that runs counter to their aesthetics, then what is their purpose and why is so much public money invested in them? The answer, of course, lies in their use value as training for the main business of film-making – feature-length (or at least, 'television hour'-length) production. This is implicit in the Film Board's rationale at the setting up of the Short Cuts scheme and there is no doubt that for film-makers the attraction is that they receive the training, gain the necessary experience and then end up with a 'calling card' for the industry proper. As we have seen, this was the route into film-making for the generation of the 1970s and early 1980s and the process is being repeated in the 1990s (though it is a matter of doubt whether this is happening with the regularity that the Film Board strategy assumes). The most spectacular example is Rathmines graduate Damien O'Donnell, who made the short film *Thirty-five a Side* in 1995, probably the most successful short ever made in Ireland in terms of awards won and accolades gained internationally. He moved into feature film production with *East is East* in 1999, a BBC/Film Four production set in Bradford's Asian community. This film has been a commercial and critical success across Europe and won a BAFTA award in 2000. In many ways, O'Donnell's success is now a benchmark for younger aspiring film-makers embarking on their first short film project.

If the main purpose of the short is as a vehicle for training and gaining experience in all aspects of film-making – handling actors, pre-production planning, producing and dealing with the business end, post-production and finally distribution and marketing – then in effect the potential of its 'institutional space' is denied. The short film is removed from the real world of film production only to be consigned to a space that simulates this world in every detail. Such an institutional space, we have argued, should allow for a more liberating environment for experiment and exploration. However, the emphasis on a training agenda means that the climate governing the production of short films mirrors that of feature film production, with the demands of the commercial marketplace and the dominance of the Hollywood narrative model dictating to a large extent the look of the films produced. In many ways, the problems that we will consider in the next chapter in relation to the 'cinema of the Celtic Tiger' (a certain conservatism in form and content and a tendency towards traditional narrative norms) are also found in the short film. Indeed, given the importance that the short film now exerts in terms of the training of young people for feature film-making, it might be said that these problems actually originate (or that they are ultimately 'trained into' the film-makers) in the arena of the short.

We can see this, perhaps, in relation to the funding initiatives that involve both the Film Board and the broadcasters in the South and the NIFC and the broadcasters in the North. In a letter to *Film West* in 1995, just as the short film-

making schemes North and South were settling down and beginning to produce results, independent film-maker David Hyndman, from Belfast's radical
Northern Visions, argued that, through the Northern Lights scheme, the NIFC
was now firmly under the control of the broadcasters. 'Enticed by the offer of
matching money from Channel Four and the BBC, the Film Council has put
its own energies and funding at the disposal of the broadcasters who now
decide what films will be made in Northern Ireland ... they call the shots' (Hyndman, 1995, p. 7). Hyndman rather overstates the situation here and the NIFC's
director, Richard Taylor, effectively refuted the charge in the next issue of the
journal (Taylor, 1995, p. 7). And yet, Hyndman had a point even if his letter did
not focus on the issue properly. The question is not one of the broadcasters 'calling the shots' directly – the schemes are designed to train young people for the
industry and therefore it is logical that the demands of the industry are paramount. It is a broader, cultural question, therefore, focusing on the issue of
dominant aesthetics and existing social, cultural and political preferences as
dictated by commercial audio-visual culture in general – in other words by the
industry. To this extent, the broadcasters, North and South, despite the broad
public service remit they work to, are as much victims of dominant norms as
are the film-makers.

Thus it can be argued (and this is implicit in what Hyndman has said) that
the emphasis on training and the arrangement with the broadcasters have had
the effect of making the resulting films look much the same in terms of visual
style, editing and narrative. The films of both the NIFC and the Film Board are
well turned out, professionally shot and edited, stylish in some regards but ultimately insubstantial and conservative, both formally and in content. Very few
of them are risk-taking in terms of their subject matter – an inordinate number of them again deal with minor rites-of-passage crises, for example, or offer
a one-joke observation on matters that are complex and divisive. Very few of
them avail of the freedom that the form allows to try and do something narratively or visually different from mainstream film drama. Thus, the appeal to a
broadcaster's sense of the audience perhaps ensures that the films do not stray
too far from existing artistic practice and norms. This is not to say that these
are bad films in themselves but merely to note that, in line with what we have
observed in relation to the feature films, their style and content is dictated by
the norms of the dominant codes. Only very rarely are these norms actually
challenged.

However, as we will see in relation to the feature films of the 1990s, the situation is considerably more complex than this observation might suggest. The
best films work the aesthetics of the form with a sense of freedom that a concentration on the visual allows. Thus, *Thirty-five a Side* succeeds simply because
its punchline joke comes at the end of a series of superbly orchestrated visual

gags that creates the slightly absurd world in which the dénouement makes perfect sense. The necessary back story and theme is told economically and comically in the opening credit sequences in which Philip's nerd-like inadequacies in a world dominated by aggressive masculinity are laid out. In this way, his short-tempered and violent father is introduced and then removed from the scene before the film is fully underway. The film has a minimum of dialogue, the story proceeding visually with comic detail filling out Philip's traumatic first few days at a new school. The macho culture of the boys, beautifully illustrated in a series of quick visual gags and culminating in the ironic sequence featuring the football anthem 'You'll Never Walk Alone', is set up so well that the outrageous deflating of it by Philip's mother at the end appears as both logical and poetically appropriate. *Thirty-five a Side* is a film-maker's short in all the best senses, then, with a serious comment about masculinity and male culture interwoven into its absurd world for those who want to see it.

Another example of the visual short story is Brendan Bourke's more sombre and existential study of the effects of emigration on a small Irish town in *Fishing the Sloe-Black River* (1995). The film is so dependent on presenting the issues visually that Bourke, a photographer by experience, decided to shoot on cinemascope. He required finance under the tax schemes to allow him to do this, making his film probably the most expensive short ever made in Ireland. The film is, in fact, a mood piece rather than a narrative as such. The conceit in the film is to imagine a small town in which emigration has been so devastating that there are no young people left. The local football team consists of the fathers who bicker and fight like the adolescent boys they are replacing. In an image that is absurd and as potent as any in Buñuel the mothers fish the river for their exiled children. However, while in a Buñuel film such absurdity is usually comically rendered for satiric purposes, here it is played as tragedy and becomes enigmatic and moving. The decision to use cinemascope is vindicated especially in one beautifully realised shot that captures this cinematic conceit. The camera is positioned above the scene and looks down on the mothers stretched in a long line along the river's edge, quiet and uncommunicating as they cast their lines into the flowing waters. It works so well because it is shot in widescreen, the effect both uncanny and poignant. The widescreen image is also utilised particularly well in various shots of the village street along which the camera prowls as if looking for signs of human habitation, the windswept litter and a lonesome dog giving the scene an air of inexplicable desolation.

It is interesting that both of these films chose the traditions of the absurd as their aesthetic, realising them differently for their contrasting purposes. Many of the short films over the years have gone for this approach. It is almost as if, accepting the difficulty of maintaining a traditional narrative momentum within the time constraints of the short film, then the traditions of the absurd allow for greater visual potential. This is clear in a number of the short films from Northern Ireland, though there is a tendency in these for the absurdity to be rendered in terms of an outrageous joke. Thus in John Forte's *Skin Tight* (1995) the joke is that the wife's revenge on an unthinking and unsympathetic husband is to make a nationalist bodhran out of a goatskin he intended for a loyalist lambeg drum. The joke in *Pan Loaf* (1995) is that the sinister crowd of loyalist men are revealed to be watching a porn video rather than planning sectarian assassinations. The joke in *Cluck* (1998) is that the naive bomber is an animal rights activist intent on liberating the chickens in a factory farm and then blowing this up rather than a hardened paramilitary with an eye on the more usual target. Even in the most celebrated of these films, the Oscar-nominated *Dance, Lexie, Dance* (1995), the narrative is premised on the 'joke' that a Protestant father has to come to terms with Irish dancing because of the wishes of his young daughter.

If this tendency towards the absurd is common, it is often mobilised for more directly polemical effect. In this regard, one of the most interesting of the 1999 shorts is Barry Dignam's *Dream Kitchen* (1999). It is a very short piece (eight minutes) shot on Beta for the Dun Laoghaire course and exists at the other end of the budget scale from the relatively well-resourced films from the Film Board and NIFC. This is kitchen sink drama with a difference. A teenager contemplates telling his parents in the family kitchen that he is gay and has fallen in love. The result, he realises, in the ordinary drabness of the kitchen, is going to be trauma, crisis, fear and lack of understanding. He fantasises another scenario altogether, in which his parents respond to the news with excitement and encouragement. The fantasy sequence is wonderfully overwrought, like melodrama on a high, with the now beautifully equipped and colourful kitchen matching the emotional excesses of his excited parents. The dialogue is delivered in a highly stylised Shakespearean language to add further to the comic and absurdist effect. The joke is that, of course, this will remain a fantasy. In its witty reimagining of the moment of revelation, with its high camp, soap opera excess, it merely confirms that in the real world he must face alienation and rejection. The drab kitchen is a symbol of the homophobic culture, built on traditional family values, which he will have to negotiate.

This is confirmation of Lance Pettitt's assessment of many of these low-budget and student films. They show, despite surface changes to the law in Ireland, that young gay and lesbian teenagers 'still have to face various kinds of social and institutionalised forms of homophobia in schools, within the churches, and in everyday domestic family situations' (Pettitt, 1997, p. 274). One of the arenas where this struggle has been documented and in which these young people have begun to fight back is in the short film, as Pettitt's analysis shows. The radical or confrontational potential of the short film is more fully realised in the low- or no-budget sector of short film-making – the sector, in other words, furthest removed from the commercial and professional end of the budget scale. This is true, also for feminist cinema in general and even for the ability of women directors to break through into film-making at all.

One of the films that Pettitt discusses is Orla Walsh's second short film *Bent Out of Shape* (1995). This short film explores the deep-seated homophobia of society in a narrative about a caring gay man, Danny, who tries to help a younger boy to come to terms with his own sexual identity and to survive the bullying from his peers that this entails. Danny's intentions are misconstrued and he falls victim to a blind and unthinking prejudice (Pettitt, 1997, p. 279). Walsh's earlier film, *The Visit* (1992), is an exploration of the relationship between nationalism and feminism in the tradition of the films of Pat Murphy and Margo Harkin, discussed in Chapter Six. In its twenty-five minute narrative, Walsh's film raises a whole set of complex ideological issues through the story of Sheila Malloy, the wife of a republican prisoner who finds herself pregnant after having an affair while her husband is in jail.

The visit in question is the one during which she will tell her husband about the affair and the decision she has made to have the baby and remain at home. She expects her husband to stick by her decision just as she stuck by his decision to go on 'the blanket protest' in pursuit of political status. As Megan Sullivan has pointed out, the film pursues its exploration through a concentration on surveillance and incarceration. This has a double focus – the surveillance and incarceration of the state and that imposed from within the republican community to 'police' the behaviour of the wives of the prisoners (Sullivan, 1998). This is the same scenario that forms a key element in Jim Sheridan's *The Boxer* (discussed in Chapter Three) but here it is handled in a much more complex and contained way. Thus, to make its point more pertinent, and to demonstrate the sheer complexity and contradictory nature of her dilemma, the film is at great pains to point out the high degree of oppression Sheila and the nationalist community feel under the constant surveillance of the state. Sheila is a republican supporter but her situation as a woman, under the constant stricture of republican ideology in regard to women ('stand by your man'), is the catalyst for a political journey in which her politics become more feminist. In this regard, Sheila's dilemma is very much like that of Goretti in *Hush-a-Bye Baby* when she tells her republican prisoner boyfriend that she is pregnant. The male agenda and the female agenda suggest deep-seated ideological differences. In other words, a whole world of contradiction opens up which both films explore but neither can resolve within a totalising narrative.

Both *The Visit* and *Bent Out of Shape* work within a social realist aesthetic (though the former, with its concentration on surveillance, is replete with complex shots of looking and being looked at which makes it visually, as well as thematically, complex). Walsh's most recent short film, *Blessed Fruit* (1999), is an altogether more visually rich piece, tapping into the tradition of absurd cinema to particularly telling effect. It replays the nativity story through a contemporary narrative of a woman, Molly, who suspects that she might be pregnant by either of two lovers and seeks inspiration in a scabrous, funny, irreverent and ultimately sacrilegious rereading of the Virgin birth. If you work on male vanity and convince your man that 'his' son is God Himself, then you can get away with anything! The film makes its points visually and employs a series of increasingly absurd fantasies to track Molly's negotiations with male and religious ideologies from a subversive female perspective.

Walsh's body of work constitutes one of the more interesting and consistent uses of the short film form for making radical or polemical statements and for challenging sedimented political and ideological assumptions. In the student films we can, perhaps, glimpse the same 'First, Second and Third Cinema' analogy that we considered in relation to feature films in Chapter Five. By and large, the bigger the budget, the closer the films get to dominant cinematic norms. Walsh's three shorts have, however, been funded by the existing arrangements with the broadcasters and they demonstrate that this does not necessarily have to be the case. Hers has been a consistently challenging vision, demonstrating now a range of approaches and skills that have fully utilised the opportunities that the short film form provides. In a sense, her vision has been the only consistent feminist vision in Irish film-making throughout the 1990s and this,

Female subversion and male vanity: Stella Feehily and Paul Roe in *Blessed Fruit*

as we have discussed in Chapter Six, is disappointing given the achievements of Pat Murphy and Margo Harkin in the 1980s.

Walsh herself noted the paucity of opportunities offered to women in the funding decisions of the Film Board in relation to its Short Cuts programme. In an angry letter to *Film Ireland* in 1998, she noted that in the Short Cuts scheme twenty-one awards had been given to date and only two of these had gone to female directors. By way of an explanation, she offered the opinion that '… it is the flawed adjudication process and not lack of talent which stops (women) getting more films made'. In terms of the arrangement with the broadcasters, she comes to a similar conclusion as David Hyndman. 'Perhaps one of the reasons is that our TV programmers are terrified to deal with drama subjects about adults and sexuality but these may be the subjects a lot of women want to write about' (Walsh, 1998). Actually, the programmers seem to have little difficulty dealing with male sexuality and male oedipal dramas which predominate in Irish cinema, as we shall see in Chapters Eight and Nine. Perhaps it is not merely the subject matter but the way in which it is approached that is the problem. Funding decisions, driven by a training agenda that is set by the commercial industry will go for those projects that are 'recognisable' within existing practice. Anything else, anything more challenging or subversive (like *Blessed Fruit*) is deemed too dangerous.

This seems to be the nature of contemporary cinema in general, where alternative modes of expression and more radical and challenging content is considerably compromised by the overwhelming commercial pressures that now dominate even a funded cinema. This is, perhaps, the final irony of state support for film-making, in Europe generally and not just in Ireland specifically. Once, funded cinema allowed for the exploration of difference from Hollywood – a response to the dominant mode that came from an exploration of cultural identity and the search for a cinematic language that was adequate to national difference. Now, funded cinema signals the struggle merely to establish a cinematic existence in the first place – a fight for cinematic survival in the substantial shadow of Hollywood and against the inexorable pressures of the marketplace that this implies. As with the feature film in Ireland, the dominance of commercial values is now so total that the space for exploration and experiment, for subversion, within the short film has narrowed considerably.

Chapter 8
The Cinema of the 'Celtic Tiger': Themes and Issues

In Syd McCartney's *A Love Divided* (1999) a major political episode that was to prove deeply embarrassing for the Irish political establishment in 1957 is rendered as a melodrama of love, commitment and personal integrity. In the Wexford village of Fethard-on-Sea, the local community, with the encouragement of the local bishop and Catholic clergy, organised an economic boycott of the Protestant community in retaliation against a Protestant woman, married to a Catholic, who refused to send her children to the Catholic school. At issue was the Ne Temere decree that demanded that the couple promise to raise their children as Catholics before the church would sanction their marriage in the first place. The case was notorious in its day and marked the most public display of anti-Protestant prejudice in independent Ireland and fuelled sectarian feeling both north and south of the border. In many ways, the film is typical of the kind of national questioning that we have identified as an aspect of recent Irish cinema, revisiting a particularly acrimonious and unpleasant episode in the recent history of Ireland to draw lessons for the present. In this way, it is one of the few fiction films produced in Ireland that has attempted to deal in a sympathetic way with the dilemmas facing Protestants in an overwhelmingly Catholic country.

What is significant about McCartney's version of such a highly charged political event is the fact that the film is immaculately filmed and acted as a highly emotional melodrama rather than as a political film. The politics have to be read out of the personal and emotional experiences of the protagonists – it becomes, in other words, a love story rather than a 'hate story' and one which approaches the political through the personal. It is popular genre film-making applied to a complex political story. Its box-office success in Ireland was substantial and vindicated the aesthetic decision to play the story as melodrama, the better to bring it into contemporary popular consciousness. In this way, it echoes Jim Sheridan's decision to make the story of the Guildford Four as oedipal melodrama, Neil Jordan's rendering of the Michael Collins story as Hollywood biopic and Terry George's version of the IRA hunger strikes as

Sectarian politics as romantic melodrama: Orla Brady and Liam Cunningham in
A Love Divided

maternal melodrama. *A Love Divided* is a perfect example, in other words, of the trend in Irish cinema since the early 1990s to play for the commercial market even when dealing with highly charged political events.

We have noted two critiques of recent Irish cinema already, one from film-maker Bob Quinn and the other from film historian and academic Kevin Rockett. Both appeared in the *Cinéaste* special supplement on Irish cinema (1999) and while there are significant differences in the political and cultural implications of their respective arguments, nonetheless, they agree on the fact that the new generation of film-makers seem less interested in either the formally adventurous film-making that Quinn has been noted for or a 'type of critical indigenous cinema which would make a significant cultural intervention in Ireland', as Rockett argues (Rockett, 1999, p. 25). Quinn and Rockett have been important voices in Irish cinema since the earlier period of film development in Ireland. Quinn's *Caoineadh Airt Uí Laoire* (1975) was, as we have seen, a significant landmark in 1970s Irish cinema and he has continued to play an important role as both film-maker and polemicist. Rockett, as a film historian and writer and also through his work as a cinema programmer and general lobbyist on behalf of Irish cinema, played a key role in the infrastructural development that has been crucial to the success of film culture in Ireland generally.

However, their reservations about the general direction of more recent cinema have found echoes with the next generation of commentators as well. Thus, *Irish Times* critic Hugh Linehan, in the same supplement, accused the cinema of the 'Celtic Tiger' of a lack of ambition or subversion. 'Conventional liberal pieties reign supreme in too many recent Irish films, while the paper tigers of church and family are rolled out and knocked down with wearisome predictability.' Acknowledging the work of the pressure groups of the 1970s, in which Quinn and Rockett played important roles, he concurs that their more critical and political conception of Irish cinema has failed to develop: '... very few, if any, of the films produced so far have managed to even tweak the feathers of the broader culture' (Linehan, 1999, pp. 46–8).

To an extent, these criticisms are justified. However, it is important to qualify them in a number of ways.

The first wave of film-makers worked in a very different cinematic and cultural climate. In the 1970s, even mainstream Hollywood cinema was in a period of transition. The collapse of the studio system facilitated the emergence of a new generation of cine-literate directors, steeped in the traditions of Hollywood film-making, who initiated a period of experimentation with the kind of genre cinema that had sustained the industry during its years of cultural domination. Cinema audiences continued to decline throughout the 1970s and there was, therefore, a sense of uncertainty about cinema that further fuelled this short period of formal and artistic experimentation. This is in stark contrast to the formal and political conservatism of Hollywood today. As well as that, many of the younger film-makers in Ireland at this time emerged from an art college background where they gained exposure to avant-garde traditions of film-making and to the theoretical concerns of the time which emphasised formal innovation and an exploration of the relationship between film and politics. The 'Third Cinema' debate of that time is a case in point. In addition, in the 1970s, many emerging film-makers learned their cinematic history from art houses that offered a wider range of film practices than was common in the 1990s. In other words, the range of 'Second' and 'Third' Cinema examples was much greater and had a more immediate impact than is the case today. It is not surprising, therefore, that as they moved into low-budget fiction film, many of these film-makers felt neither constrained by a dominant 'native tradition' nor compelled to adhere to a global narrative formula. Looking back from the new century the freshness and almost naive exploration of film form that characterises so many of these first-wave films now looks impressive. The social and political context, outlined in Chapter Four, adds to the general sense in the films that a new aesthetic was being explored to meet the needs of a changing society. The harder political edge and formal experiment that characterised the best of these early films now look like the rudiments of a nascent 'Third Cinema' according to the Solanas formulation of the 1970s.

That this was to be eclipsed by the more commercial context of the 1990s is a characteristic of cinema everywhere. The great 'Second Cinema' tradition of Europe has itself taken something of a battering, the cinemas of Germany and Italy in particular increasingly resembling localised versions of commercial cinema. Third Cinema worldwide has declined with the eclipse of the radical left politics that sustained it. The 'geography' of oppositional cinema, as Chanan puts it, has changed (Chanan, 1997). Even the exhibition spaces available to more radical cinema have declined significantly. The great revival in film audiences in the USA and Europe from the mid-1980s on has been fuelled by a return to monopoly practices by the main Hollywood studios. The multiplex revolution has increased audiences for mainstream Hollywood films but has done so at the expense of all other kinds of cinema. The irony here is that even a director like Martin Scorsese, operating out of the heart of the American industry and using the stars of the Hollywood system, is now an 'art house' director. While a new Scorsese film is still a considerable cultural event for art house filmgoers and critics, the multiplex audience greets it with resounding indifference. His films, thematically and formally, appear too radical and too demanding compared to the Hollywood blockbuster. Certainly, for part of the 1990s, Scorsese ploughed a determinedly 'Second Cinema' path with films like *Age of Innocence* (1993) and *Kundun* (1997). But even a return to the contemporary urban environment of New York has not returned him to commercial success. *Bringing Out the Dead* (1999), with a cast of leading Hollywood character actors (including Nicolas Cage and Patricia Arquette), has had only a limited release in Europe and has hardly registered in terms of box-office returns.

In Ireland, the situation facing contemporary indigenous film-makers is, therefore, extremely difficult. Despite the plurality of funding arrangements put in place from 1993 onwards a younger generation of film-makers who might wish to retain some of the political edge of the earlier period have had to occupy a more obviously commercial space than their predecessors, with little guarantee of a wide distribution for their films. In many ways, the low-budget end of Irish film-making represents a kind of film that formerly may have been made as television drama but even here the gap between 'film' and 'cinema' on one hand and 'television drama' on the other has narrowed considerably since the 1970s (Hill and McLoone, 1996; McLoone, 1996, pp. 76–106). The fact that many of these films are seen only on the festival circuit and then on television represents as much the constriction of distribution and exhibition opportunities as it does their limited artistic horizons.

In Hugh Linehan's criticism of the films there is an exasperation and irritation with the recycling of old themes – 'the paper tigers of church and family'. However, it could be argued that Linehan himself is guilty here of the same kind of complacency that he criticises in others. Given the trauma that church/state relationships went through so recently in Ireland and the revelations about abuse and misdemeanours of all kinds that have been the stuff of news and current affairs in the 1990s, it is hardly surprising that this continues to be an obsession with film-makers, even twenty years on from *Our Boys*.

The family has been the site of dramatic conflict since the ancient Greeks and it is difficult to see why it won't continue to be so, as Thomas Vinterberg's *Festen* (1998) so admirably proves. To be fair to Linehan's argument, it is the style and approach of the films that he really objects to rather than the subject matter *per se*. Thus the films that he praises, Gaspar Noé's *Seul Contre Tous* (1998) and Vinterberg's *Festen*, are part of what might be deemed 'transgressive' cinema – the tradition of '*épater le bourgeois*' that was the preoccupation of Buñuel during a career that spanned fifty years. These films, especially Noé's, are extreme in their brutal attempt to shock audiences and there is no doubt that there is little in the indigenous Irish cinema that resembles their aesthetics of confrontation.

One possible exception is Alan Gilsenan's *All Soul's Day* (1997). This elliptical and confusing narrative mixes multiple and diverse pieces of visual evidence to follow a mother's investigation into why her daughter was murdered by her seemingly sensible and balanced boyfriend. The narrative allows for (or requires) the use of surveillance video, 8mm home movie, home video footage, and a confessional audio tape intertwined in a complex manner to suggest multiple narrative perspectives. The mother meets with the murderer in prison and her daughter's story unfolds through these multiple discourses. The audience is challenged by both the form and content of the film. Which of the multiple discourses represents the truth about the daughter, her family and her boyfriend? Is the young woman's death a mercy killing to be understood if not condoned (a question Noé also asks of his audience in rather brutal fashion)? Is this film a critique of voyeurism (the camera lingering over the exposed female body visually underlines the manner in which the young woman's life and thoughts are laid bare) or an attempt to exploit it? The revelations about paternal incest in the film and the unravelling of the family that ensues are strangely reminiscent of the family disintegration in *Festen*. The final dénouement is as unsettling as it is entirely predictable. In the warped logic of the murderer's mind the falsity and hypocrisy of this seemingly happy family requires that all traces of it be expunged.

Gilsenan's film does not have the confrontational edge of Noé's or Vinterberg's films. It quietly irritates rather than shocks. However, in its relentlessly low-budget aesthetics it echoes the Dogme group's 'return to basics' and cost a fraction of the budget for *Festen* (the final cost was as little as IR£70,000). In its determinedly avant-garde exploration of film itself, it harks back to an era of experimental cinema that is rare today. And inevitably, Gilsenan's film has been little seen so far, either in Ireland or elsewhere.

If one accepts that the funding strategy is to provide for a diverse production climate in Ireland and that to achieve this Irish cinema and cinema about Ireland must be seen as complementary, then the record is far from bleak. The films of Neil Jordan in particular have pushed and shocked audiences as much as those Linehan mentions. *The Butcher Boy* (1997) in particular has an unsettling effect on the audience because it positions the viewer in an awkward, even complicit, position through the sympathy it elicits for its disturbed hero. The sexual frisson caused by *The Crying Game* (1992) is still being felt in film studies long after it has subsided for audiences. The great controversies generated by *Michael Collins* (1996) touched a raw nerve in the Irish psyche and its huge commercial success in Ireland demonstrated that popular audiences could be found for a cinema that uses a commercial format to raise interesting questions. Jim Sheridan, of course, proved this earlier with the success of *In the Name of the Father* (1993).

However much we might regret the lack so far of a more challenging and more combative cinema from the low-budget end of the production scale, nonetheless, the cinema that has emerged is not socially neutral. It is a product itself of the society that produced it and if it exhibits certain characteristics of that society, then it tells us something interesting about it. Indigenous cinema exists in an in-between world of the local and the global. It may reflect in a low-budget way the aesthetics of the global commercial cinema but is, nonetheless, reflective of particular societal pressures that are native. The dialectical strains that result are what make this cinema interesting, as much in their negative as in their positive registers. Their characteristic themes and concerns are, therefore, well worth teasing out. Even if these films are not politically engaged, they can be engaged with politically.

Hugh Linehan is right to locate the family as the major preoccupation of recent Irish cinema. As we shall see, a recurring motif is the sense that the Irish family is incomplete, with either the mother or the father missing from the drama, with disastrous results in terms of generational conflict. The main neurosis afflicting the Irish family and influencing such conflict is often child-abuse in general or incest and child-abuse within the family in particular. There is both a material and a metaphorical dimension to this. The 1980s and the 1990s have been noted for a procession of scandals and revelations about child abuse in Ireland, both institutional abuse (often involving the clergy and religious orders) and abuse in the family revealed in the unburdening in adulthood of people who were so abused. This reality from society at large is often rendered in films as a metaphor for the instability of both family and nation, and as a metaphor it is both suggestive and deeply worrying. The number of films that touch on these themes is remarkable: Neil Jordan's *The Butcher Boy* (1997) (and incest in *The Miracle* [1991]), John Carney's *November Afternoon* (1996) and *Park* (1999), Alan Gilsenan's *All Soul's Day* (1997), John Boorman's *The General* (1998), Colm Villa's *Sunset Heights* (1997) and Jimmy Smallhorne's *2 By 4* (1998). If we add to this male violence within the family, as in Gerry Stembridge's *Guiltrip* (1995) and a whole host of films that play out oedipal themes of all kinds, it seems as if, in Ireland, the most dangerous place for the child to be to be is within a family. Here we will take a broad overview and then consider some key films later.

Coming-of-age and Generational Conflict

In Frank Stapleton's *The Fifth Province* (1997), an amiable satire on film-making, the imagination and the creative process, there is a witty aside on the 'great themes' of recent Irish cinema. Aspiring writer, Timmy (Brian O'Byrne), goes to a seminar on scriptwriting (held at the appropriately named 'Innisfree' hotel) and catches the increasingly deranged talk given by European expert, Diana de Brie (Lia Williams). 'When it comes to the story, I'll tell you want we don't want', she begins. 'We do not want any more stories about … Irish mothers, priests, sexual repressions and the miseries of the rural life. We want stories that are upbeat, that are urban, that have pace and verve and are going somewhere.' The first joke, of course, is that Timmy is a sexually repressed young man, living in rural Ireland, dominated by an off-screen mother who hectors him about doing the chores and zealously patrols his sexuality ('Timmy, is there a woman down there with you?'). Timmy, of course, wants to write about all this. The second joke is that, of course, the demented words of Diana de Brie have been heard so often before in every corner of the land, seemingly to no avail as far as recurring themes are concerned.

The film is poised somewhere between low-key Buñuel and a less frenetic Flann O'Brien, replete with cinematic references and in-jokes that creates its amiable and largely benign humour. Nevertheless, it manages to satirise and at the same time re-create the perennial oedipal conflicts of the Irish male that are a feature of so much of the cinema that it gently parodies – including maternal fixation and symbolic matricide. The father is missing, of course, and in Timmy's imagination, the mother looms large. As his hapless and ineffectual psychiatrist and father-confessor says to him, 'You have a powerful imagination. Maybe this terrible mother of yours … maybe she's terrible because you imagine her that way.' The latent misogyny and symbolic matricide that is so much a part of the creative imagination of this displaced Irish male is encapsulated in Diana de Brie's demented rehearsal of the shower scene from Alfred Hitchcock's *Psycho* (1960) – 'The stabbing and the dragging; the stabbing and the dragging,' she moans in ecstasy.

David Keating's *Last of the High Kings* (1996), based on Ferdia Mac Anna's novel, illustrates a number of key themes that have emerged in recent years and which are gently parodied in *The Fifth Province*. This is basically a 'coming-of-age' film, set in the summer of 1977 just at a point when the modernisation process in Ireland was slowing down and the Irish economy was hit by a stagnation that was to drag on for the best part of a decade. As in all such films, the protagonist is caught between two worlds – that of family and childhood on one side and the beckoning adult world beyond. Frankie Griffin is seventeen and spending the summer of his Leaving Cert examinations dreading the results and worrying about his future. His is an amiably dishevelled family (rather than a dysfunctional one) in which his well-intentioned but rather ineffectual father, an actor, is away from home a lot of the time and his mother is an unpredictable but assertive woman of very pronounced traditional views (staunch Catholic, arch republican and unbendingly anti-British).

Against this ramshackle family life, Frankie struggles to achieve his own identity. It is a summer of both stasis and change. His mother's political allies in Fianna Fáil return to power in an election, mouthing the nationalist banalities of the past. (This is the government that many economists blame for mishandling the economy so spectacularly that Ireland was plunged into an unnecessarily deep and protracted recession [Ó'Gráda, 1997, p. 30].) More importantly for Frankie, though, he loses his virginity, falls in love (events clearly not related to each other) and Elvis Presley dies. When his examination results come through, he has done well enough to go to college and his future beyond his parental home begins to take shape.

The film is comically poised at a moment of change when the old and the familiar and the new and the unknown coexist, struggling for ultimate supremacy. Change will eventually win this struggle and after his first sexual experience, Frankie notes, 'Nothing will be the same again.' In relation to the death of Elvis, Frankie's pal, an Elvis-obsessive, declares, 'It is the end of an era.'

This kind of sentiment is, of course, a standard aspect of the coming-of-age film and when set in the recent past the events are inevitably viewed with the benefit of hindsight. Thus in American movies set in the early 1960s, like George Lucas' *American Graffiti* (1973) or John Milius' *Big Wednesday* (1978), the nostalgia is viewed through the prism of the Vietnam War and with the knowledge of the horrors to come. In Lucas' film, this knowledge contributes to the air of sadness and sense of loss that permeates the whole film and severely undercuts the optimism with which the characters view their future. Despite its setting in the early 1960s *American Graffiti* is very much a product of the disillusioned 1970s. What is remarkable about *Last of the High Kings* is its unqualified optimism and the sense that the future is there to be grabbed, moulded and remade. Hindsight affirms that tomorrow will, indeed, belong to the young and in this way the film is a true marker of the mood in Ireland in the 1990s as much as it is of the transitional period of the 1970s. And just as *American Graffiti* can be read as a metaphor for America as well as a nostalgic look back at a specific moment in recent history, so too *Last of the High Kings* invites a metaphorical reading as a statement on the transition from a traditional to a modern Ireland.

The film is not, of course, a political film in the strict sense, nor is it a po-faced 'state-of-the-nation' tract. It is a comedy and one that deliberately demands a series of over-the-top performances from its adult leads. Catherine O'Hara is sometimes demented in her portrayal of Frankie's overbearing mother, Gabriel Byrne hams it up as his actor father and in a side-splitting cameo, Stephen Rea is outrageous as a fantasising Dublin taxi-driver with an accent three times thicker than any to be found in the backstreets off O'Connell Street. As a metaphor of the nation, the Griffin family is eccentric and slightly askew rather than dysfunctional or abusive. The exaggerated behaviour of the parents is the perception of the better-adjusted son. It is he (and thus the younger generation that he represents) who brings about reconciliation and stability at the end. The mother's faintly ludicrous sectarian politics, the taxi- driver's self-deluding fantasies, the sexually repressed hypocrisies of Colm Meaney's Fianna Fáil politician and the perversities of the Catholic priest belong to the old Ireland that, like Elvis and like Frankie's virginity, has passed away.

Tomorrow will belong to the young: high optimism in *Last of the High Kings* (Irish Film Archive of the Film Institute of Ireland)

But is the optimism and general amiability of *Last of the High Kings* merely self-satisfied smugness? In some ways, the knowing and slightly ironic tone of the film comes across as complacent. Frankie's home life might be slightly ramshackle and unconventional but it can only be so because it is comfortably middle-class. His worries are those of the teenager – sex and the future – rather than the life-and-death struggle of the inner city that is never seen. His mother's sectarianism is amusing and ultimately harmless but only because she lives in Howth overlooking Dublin Bay and not in Belfast overlooking the Shankill Road. The film is about a certain kind of middle-class Dublin, a certain kind of comfortable Ireland. It speaks of the past from this perspective in the present. If it evinces a kind of middle-class smugness then it does so as a reflection of the middle-class smugness, of contemporary Ireland. We shall look at another aspect of its contemporary view of the past later.

It is hardly surprising, given the youthfulness of the Irish population and the youth of many of the first-time directors who have emerged in the last decade or so, that the coming-of-age and generational conflict themes should be recurring motifs in so much recent cinema. As far back as 1987, Fergus Tighe produced the first 'Leaving Cert summer' film with *Clash of the Ash* (interestingly less optimistic then than Keating's film of a decade later). In Owen McPolin's *Drinking Crude* (1997), the protagonist, Paul, spends his Leaving Cert summer on the road in Ireland cleaning out the insides of oil storage tanks. This is an odd excursion into an unknown environment on the fringes of industrial Ireland that ends again in the triumph of youth over the jaded expectations of an older generation. Paul's journey of self-discovery appropriates another cinematic trope of the road movie: the gathering together of an alternative family on the way. This begins when he is rescued from penury by Al, a streetwise Scottish labourer who becomes a surrogate father for Paul and teaches him the business of cleaning oil tanks and the skills necessary to survive on the road. Later Al and Paul are joined by young mother Karen and her baby, fleeing from an abusive husband. Certainly, this is no Josie Wales but the building of an alternative family conceived outside the strictures of an unfeeling and uncaring society is a familiar device for encapsulating an alternative imagining of the nation (as we noted in the films of Joe Comerford).

The most interesting of these films is Johnny Gogan's *The Last Bus Home* (1997), which uses the metaphor of a punk band to articulate the reimagining of the family/nation which an angry and determined younger generation is engaged in. This is the most directly political of the youth films and manages a delicate balance between the opposing forces. On the one hand, it retains a healthy scepticism about the new dawn offered by the youth of Ireland while at the same time is unstinting in its criticism of the Ireland of the older generation that they aim to disrupt and supplant. Punk rock, of course, carries its own set of anti-establishment codes and what the film values is the manner in which the young people come together under these codes in response to the failures of their parents' generation.

The film opens in 1979, on the day the Pope celebrated Mass to over one million people in Phoenix Park in Dublin. There is an impressive sequence near the beginning that beautifully illustrates the generational conflict at the centre of the film. Gogan shows the empty streets of the Dublin suburbs on the afternoon of the Mass, its eerie silence and utter desolation eloquently commenting on the desolation felt by young punk Reena (Annie Ryan) as she wanders the streets alone. However, anyone who has stayed away from the park has already made a political statement of some significance and in this way, the members of the punk band find each other and begin to build their alternative family. (The band call themselves 'The Dead Patriots', which may be a nod to The Dead Kennedys but is significant enough in itself.) The film tracks their progress over the next few years, dealing with the implications of the economic downturn, especially the renewed threat of emigration, and struggling with a rock business disinclined to support their music while only too eager to exploit the band when possible.

The film, then, is another exploration of young people's struggle to find their identity and mark their difference from their parents' generation. What is interesting about the film, however, is the fact that the band itself neither represents unblemished virtue nor does it have access to all the answers. The drummer Petie's quest for personal identity involves coming to terms with his gayness and when his parents reject him, he seeks comfort in the alternative family of the band. However, homophobia is not generation-specific and when the lead singer – loud, brash, self-centred Jessop (Brian O'Byrne) – rejects his friend publicly, feeling threatened himself by his homosexuality, the result ends in tragedy. This is a realistic corrective to the 'can-do' optimism of some of the other youth films. In the rather sad coda which ends the film, set a few years later when the surviving band members have settled into the yuppie world of contemporary Dublin, the former punk rebels have made their peace with the consumerist society slowly emerging in the wake of economic regeneration, their rebelliousness totally recuperated to the new orthodoxy.

The Last Bus Home seems, therefore, to say something interesting about punk music in particular and generational revolt in general. Under the brashness of punk music, its 'gobbing' and two-finger salute to the world, there is an emptiness and a political vacuum that complements a basic self-centredness. Like the parents' generation that the punks set out to scandalise, there is at root a desire to succeed and to make money. Within the alternative 'family' of the punk band lurk the same values of hypocrisy, prejudice and intolerance.

Another interesting aspect of *The Last Bus Home* is that it is set in the

The nation as punk band: The Dead Patriots in *The Last Bus Home*

working-class suburb of Tallaght, and while class conflict is touched on around the edges of some of the other films, it is here a central theme, giving an added piquancy to the end coda. Not only is punk seen as a fake rebellion to the bourgeois conformity of society, its rapid recuperation by that society confirms the absence of any political alternative. There is a deep sense of sadness in the end about the thwarted hopes of the punk revolt that were captured so well in the opening sequences. It is a refreshing perspective on the disillusionment of the 'pop revolution' and proves that ageing hippies do not have a copyright on failed revolutionary dreams. In this regard, Johnny Gogan's film is not only one of the most astute comments yet on the smugness of the 'Celtic Tiger' society, it is also one of the first revisionist films about the punk era.

Oedipal Conflicts and Maternal Narratives

Very often, as we have noted, the crisis of identity faced by the young protagonist is exacerbated by the fact that one of the parents is missing and, in the case of the father, is either dead or hopelessly ineffectual. In Martin Duffy's *The Boy from Mercury* (1996) the father is dead and part of young Harry's crisis is occasioned by having to accompany his mother so often to pay homage at the graveside, reinforcing for the boy the fact that his family is 'incomplete'. In Paddy Breathnach's *I Went Down* (1997) the dead father is replaced by the father figure of Dublin gangster, Bunny Kelly (Brendan Gleeson), who takes on the role of teaching the young Git Hynes (Peter McDonald) the skills necessary to survive in Ireland's gangland turf wars. The exploration of Irish-American identity in Paul Quinn's *This is My Father* (1998) is initiated by Kieran Johnson's (James Caan) desire to find out more about the Irish father his mother has never talked about but who turns up in an old photograph to cast an enigmatic presence over the jaded Kieran. In Alan Parker's adaptation of *Angela's Ashes* (1999), the father Malachy (Robert Carlyle), is an unreliable drunk for most of the time he is around and then one day just disappears. And even in Damian O'Donnell's highly acclaimed, extremely funny and irreverent short, *Thirty-five a Side* (1995), the father's absence in prison occasions the crisis for young Philip that is so splendidly resolved by his resourceful mother. In *Last of the High Kings*, Frankie's actor father is away for much of his pivotal summer and this throws the conflict with his rhetoric-spouting mother into sharper relief. In the most celebrated of these films, Neil Jordan's *The Miracle* (1991) the mother is supposedly dead and the conflict between the ineffectual father (Donal McCann) and his teenage son is played out against his secretiveness about her and her enigmatic absence. The fact that the mother turns out to be the older woman that the son has sexual fantasies about only completes the oedipal circuit by broaching the final taboo – mother/son incest. The miracle in the film is the fact that the boy comes through all this relatively intact and can, the narrative suggests, finally acknowledge his sexuality in relation to the girl who loves him. In Margo Harkin's *Hush-a-Bye Baby* (1989), Thaddeus O'Sullivan's *December Bride* (1990) and Gilles MacKinnon's *The Playboys* (1992) the father, as Luke Gibbons has pointed out, 'hovers in the background, or is adrift from the action, or cannot be identified at all' (Gibbons, 1992, p. 13).

Indeed, there are so many missing fathers in recent Irish cinema that one can be forgiven for concluding that this, in some deeply significant way, represents a crisis of paternity in Ireland. The fact that nearly all these films (the exception is *Hush-a-Bye Baby*) are the work of male writers and directors is surely significant. Of itself, generational conflict is nothing new for Irish culture and in rural Ireland, especially, the social economy of landholding gave this a particularly oedipal character. In Chapter One, we discussed the material reality of landholding in post-Famine rural Ireland and noted the paramount importance of not subdividing the land. Only one son inherited the land so any others were forced into the church, emigration or celibacy. Tom Inglis has noted the often antagonistic nature of father/son relationships in Ireland and argues:

In fact the cold relationship between father and son can be linked to the rise in the new stem-family practices whereby sons were prevented from marrying by being denied plots of land subdivided from the family holding. The farm began to be handed over intact to just one son. But which son that was to be was not made clear for years. This was a strategy by which postponed marriage and permanent celibacy were maintained. (Inglis, 1987, p. 184)

The domestic sphere became the domain of the mother and she took over the responsibility for the social regulation of both her sons' and daughters' sexuality. The inheriting son waited for the father to die. Generational conflict, therefore, was not linked merely to the condition of adolescence. Unmarried children often remained in the home well into middle age before the parents died and therefore existed in a state of permanent adolescence (or, in psychoanalytic terms, remained in 'the half light of the imaginary' [Mulvey, 1975]). In Pat O'Connor's *The Ballroom of Romance* (1982) the essential sterility of this life is shown by the fact that the dancers assembled in the ballroom are nearly all middle-aged (and older), still looking for a partner. There is, of course, no romance involved in the rituals of the ballroom. Inglis also points out that the bachelor drinking group is part of the social regulation of sexuality. Extreme control is exercised over the body and the passions, in contrast, he argues, to the general European pattern 'in which drinking is associated with festivity and letting go: with mocking and breaking the rules by which people are limited and controlled' (Inglis, 1987, p. 182). In the *Ballroom of Romance*, the drinking group operates as a regulatory rather than as a liberating mechanism – a group of men living in an arrested state of adolescence in which the male drinking group is a process of desexualisation, the sublimation of denied sexuality into drinking. The desperation in these lonely people is then mediated through their oedipal obsessions. Bowes Egan (John Kavanagh) proposes to Bridie (Brenda Fricker) by way of his mother: 'She won't last the winter, Bridie, and then we can get married.' As with the characters in *The Kinkisha*, there are no flowers and Valentine cards in romantic Ireland. The theme of patricide itself finds its most famous expression in Synge's *The Playboy of the Western World* (imagined rather than real but an imagining that stems from suppressed desire and ambition).

If the sexually mature son has to stay celibate and remain at home long into adulthood, he maintains a dependence on the mother who regulates and suppresses his sexuality to the greater social good. This dependence on the mother and the presence of the father as the barrier to his fulfilment create multiple oedipal crises for the son. Inglis also points out that the result of the delayed marriage for both the man and the woman is that their eventual union becomes a social arrangement rather than an emotional commitment (the son arranges a marriage as he might the purchase of a cow, as Inglis so graphically describes it). There is a coldness and a formality about marital relationships as well (Inglis, 1987, p. 184). It is difficult to see that the desperate clutching towards each other that is characteristic of all the ageing couples in *The Ballroom of Romance* will ever lead to anything warmer in human terms. The banner that hangs over the stage in the ballroom – 'Happy Homes for Ireland and for God' – is both ironic and very cruel.

In this world of social and sexual regulation, populated by lonely and desperate people, it is hardly surprising that oedipal conflicts of all kinds should feature so prominently in the culture it produces. It is a recurring theme in the films of Neil Jordan, for example, and the emblematic figure of his musician father hangs over *Angel* (1982), *Night in Tunisia* (1983), *The Miracle* (1991) and *The Butcher Boy* (1997). It is also a key motif in the cinema of Jim Sheridan and if his 1993 version of the Gerry Conlon story, *In the Name of the Father*, highlights this in the very title, oedipal tensions are no less important to his other work, both as director and writer.

The crisis of paternity noted in recent Irish cinema has its roots, therefore, deep in Irish social history and can be located, not in the structures of ancient peasant society, but in the nineteenth century in a process of Catholic modernisation. It is hardly a surprise, then, that Irish culture commits symbolic patricide with such regularity. However, there is more at stake here than the fact that all these films display a kind of spontaneous eruption of the repressed. These are, after all, films made in the last ten years or so, from or about a country enjoying enormous economic growth. They have emerged from diverse production contexts (medium- as well as low-budget films, some produced entirely in Ireland and some from outside). What contemporary eruption do they signify?

Luke Gibbons has characterised the coincidence of the 'maternal narratives' as a reaction to the traumatic events of the 1980s. Throughout the abortion and divorce referenda and in the tragedies at Granard and Cahirciveen, the voice of women was effectively silenced by the patriarchal voice of 'faith and fatherland'. These 'fatherless' films operate, then, as politically charged and alternative national narratives in which the father is silenced and paternity is thrown into crisis. They are, in effect, symbolic representations of a resurgence of women's voices that culminated in the election of Mary Robinson to the Presidency in 1990 (Gibbons, 1992, p. 13). The interesting dimension to this is that the women of Ireland, the mothers of Ireland, who played such a key role in limiting modernisation to the needs of the church in Ireland's 'long nineteenth century', are now seen to be the force that has arrested the attempted resurgence of the 'faith and fatherland' ideology that sustained it. Women, in other words, gave important ideological support to the revival of the stalled modernisation programme in 1990s Ireland. This is certainly persuasive in the case of those film narratives that actually involve direct questions of paternity and childbirth, but there is still the more general question of the missing parent cycle in a wider sense. If the Irish mother of Catholic Ireland has been replaced by the women of 'Robinson's Ireland' – and in summing up her victory, Mary Robinson herself characterised what happened as 'the women of Ireland stopped rocking the cradle and rocked the system' – then how does it link into the generational conflict film?

If the father is missing, then the mother in her domestic domain is even more powerful. As in *Last of the High Kings,* she commands her domain with complete authority. However, Frankie's domineering mother is pushed beyond the boundaries of parody, with Catherine O'Hara's performance becoming increasingly more extreme. The Irish mother is being parodied out of existence and by extension so too is the Ireland that she has come to represent. It is all exaggerated, of course – her anti-Protestantism, anti-Britishness and her sentimental nationalism. This portrayal is a knowing overblown parody – the ironic mode mobilised to justify symbolic matricide and to signify the death of Mother Ireland. It is part of the film's overall optimistic portrayal of the passing-on of one generation and the assumption to power of the next. It is very much a 1990s film about a transitional moment in the 1970s. While the deep-structured oedipal tension is undoubtedly at play, in the context of contemporary Ireland, the impact of modernity and the attitude that this induces in relation to the memory of the past – of the parents' generation – is another crucial factor. In this film there is a benign, if resigned, amusement towards the mother's excesses – a tolerance bred from a position of comfortable (male) knowledge that the values that she represented have already passed away. A generation closer to the period when these values held influence, the attitude is a lot less tolerant – hence the desperation and starkness of a film like *The Ballroom of Romance.*

We have noted in Chapter Two that the Irish mother as a cinematic stereotype had a basis in the social relations of rural Ireland and that this stereotype was used in strategic ways in early Hollywood cinema as part of a process of assimilation for the Irish-American. She was often a widow, of course, and again this reflected a certain social reality. The working conditions for the Irish immigrant, especially in the USA, were so bad that life expectancy among Irish males was poor. The Irish mother was often called upon to provide for the family as well. Survival skills were as important as the ability to act as a moral authority and in this sphere she performed the role of the father, providing the strength, resilience and practical decision-making that were necessary to survive the tribulations an uncaring world threw at the family. In Angelica Huston's *Agnes Browne* (1999), based on Brendan O'Carroll's novel *The Mammy,* the opening sequence shows Agnes (played also by Huston) and her friend Marion (Marion O'Dwyer) in the social security office organising the paperwork necessary for Agnes to claim a widow's pension. The joke is that

Agnes' husband has just died that afternoon. It is Marion's job to see that Agnes has her priorities right. The subsequent funeral is a series of disasters and confusions that end up with Agnes and her friends standing over the wrong grave. The death is a bit of a joke in other words and in conversations with Marion we learn that her husband was also useless, sexually and socially. In fact Agnes' seven children seem to share her lack of grief as well. As Agnes walks to work there is a ritualistic passing-on of condolences from her neighbours that similarly lacks emotion. All this is in stark contrast to the high emotional melodramatics that lead up to and follow the death of Marion later in the film. In the world of female and family survival the father just doesn't count. The rest of the film traces Agnes' growing confidence in both her social skills and in her survival strategies. Set in working-class Dublin in 1967, it again evinces a 1990s complacency. The fact that Agnes' predicaments are sorted out in a fantasy form – through the intervention of her idol, Tom Jones – is another rather strained contemporary device.

In the sense, then, that it attempts a knowing contemporary take on the past, it is similar to *Last of the High Kings*. But if the latter is a view of the mother (and Mother Ireland) from the perspective of the young male who needs to pass through his own oedipal crisis before, as he expects, he can inherit the earth, then *Agnes Browne* is a proto-feminist film that looks at a changing society from the perspective of women. The mother here represents the future, not the past, as in *Last of the High Kings*. The men are uniformly repressive and exploitative, selfish and unreliable or just downright frustratingly inadequate. The film does play a little with the character of Pierre, Agnes' French admirer, who sets up a *boulangerie* in the market street. He wanders through the film dressed in his baker's whites, resembling a kind of 'knight in white'. He promises to bring a touch of continental sensuousness to Agnes' life (and a bit of continental modernity to the drab cuisine of traditional Dublin). Yet, Pierre never quite delivers as well and it is to the film's credit that it resists the temptation to have Pierre ride to Agnes' rescue in the end. It is a combination of Agnes' own determination and the inventive resilience of her family that brings about the vanquishing of the moneylender. The Tom Jones intervention is the film's nod to a sort of 'magic realism' that is itself rather undercut by the fact that the contemporary Tom Jones himself plays his much younger self.

The film works best in the way that it conjures up a kind of 'parliament of women', accessing women's discourse and privileging the ruminations of women on the peculiarities of a male-ordered universe. This is especially so in the relationship between Agnes and her best friend, Marion. There are scenes here of female support and solidarity that are impressive and often moving. The performance of Marion O'Dwyer is especially good and, for the Irish audience at least, her role is pivotal since it otherwise requires quite a leap of the

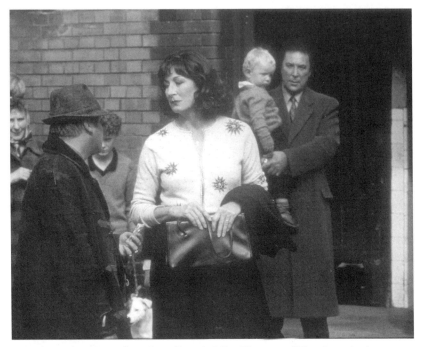

Organic community and magic realism: Anjelica Huston and Tom Jones in *Agnes Browne* (Irish Film Archive of the Film Institute of Ireland)

imagination to accept Anjelica Huston as a Moore Street fruit and vegetable trader. Despite the tragedy at the centre of this relationship, the film achieves another kind of 'can-do' optimism, this time about the future of women in Ireland – the Robinson generation which came into its own in the 1990s. However, it does so by conjuring up an idealised view of working-class community life that exudes nostalgia for a non-existent time when such organic communities offered broad mutual support and solidarity. There is little here in the way of the anger, resistance, alienation and despair which were more realistically aspects of working-class Dublin life in the 1960s and which might register with the realities of contemporary Dublin. There is again a sort of self-satisfied complacency at the centre of the film and a hopelessly romantic view of urban hardship and poverty that cuts across its feminist message.

These two films, then, are set in a period when the perception of a changing Ireland was the dominant zeitgeist and both look at the mother figure in Irish society from this perspective. Although set in the past, the films evince a distinctly 1990s optimism about the future, based on the perceptions of how the future did develop onwards from this past. *Last of the High Kings* eliminates the mother figure by parodying her out of existence and clearing the way for the young male (a descendent of the last of the high kings of Ireland, as his mother refers to him) to assume his rightful place in a changing world. *Agnes Browne*, on the other hand, eliminates the father and declares that the future belongs to the women of Ireland. Despite their telling moments and the interesting way in which they raise questions about how the past is remembered from the present, they both suffer from an excess of complacent optimism that reflects a certain knowing smugness characteristic of contemporary Ireland.

A film that lacks any sense of this is Alan Parker's adaptation of *Angela's Ashes* but only because the film makes no kind of register with contemporary Ireland at all. There are some superficial similarities to both *Last of the High Kings* and *Agnes Browne*, in that the absence of the father pushes the mother into the centre of the narrative. Although the film attempts to paint a sympathetic picture of the father Malachy (Robert Carlyle), at least as far as the memory of his son Frank is concerned, it is obvious that he is completely inadequate in the struggle for survival. When he eventually disappears there is little in the way of grief or distress. For Angela (Emily Watson) in particular there is no emotional loss in his going – it is almost a relief that there is one less mouth to feed. There is a major problem, though, with the way the film then presents Angela's struggle for survival. Frank McCourt's memoir of the poverty of de Valera's Ireland, on which the film was based, is wry, ironic and bitter and its readability depends on this authorial voice which at all stages in its horrific narrative mediates the experience for the reader. We can survive or endure the narrative because this voice fills in for us a contemporary register. It is this voice that, after all, rose from Angela's ashes to tell the world, with all the bitterness and anger it can muster, about the terrible indignities that were visited on her and her family. It is this voice that is Angela's legacy. In the film, it is this voice that is missing and which crucially disables the film. We get pictures of the narrative but the authorial voice cannot be pictorialised in the same way as the bare bones of the narrative.

The difference between McCourt's literary language and the pictorial bluntness of Parker's images (and there is no doubting the admirable beauty of these) is well illustrated by Nick Roddick in his review of the film. Despite the fact that the family rallies around Eugene after the death of his twin brother Oliver, McCourt succinctly observes 'He died anyway' – a devastatingly ironic and bitter three-word paragraph that it is impossible to render on to the screen pictorially. As Roddick observes 'The words also appear in the film (in voiceover of course), but by then we have already seen Eugene's lifeless head on the pillow, and the effect is quite different: the information has already been conveyed, the punchline-structure loses its drama, and the irony vanishes' (Roddick, 2000, p. 41). This irony is, of course, the book's resistance and fightback – without this the audience is left to wonder about the total resignation in the film and to suspect that no resistance was ever offered, could be offered and isn't being offered to this kind of social oppression. In this regard, the film comes across as particularly reactionary and regressive. What is the point of *Angela's Ashes*, if not to register anger and resistance to oppression?

The film, then, lacks the bitter and desperate anger of the source material and is too far removed from the events to evince the desperate anger of *The Ballroom of Romance*. In the manner in which it addresses a contemporary audience it lacks also the ironic knowingness and humour of *Agnes Browne* or *Last of the High Kings*. It makes little connection to contemporary Ireland, then, because it has no real emotional impact, one way or another. It is a series of pretty pictures of Irish poverty, devoid of any kind of engagement – an efficient and mechanical piece of film-making that says nothing more than 'this was in the book, here it is now up on the big screen'.

Of course, the fact that the majority of these films are written and directed by men may also have another, deeper significance. Despite the optimism of *Last of the High Kings*, for example, could not the rather overblown portrait of the mother, together with the overt and challenging sexiness of the girls in Frankie's fantasy, not also reflect a containment exercise that reveals deep fears of assertive women? In this case, the oedipal conflict being worked through is a castration anxiety. As the old patriarchal nationalist consensus withers, and with it the limited domestic and maternal role assigned to women, then fears of losing the actual or potential male inheritance are expressed in cautionary tales about these assertive women. There is a long tradition in Hollywood cinema of such 'castrating women' narratives, most commonly associated with the femme fatale character of the film noir cycle of the 1940s and 1950s, but periodically resurrected ever since (Kaplan, 1978). The films of Neil Jordan are particularly susceptible to this reading. In the complex web of transgressive themes in *The Crying Game*, the only uninterrogated aspect of the film is the portrayal of the one ('real') woman in the film, the IRA woman Jude (Miranda Richardson). Her character hardens (or is masculinised) as the narrative proceeds, in contrast to Fergus (Stephen Rea), who softens as he is 'feminised'. Jude's final appearance, as a power-dressed and determined terrorist with gun in hand, is the most traditional of 'castrating women' stereotypes. Indeed, male redemption in this film is at the expense of the woman who has to be eliminated before any kind of resolution can occur for Fergus and Dil (Jaye Davidson). The regressiveness of this portrayal is in inverse proportion to the progressiveness of the film's exploration of male identity and sexuality. Even in *The Butcher Boy*, Francie's nemesis is Mrs Nugent, whose main crime is an assertive upward mobility. Her 'punishment' far outweighs her 'crime'.

Generational conflict in recent Irish cinema works, then, much in the way that it works in cinema in general but with the added complications of a particularly male set of oedipal complexities that find their roots deep in Irish social history. Some aspects of these crises can be located also in the turbulent recent experience of church/state tensions in Ireland and a crisis brought on especially by the greater intrusion of women into a traditional patriarchal culture. This is especially so in relation to sexuality, reproduction and legislative control of the woman's body as a result of the particularly fractious abortion debate. However, there is one final way of considering generational conflict in these films, suggested by the metaphor of the family as the nation. Here, the question is the relationship between national or cultural identity and the influence of outside forces on the particularities of Irish culture.

Chapter 9
Cultural Identity: The American Friend and the European Neighbour

The process of reimagining the nation inevitably touches on the kind of cultural identity that is experienced, valued or promoted by the younger generation. Ireland is now a long way from de Valera's notion of 'frugal self-sufficiency' and its economic advance has been the result of massive inward investment from Europe, Asia and especially the USA. The price paid for this is that the country has entered the global economy and the global marketplace of popular culture. Many of the films discussed here have been reflections on the cultural implications of this change.

Central to this sense of identity is the looming presence of American popular culture and the implications of this forms one central thread of Neil Jordan's multilayered *The Butcher Boy*. In most of Jordan's films, American music, especially the jazz-inflected music of the father-musicians who populate his films, plays an important role in defining the relationships within the nation/family as well as the relationship between the indigenous and the international (Pramaggiore, 1998). The problem with American popular culture is that its dominant position in Irish culture can be read in either of two ways, as we discussed in Chapter Four.

On one hand it can be seen to represent a form of cultural imperialism that thwarts the development of indigenous culture and merely reaffirms that prosperity in Ireland has been gained at the expense of national difference. On the other hand, the essentialist identity proposed by Catholic nationalism and the Gaelic revival was so insular and stifling that the greater encroachment of American popular culture has been positively liberating. It has to be said that the balance of recent Irish cinema would seem to favour the latter, though the contradiction is never really lost sight of. Again, this is most thoroughly worked through in *The Butcher Boy*. However, Elvis, Thin Lizzy and other icons of rock music are central to the young people in *Last of the High Kings* and contrast greatly with the sentimental rebel ballads favoured by the older generation. Similarly, in *The Last Bus Home*, punk music is offered as the most effective riposte to the religiosity of the parents praying with the Pope in Phoenix Park.

The theme is again central to *The Boy from Mercury*, where Harry escapes the malaise of his incomplete family by losing himself in American sci-fi films and Westerns while his older brother gyrates in the kitchen with a broom to the sounds of rock and roll. In a culture which validates the afterlife more than the material world and which spends most of the time venerating the past and the dead it is hardly surprising that young Harry should fantasise that he is really from Mercury and merely passing through Earth temporarily.

Some earlier films also played with the impact of American culture in Ireland, most notably Thaddeus O'Sullivan's short film *The Woman who Married Clark Gable* (1985) and Peter Ormrod's feature *Eat the Peach* (1986), the narrative of both being initiated by an encounter with American cinema specifically. As we have seen, the influence of Hollywood is global and in this regard its impact on Ireland is consistent with other cultures. One can detect a similar thrust in the New German Cinema of the 1970s. Thomas Elsaesser quotes a pertinent remark by Wim Wenders: '... asked why American music, comics and movies had been his "life-savers" in adolescence, Wenders replied: "Twenty years of political amnesia had left a hole: we covered it with chewing gum and Polaroids" ' (Elsaesser, 1988, p. 239). Elsaesser argues that the New German Cinema pushed through this amnesia and by the time it had achieved considerable international success it 'appeared set to have its identity firmly located in a brooding obsession with Germany's own unredeemed and irredeemable past as a nation' (ibid.). These two movements are, of course, interlinked. While Elsaesser is surely right to locate this brooding, in psychoanalytic terms, in the loss of a father figure (a generation's loss of the positive identifications which the previous Nazi generation could not provide), nonetheless, the catalyst for this identity crisis is the presence of American culture. Thus Wender's work, and that of Fassbinder, continually echo, reference and critique the 'American friend' in German national psyche.

In terms of Ireland we can see a double response to the past. In many films there is a sense of brooding, if not quite on a 'unredeemed and irredeemable' past, at least on a Catholic nationalist past that is strongly problematical for the younger generation and a past which continues to have an impact on the present in the most traumatic ways. Many of the film-makers from the first wave, including Quinn, Comerford, Black, Murphy and O'Sullivan, have returned again and again to themes that attempt to explore the meaning of the past for contemporary Ireland in much the same way that Elsaesser identifies in New German Cinema of the 1970s/1980s. On the other hand, the younger generation has mastered many of the tropes of American popular culture, especially, of course, rock and pop music. In time, they may also master the tropes of cinema. They feel they have inherited the world already from their traumatised parents and can breezily cast aside their neuroses and learn to live with an American popular culture that their emigrant ancestors helped to build in the first place. Their films are, there-fore, much less brooding and much more assertive about the new Ireland that they inhabit. Underneath the breezy surface, however, we can locate an anxiety also about this generation's relationship to their parents and the preceding gen-erations. Their method of dealing with this anxiety is to attempt to erase the parental figures, either through parody or displacement. The way in which they do so tells us much about the prevailing ethos of this new Ireland.

The picture, then, that emerges from the generational conflict films is one of incompleteness. The conflict is occasioned not by the presence of traditional, conservative parents but rather by the absence or inadequacy of one of them. It is almost as if the films read Ireland's older generation as the one in need of rescue and repair. The task of re-establishing stability to the nation will fall on the shoulders of the young precisely because they are unencumbered by the neuroses and inadequacies of their parents. In all of this, American popular cul-ture provides the images that allow these displaced children from the fractured family of the nation to begin again to dream and to imagine.

There is another interesting recent development in Irish cinema's explo-ration of this American theme. Over the last few years, a number of Irish and Irish-American films have been concerned to probe the relationship between the two countries through the presence of the Irish diaspora and the implica-tions of the large-scale emigration to the USA. This is an important theme in Cathal Black's *Korea* (1995) but has emerged in recent years in a series of films originating in the USA itself. Paul Quinn's *This is My Father* (1998) explores the Irish roots of a troubled second-generation Irish-American, while Eugene Brady's *The Nephew* (1998) looks at the impact back in Ireland of the return-ing Irish-American, this time with the added frisson that the returning nephew is also African-American. Most of these films, however, look at the fate of the new Irish immigrant of the 1980s and 1990s. Elizabeth Gill's *Gold in the Streets* (1997), Jimmy Smallhorne's *2 By 4* (1998), George Bazala's *Beyond the Pale* (1999), Bryan Baker and Anthony M. Davis' *Characters* (1999), Bill Muir's *Exiled* (1999) and Nelson Hulme's *Sunburn* (1999) all explore the experiences of recent Irish immigrants in New York. We will look at *2 By 4* and *This is My Father* in more detail below, as they encapsulate many of the themes (oedipal tensions, the 'family' of the nation, the interface between Ireland and America and questions of sexuality) that we have been outlining here. However, the overriding impression from the rest of these films is that the new Irish are, by and large, young, gormless and wet. Their milieu is the bar and their culture is that of drink. Their obsession with getting laid is matched only by their com-plete inadequacy at achieving it. They encounter aspects of American life – sex, drugs, individualism, survival, crime and personal responsibility – that Ireland has ill-prepared them for.

Certainly, there are some interesting details in many of the films. In *Sunburn* there is a contrast between the selfish individualism of Davin (Cillian Murphy), who buys into the American dream totally (symbolised in the old convertible that he purchases), and the sense of family duty and group loyalty that characterises the other Irish students he spends the summer with. In *Beyond the Pale*, the American dream itself is shown to have diminished into an alcoholic haze in the shape of failed writer, Tom Finnegan (played by Malachy McCourt with a relish for the Irish stereotype) and in the seriously troubled drinking of the newly arrived Seamus. The all-round stupidity of the male is the final message of *Characters*. The film is shot in long takes with a minimum of editing and progresses through dialogue rather than action. This dialogue reveals the inadequacies of the two recent arrivals, Bryan (Bryan Baker) and Edward (Ed Beausang) and conveys well their propensity to fantasise rather than do. This inadequacy is matched by that of the two American goons employed to look after the young woman that Bryan falls for. They may be vicious but are, ultimately, just as gormless as the Irish lads are. Both sets of males live a fantasy existence where the promises of the American dream, although differently ingested, result in the same kind of displaced (and misplaced) inadequacy.

The darkest of these films, because it is the most ambitious, is Bill Muir's *Exiled*. Young Dubliner and minor criminal Brendan (Paul Ronan), on the run from the Dublin police, arrives in New York to stay with his Belfast cousin Sean (Ronan Carr). Sean introduces Brendan into the subculture of New York's Irish-American community, the 'thirty-third county', as he describes it. As in the other films, this subculture consists of bars, drinking and the pursuit of sex. However, the film follows the contrast between Brendan's Dublin background, where he is a petty criminal, and Sean's Northern environment, where he is a political activist. In contrast to the other films, therefore, Muir shows that this subculture also consists of overt (and particularly unforgiving) republicanism. Sean is heavily involved in a conspiracy to smuggle arms to the IRA in Belfast. One of the film's ambitions is to suggest how far the North and the South have drifted apart and now have their own contrasting priorities. As Brendan says, rather laconically, 'There's no mist rolling down the hills in the housing estate I live in.' The male bonding between the cousins is carefully teased out and this family loyalty again becomes conflated with national commitment. Thus, the conflict of loyalties that confront Brendan when he is caught between Sean's IRA, which enlists him to help in an arms-smuggling job, and the FBI, who blackmail him over his criminal past, is stark. The world of graft, illegal immigration, corruption and male violence (sexual and political) is laid on rather menacingly and Brendan's attempt to find love as well as comradeship leads from treachery to retribution and tragedy.

The most striking aspect of these films, however, is the very fact that they are appearing in such numbers at this moment. This surely reflects both the expansion of the notion of Irishness that we alluded to in the introduction and the urgency with which the whole question of Irish emigration is now being addressed. It is also significant that they emanate largely from the USA itself and that they are mostly concerned with the 'new Irish', the products of modernised Ireland who have had the benefits of both a better education than previous immigrants and the second-hand knowledge of things American that comes from a greater exposure to American popular culture. It is interesting that these films seem to suggest that none of this has prepared them any better than their predecessors for the challenges of life in America. Brad Pitt's charismatically efficient IRA man in *The Devil's Own*, discussed in Chapter Three, is a long way removed from the anxious immigrants of these films.

American Dreams and Nightmares: *This is My Father* (1998) and *2 By 4* (1998)

The cross-fertilisation of Ireland and America is well illustrated by the Quinn brothers' collaborative *This is My Father* (1998), directed by Paul, shot by Declan (who also won a cinematography award at 1998's Sundance festival for *2 By 4*) and starring Aidan, all of whom have spent some of their younger years and received part of their education in both Ireland and the USA. (Declan's first film as Director of Photography was Fergus Tighe's *Clash of the Ash* [1987].) The film is an attempt to explore the cultural significance of an Irish-American experience that goes beyond the merely physical. The point about Ireland is that these close physical and familial ties are only part of the story. The influence of American popular culture in Ireland over the years has been so profound that it has penetrated deep into Irish consciousness. The Irish, perhaps more so than other Europeans, have inhabited the imaginative spaces of the USA for so long, and been involved so deeply in the myth of the promised land or the land of opportunity that the American dream is deeply embedded in Irish cultural identity. The recent wave of films merely offers an imaginative perspective on, and attempt to put a human face to, the reality of this special relationship. In fact, in mainstream American cinema, there has always been an interest in the culture of Irish-America and this has also manifested itself recently in a range of films which probe, to a greater or lesser degree, aspects of this culture from within.

Thus, Ron Howard has paid homage to his Irish roots in the epic folly of *Far and Away* (1992) and has pursued aspects of Irish-American identity in the fire-fighter thriller *Backdraft* (1991). During the last ten years or so, there has been a steady stream of American films that have investigated the heritage of Irish ethnic identity in American communities. The most celebrated of these was Edward Byrne's *The Brothers McMullen* (1995), but the theme has appeared in comedy form in Chris Columbus' *Only the Lonely* (1991), in which Maureen O'Hara returned to the screen to play the other side of her feisty colleen of *The Quiet Man*, the domineering Irish widow/mother who is still regulating her middle-aged son's sex life. In Ted Demme's *Monument Avenue* (1998) Irishness is pursued through the filter of a local street gang. These are a more vicious and more racist group of 'angels with dirty faces' than their celebrated predecessors, merely existing in the modern world in a life of thwarted ambition and limited horizons.

If these films are concerned with the fate of Irish ethnic identity in the USA, *This is My Father* is concerned with the emotional and psychic interplay between Ireland and America. The motivation for Kieran Johnston's (James Caan) visit to the land of his parents is, inevitably, a crisis over paternity. Kieran is a childless widower who has never known his father. His mother, now lying near death in a coma, has never discussed the matter with him in any detail. There is, therefore, a 'lack' at the centre of his life. He leads a lonely, vague and directionless existence as a High School history teacher who has even less motivation than his students do. When he discovers an old photograph of his mother as a young woman with a slightly older man he presumes that this is the missing link in his sad and empty life.

Paternity crises in Ireland and America: James Caan in *This is My Father* (Irish Film Archive of the Film Institute of Ireland)

There is another paternity crisis at play as well. Kieran's nephew Jack (Jacob Tierney), son of his divorced sister, is also suffering from the absence of a father (flunking at school, taking drugs) and when Kieran decides to go to Ireland to find out more about his father, he is persuaded to take the surly Jack with him. This contemporary tale of angst and lack of direction provides the frame within which the story of Kieran's parents is told in flashback. The main story, then, is set in rural Ireland in 1939 and concerns the inappropriate and ultimately tragic romance between a simple farmer, also called Kieran (Aidan Quinn) and Fiona Flynn (Moya Farrelly), the feisty daughter of local landowner the Widow Flynn (Gina Moxley). Kieran is described as a 'poorhouse bastard' who has been told that his father was a French sailor, a similar yarn foisted by Fiona on her own son in later years. The second layer of paternity crises, therefore, resides in the historical tale of Kieran's and Fiona's doomed romance. At one point, Fiona tells Kieran, 'I miss my father. He was the only one who could make Mammy happy.' This might account for the Widow's generally mean disposition and her bitter response to her daughter's affair with Kieran though, in fact, the character is a slightly exaggerated cinema stereotype of the Irish mother/widow. In line with many of the cameo parts in the film, Gina Moxley plays this character with a certain amount of actorly excess. However, this emphasis on missing fathers seems to push the story towards an ambitious layering of oedipal conflicts and displaced psyches.

This is one of the problems with the film. Its ambitions and its schematic structure are never fully realised – the scale of the film is too small for the ambitions. Certainly, there is much to admire in the way it sets out to do this. For example, it is obvious that the Quinns intended to visualise the three separate worlds of the film in different ways. The framing story, set in the Chicago suburb of Aurora, is shot in muted browns, suggesting the lack of colour and excitement in the lives of these troubled and anxious Irish-Americans. The film then plays nicely with the landscape when the characters decamp to Ireland to begin their search for the contemporary Kieran's roots. The film shows the Irish countryside through the constricting vista of the car windows as Kieran and Jack travel west towards Fiona's home village. They arrive at their destination at night. When Jack wakes up next morning and pulls back the curtain, generic conventions suggest that what he will see is the famed beauty of rural Ireland, the world of *The Quiet Man* (or even *Waking Ned*). Instead, Jack mutters incredulously, 'We've landed in Chernobyl!' and the scene cuts to a shot of squat furnace chimneys blighting the horizon. Other aspects of contemporary Ireland are equally demythologised. Right at the end of the film, Jack runs through the flat, elemental bogland to say goodbye to Maria, the Irish girl he fancies. The camera tracks with him as he leaps and bounds over the ancient sod. However, on arriving at her house she emerges from a very modern and expensive bungalow. The chimneys and the bungalow are the signifiers of a modern, utilitarian Ireland far removed from the romantic pastoral of legend.

Where this kind of romantic landscape does reside is in the past and here the cinematography opens out into vistas of beautiful scenery. In fact this opening-out is signalled in the words of the old woman who tells Kieran the story of his parents, '… and the world was different then'. The scene cuts to a shot of the romantic landscape, perhaps exactly the kind of shot we might have expected earlier when Jack drew the curtains. The problem, though, is that this beautiful Ireland is the backdrop to a set of religious, social and class prejudices and oppressions that leads to the tragedy of Kieran O'Day, the contemporary Kieran's father. This is underlined when the young Fiona surveys the landscape and says 'God, I hate the country!' In fact the film has again signalled this in visual terms earlier. Kieran looks at an illustration in a book of a tree in full foliage standing on a small hillock surrounded by the landscape. There is a quick cut from the dull reproduction in the old book to the lushness of the same tree in its location in Ireland. The irony of this is that this is the 'fairy' tree that the guilt-ridden and rejected Kieran O'Day will eventually hang himself from.

The repressive world of rural Catholic Ireland is again conjured up through its repression of desire, sexuality and emotion. The dance sequence in which Fiona, casual and provocative in a red dress, stirs up the emotions and thwarted sexuality in the men illustrates this well. As the villagers (from the oldest to the youngest) dance a reel together, the parish priest patrols down the centre of the dancefloor. The festivities are relieved of his repressive presence when, with a shake of the moneybox to weigh up that night's take, he leaves. However, the ensuing fight between Kieran O'Day and some local lads over Fiona allows the priest to return to the subject at Mass the next day. Castigating the 'drinking, cursing and fighting' (stimulated by 'fast music to stir up the passions') that ensued after he left, he condemns the whole community to a pilgrimage to Croagh Patrick as penance.

While the priest worries about the couple's immortal souls there is also a social dimension to this repression. The whole community is either scandalised or highly amused at the unlikely pairing of the outgoing, vivacious and (relatively) wealthy Fiona and the landless, simple 'poorhouse bastard' Kieran. The Widow Flynn suspects he is after her land and Kieran's adoptive parents, the poor Maneys, fear that this dangerous liaison will result in the Widow evicting them from the humble home they rent on her property. Indeed, there is a leap of faith required here for the audience as well, for Fiona's attraction to Kieran is largely unexplained. This suggests that the film is asking its audience to view the two lovers in more metaphorical ways. Kieran, of course, is the very essence of the simple Irish farmer, even if his own roots are obscured behind the epithet that is used to describe him. His horizons are bounded by the daily grind of menial farm labour, looking after the Maneys and attending to his religious duties. He does tell Fiona that he once nearly went to America but when Mr Maney came after him to the boat and told him to come home again, he acquiesced tamely.

If Fiona's love for Kieran is largely unmotivated within the film, so is the personality of Fiona herself. She is similar in her own way to Rose in *Titanic*, unusually 'modern' and sophisticated for someone who has emerged from a particularly oppressive social and class background. She is sensuous and confrontational in her red dress and her flirtatiousness. She is progressive in her attitudes to sexuality and religion and open and liberal in her class attitudes (to the 'peasant' Kieran and to the travellers/tinkers that the rest of her community distrusts). In this regard, she is potentially a more liberated and liberating 'feisty colleen' than Mary Kate in *The Quiet Man*. Where does such an assertive seventeen-year-old come from in this Ireland of nuns, priests and petty bourgeois pretensions? The film provides some fleeting clues. She obviously hates the country and her education in Galway suggests that hers is essentially an urban sensibility. She is also a person of the cinema and her heroine is Greta Garbo. As she says to Kieran regretfully when a car problem thwarts their trip to Galway, 'I wanted to take you to the cinema – to see Greta Garbo in *Camille*. It'd change your life forever.' The implication is that the cinema has changed Fiona's life for ever, providing her with the chance to dream and with the models of desire that the dead grip of Catholicism otherwise denies her. The reference to Garbo, picked up again later when Kieran and Fiona meet the American airman Eddie Sharp (John Cusack), is suggestive in this regard. Roland Barthes has said of Garbo's face:

> Garbo still belongs to that moment in the cinema when capturing the human face still plunged audiences into the deepest ecstasy, when one literally lost oneself in a human image as one would in a philtre, when the face represented a kind of absolute state of the flesh, which could neither be reached or renounced. … Garbo's face represents this fragile moment when the cinema is about to draw an existential from an essential beauty, when the archetype leans towards the fascination of mortal faces, when the clarity of the flesh as essence yields its place to a lyricism of Woman. (Barthes, 1957/70, pp. 56–7)

Barthes is here describing a process by which the cinema fetishised the female body, responding to the latent castrating threat that women posed by elevating her to a position beyond the merely corporeal, where the threat is neutralised in an abstraction (Mulvey, 1975). The point, though, is that to do this, the cinema has to acknowledge the threat in the first place, to *show* the desires of the woman and the 'absolute state of the flesh'. Fiona, then, learns about the flesh, and about the possibility of expressing the pleasures of the flesh, from the cinema. If she must look for inspiration from an idealised image of 'Woman', then she'd rather have Greta Garbo than the Virgin Mary. American cinema is her escape from the repression of life in Ireland. America itself comes to represent the land of freedom where dreams can become reality and desire can be expressed rather than patrolled by a celibate clergy.

However, what makes the film interesting is the way in which the uncertainty of its approach to these issues results in a kind of overflowing of ambition that swamps achievement and yet leaves a whole set of suggestive loose ends. For one thing, there is a tendency to absurdity in the film that pulls against the emotional melodrama of the central tragic love story of Fiona and Kieran O'Day. There are lots of incidental examples of this absurdity. Like Gina Moxley's Widow Flynn, they are implicit in a whole range of cameo roles played by a strong cast of character actors who attack their minor parts with gusto.

For example, Seamus Kearney, the son of the old fortune-teller who narrates the flashback story, is played by Colm Meaney with a mincing campness that borders on the surreal. Why he should be so camp is neither 'explained' nor developed, an incidental detail that is so obviously exaggerated that it simply cannot be contained within the narrative. Like the film's playing with audience expectations over the shot of the landscape it seems to be a further extension of the film's demythologising of Ireland. It can, of course, be read as a result of his own 'fatherless' condition and here it might link to the film's overall discourse on the crisis of paternity. Kieran Johnston is dissatisfied and unfulfilled because of the lack of closure that his father's story might bring. Jack is slowly developing into a juvenile delinquent as a result of his divorced father's absence. Kieran O'Day's untutored simplicity and vulnerability is the result of a lack of paternal guidance and strength. Fiona's overt and uncontainable sensuousness is the result of a lack of strong paternal authority and finally, Seamus Kearney's mincing campness establishes him as a 'mammy's boy' deprived of the strong virile influence of a father. This essentially patriarchal schema is a possible reading but it seems so at odds with the film's humorous exaggeration, its underlying playfulness, that to read it as such requires the audience to look past the film's tendency to mischief. This tendency is again evident in the portrayal of the fathers who *are* present, the parish priest, Fr Mooney and the troubleshooting fire-and-brimstone Fr Quinn (Stephen Rea), brought in after the fight at the dance to sort out the village sinners. Rea's performance here is reminiscent of his cameo in *Last of the High Kings*, full of bluster and exaggeration. His concern with the sexual peccadilloes of his parishioners is voyeuristic and deeply perverted even if his thundering rhetoric reduces Kieran to abject submission.

The most bizarre and 'uncontainable' scene in the film is the cameo appearance of John Cusack as Eddie Sharp, the American aerial photographer (for *Life* magazine, wouldn't you know) who literally drops in on Fiona and Kieran on the beach. With his very contemporary screen persona, Cusack looks like he came straight from the set of another movie. It is as if, since Kieran and Fiona can no longer go to the cinema in Galway because of car trouble, then American cinema must come to them on the beach. If there is a contrast here between American modernity and the pre-modern world of rural Ireland, then the relationship is posed almost like that of a 'cargo cult'. Sharp drops in, plays American football with them (Kieran's version is very much GAA) and puts on the music that allows the Irish couple to dance and cement their feelings for each other. He literally drops in the dreams and aspirations that release the couple from the strictures of their miserable Irish existence and offers them both hope and fulfilment. Fiona, of course, is already well integrated into the dreams of America, her sensuousness and assertiveness already at odds with the conservatism of her society. Kieran, on the other hand, is so repressed by his lowly status (even within such a poor society) and by his unthinking resignation in the face of hardship and scorn that Eddie Sharp represents that which is barely comprehensible. 'Skyscrapers, how are you', he mumbles, as Fiona and Eddie discuss the wonders of America.

Eddie, however, will rescue neither Fiona nor Kieran directly. His role is as a sort of facilitator for the Irish couple, providing the popular culture which they themselves inhabit to affect their own relationship, their own release from frustration and confinement. His spontaneity and individualism, his unorthodox and supreme self-confidence are offered as vindication of those traits in Fiona that she will bring, through her love, to the repressed Kieran. The next morning, having fixed their car and their love for each other, Eddie has flown off (into his own movie) while Kieran and Fiona sleep the sleep of young love confirmed. The narrative excess of this sequence is both comical and absurd, a highly suggestive interlude from the inevitability of the tragedy that is unfolding. Certainly, the scenes are anchored narratively by the fact that Eddie takes the photograph of Fiona and Kieran that over half a century later will bring the other Kieran to Ireland in search of his father but this device to establish the film's 'MacGuffin' hardly justifies the scene's excesses.

The film ends with Kieran passing the now framed photograph around his high-school class, more settled and content now that he can say 'this is my father'. His family is now complete. The photograph, though, represents not just an alternative future that Kieran's family might have had. It represents an alternative imagining of Ireland that also might have been – an Ireland at peace with itself, freed of the social, class and religious repression that eventually blighted the lives of Kieran and Fiona. Above all, the photograph symbolises an encounter between Ireland and America that is ambivalent and elliptical as it has resonated down the years. To deal with this resonance there is a sense in which the film attempted to offer a love story in contemporary Ireland parallel to that of Kieran and Fiona in the past. As the surly Jack walks around his grandmother's village, he is accosted by two young girls, Maria and Nuala, who harass him and eventually entice him out of his own morose introspection. They are as sassy and assertive as the young Fiona had been sixty years earlier. Jack, however, though amiable enough, lacks any of the self-confidence and brashness of Eddie Sharp. He wanders the town in a mood of sullen introspection and, if anything, he resembles his Irish grandfather's simple reticence.

The girls tease him about America – 'Is it true that every American has a gun?' – and retort to his gibe about violence in Northern Ireland by proclaiming with consummate irony, 'Don't you know that it's an eight-hundred-year struggle to repel foreign invaders?' Jack and Nuala eventually get together but this subplot just stops with Jack's goodbye kiss. As we have seen, the way in which this scene is shot, with its the emphasis more on a visual play with the bog landscape and the modern bungalow than on the intimacy of new love, seems to downplay any significance in the relationship. Certainly, there is a suggestion that the new Ireland is a much more confident and assertive place, as if the Fionas have prospered at the expense of the Fathers Mooney and Quinn. Jack is no Sean Thornton, come to rural Ireland to find the peace and tranquillity that urban America denies him. This land of 'Chernobyl' chimneys and prosperous bungalows is not Innisfree and this village, whatever else it might be, is the place where Jack's grandfather committed suicide. Maria and Nuala do not need the help of American cinema to dream and aspire. Their attitude to America is altogether more sceptical and ironic. There is no need, either, for Maria to leave the comfort of her modern contemporary lifestyle to seek her fortune in America. In the end, the young lovers kiss and promise to write. The emotional and psychological dependence of Ireland on America has now become a matter of mere penpals.

As a contemporary parallel narrative, therefore, the subplot involving Jack is suggestive but, like so many other details in the film, it doesn't develop. *This is My Father* is, then, a strangely incomplete film, unsatisfactory in terms of narrative coherence and yet, for all that, most interesting and most suggestive exactly in those unruly narrative excesses that escape final closure.

Jimmy Smallhorne's *2 By 4* is a very different kind of exploration of the interface between Ireland and America. It is a low-budget film that was financed entirely in the USA and, except for some brief Dublin scenes that appear in the film's nightmare sequences, was shot entirely in New York. The film is set in the contemporary Bronx among the building workers of the Irish community, mostly young recent immigrants. It is, in fact, one of the few films to deal with the actual working life of the blue-collar Irish. If, like many of the films discussed earlier, it shows this life through the drinking and general male bar life of the city, at least it also shows that these young workers toil long and hard for their money. In fact, there is a scene which acknowledges the importance of the Irish labourer to the success of the American way. As a truck carries the group of workers through the city to the site they are working on, they discuss various celebrated buildings, including the Empire State Building, that owe their existence to the army of Irish labourers that the city called on over the years. There is a genuine pride in the results of such manual labour that goes some way towards reinserting the dignity and importance of countless generations of Irish labourers to the glory that is contemporary New York.

However, in line with the film's hard-edged realist aesthetic, this scene is not allowed to tumble over into a kind of nostalgic sentimentality. The life that these young workers lead is tough and demanding. It becomes clear, for example, that they are being exploited by their own Irish boss, Trump (Chris O'Neill) despite the fact that he also takes a dominant role in preserving their ethnic identity (running the Irish bar they drink in and organising them into a hurling team for recreation). The other aspect of their life that is remarkably portrayed in the film is their determinedly contemporary existence despite the trappings of ethnic Irishness. These men relax by doing drugs and alcohol – coke and poker parties being a speciality. They get their sex from hookers. There is no sentimental ethnic solidarity either across different ethnic divides and the Irish workers are shown to be unthinkingly racist in their attitudes to other minorities. The film's final dénouement is initiated after a particularly ignorant display of racial abuse by the main protagonist, Johnnie (played by the film's co-writer as well as director, Jimmy Smallhorne). The tendency to nostalgic Irishness, therefore, is comprehensively undercut by the realistic harshness of urban living.

The film is well served in this regard by Declan Quinn's cinematography. Indeed, for such a low-budget film, the cinematography is extremely evocative and catches well the neon glamour of the bars and clubs that the characters inhabit. There is, overall, a hard-edged coldness about the life that the characters lead but one gets a real sense of the hedonism of their nightlife as it is visualised in the smoky blues and reds of the bars and clubs.

All this is, of course, background for the central story of Johnnie, Trump's nephew from Dublin, who works as his foreman on a building project financed by the city's Hasidic Jewish community. Trump looks after Johnnie as a surrogate father – 'You were always there for me, Trump,' he says at one point, and this is to prove highly ironic as the narrative unfolds. However, Johnnie is deeply dissatisfied for reasons that he can't quite fathom and finds it hard to adapt to his new environment because of some unresolved tension in him that he can't quite identify. He suffers from a recurring nightmare that remains just beyond his consciousness and which leaves him, waking and shaken, clinging to the wall of his apartment. Johnnie (and the audience) begins to suspect that his trauma is a sexual one that lies deeply buried in his childhood experiences in Dublin.

As the nature of this tension begins to become clear, the film's exploration of identity in general shifts focus on to an exploration of male sexual identity in particular. This deeply repressed oedipal memory begins to haunt his increasingly drug- and alcohol-addled consciousness and affects his relationship to his girlfriend, Maria. He begins to suspect that his sexual orientation is gay but that there is some repressed horror that prevents him from acknowledging this. The film then does a complete shift in its perspective. This is signalled in a quite remarkable scene in the building site as the workers await Trump with their wages. The biggest and most inarticulate member of the crew, Joe from Kerry (Joe Holyoke), admits that he writes poetry. Despite the sarcastic ribbing of the rest, Joe eventually agrees to read out one of his poems. His colleagues remain silent in rapt admiration as Joe reads his poem on dreams and aspirations. Thus the hard-nosed Irish navvy, trained by a confluence of social and religious factors in Ireland to deny emotion, expresses in a poignant moment of male vulnerability his most secret thoughts. This scene prepares the audience for a similar expression of male sensitivity and emotion involving the troubled Johnnie, which again is quite remarkable in an Irish 'paddy' movie.

Johnnie finally acknowledges his troubled sexuality when he picks up the equally troubled Christian (Bradley Fitts) and they make love in his apartment. This scene is shot in a warm and hazy glow of soft lights and candles, and is remarkable for the way in which it shows the lovers engaged in a sensitive exploration of each other rather than in hard-core sexual activity. In its visualisation, and in the manner in which the two men relate to each other, the scene recalls the male sensitivity of the poetry reading and achieves the same kind of frisson in establishing a completely different imagining of the blue-collar Irish.

However, Johnnie's recurring nightmare subverts this relationship as well. Only after he masochistically gets himself beaten up by the Latinos that he racially abuses does this bleached-out memory of Ireland comes into focus. As a child, Johnnie was sexually abused by his surrogate father, Trump. Thus, another male oedipal crisis reverberates with the symbolism of the abusive and incomplete family/nation and a crisis of cultural identity is rendered as a crisis of sexual identity. The parental generation is here linked inextricably to a great trauma and repression that has badly scarred the young. This oedipal metaphor for some kind of national crisis is certainly ambiguous, maybe even troubling. If the Ireland of Kieran Johnston's parents was an Ireland of social and sexual repression that resulted in the dissipation of so many of its children and left the scars deep in the psyche of the Irish in America, for Johnnie, Ireland literally fucked him up. His final, violent showdown with Trump may have given him momentary release from the unsettled and disjointed existence but it is hard to see that Johnnie will ever find stability again. In its metaphorical sense too, the ending of the film is deeply ambivalent.

Is Johnnie gay because he was sexually abused? Alternatively, is his problem in accepting his natural gayness the result of child sex-abuse? The problem here is one that we have encountered before – gayness, metaphorically, works to illustrate the disjunction of the family and the nation. However, as a metaphor, it can only work if gayness is somehow accepted as 'deviant' rather than as normal. Despite the evidence elsewhere in the film – the love scene or the poetry reading – there is, in the end, a feeling of negative stasis about the film. Ireland here is presented as a nightmare and the American dream turns out to be a bare existence of troubled and unsettled psychosis.

European Aspirations and American Narrative

The irony of this new-found interest in Irish-American identity is that it has begun to happen precisely at a time when Ireland is moving closer economically and politically to Europe. Though less obvious than the American theme, many recent Irish films have attempted to explore this European aspect of cultural identity. The scenario of Valerio Jalongo's *Spaghetti Slow* (1997) is based on a reality of Dublin life every summer. Such is the popularity of the city for young Spanish, French and Italian students wishing to improve their English that the streets are filled with hoards of young Europeans loudly proclaiming their presence, sometimes to the considerable chagrin of hard-bitten locals. In *Spaghetti Slow*, basically another summer coming-of-age film, a young Italian boy, Simone, arrives to spend a few weeks in Dublin staying with the Ferguson family. The fact that Simone comes from a wealthy Italian family and the Fergusons are modest working-class Dubliners allows the film to probe comically, though without any great political astuteness, the differences between the European bourgeoisie and the Irish proletariat. When Simone meets the Ferguson's troubled teenage daughter, Alison – a 'Goth' with death-mask face and dressed all in black – he is immediately smitten and takes off with her into rural Ireland on a journey of self-discovery and sexual awakening. This is an amiable, if rambling piece, which charts a familiar course through rebellion against overbearing and cold fathers, generational differences, cultural differences, the fumbling of young love and family reconciliation. The European aspect of the film is interestingly set up but the film is best summed up by Alison's injunction, 'Abandon yourself to the fantasy of the moment.'

The film was financed through an elaborate set of European and Irish funding arrangements and this might account for its lack of political or narrative focus. It is a trait of many of the Irish-European films, like the equally rambling first feature from Sue Clayton, *The Disappearance of Finbar* (1997), which, despite many impressive moments, manages to stretch its journey of self-discovery from working-class Dublin through Sweden to the borders of Finland and the Arctic Circle. Not all European funding results in this kind of so-called 'Euro-pudding' (for example, the modestly impressive *The Last Bus Home* was funded through the same route) but the exploration of Irish-European identity has not, as yet, produced a truly memorable film.

There is one important area where the competing pull of Europe and America has had a profound influence and that is in the formal and narrative characteristics of Irish cinema. This can be illustrated by looking at Paddy Breathnach's two feature films, *Ailsa* (1994) and *I Went Down* (1997). The former is a cool, even detached study of one man's obsession with the young woman in his apartment block, shot in the middle-class apartment area of suburban Dublin. It is composed of long takes and measured scenes, tracking the inner workings of the protagonist's mind. Its version of Dublin is a long way from the expected representation – neither Sean O'Casey nor Roddy Doyle – rendering it more like a sophisticated European city of leafy suburbs and existential angst. In fact, Breathnach has fashioned a European art movie, character-driven with a minimal amount of action.

His second feature, the blackly comic *I Went Down*, is a combination of gangster thriller and road movie and it carries some of the thematic content of these. The gangster element allows for a picture to emerge of the seedier side of the economic miracle, the underworld of organised crime where deals are done and debts repaid in backstreet pubs and clubs and where violence is a constant threat. The road movie element typically allows for the characters – the *ingénu* Git Hynes and the experienced petty criminal, Bunny Kelly – to work through their respective voyages of self-discovery, playing out the father/son theme against a downbeat rural Ireland of boglands and cheap hotels. The film is poised between action thriller and character study and impressive and funny as it is, its narrative thrust is sometimes uncertain and its mood unpredictable.

Breathnach's two films are deliberately poised, however, to achieve a style that is far removed from the frenetic pacing of mainstream American cinema and any uncertainty the viewer might feel about the films' formal qualities results from the director's wholly admirable desire to work out a style adequate to his own purposes. In a sense, there is an exploration in the two films of film form itself, not in the avant-garde traditions of the 1970s, but in the context of a new film culture emerging under both American and European influences which is attempting to find its own cinematic identity.

Most of the indigenous films discussed here are character-driven or are poised between action and character, and for some critics in Ireland this is why so few of the lower-budget films get into mainstream distribution. Television scriptwriter, Eoghan Harris, for example, expressed his distaste for European or European-influenced cinema quite forcibly in an interview to the journal, *Film Ireland*. 'What's wrong with Irish cinema is that Irish screenwriters have no sense of narrative line. They have no respect for the Hollywood narrative line ... there is an absolute contempt for plot and plot devices. Indeed the same can be said for France, where they have what I call the "je mange, je pense" kind of films' (Burke, 1995, p. 24).

However, what is impressive about the films of Breathnach and which can be seen as a feature of so many of the younger directors, is precisely that they have no respect for the Hollywood narrative line – the 'je ne pense jamais' kind of film. To that extent, Breathnach's *I Went Down* shares similarities with independent American cinema (especially the Coen brothers) and even the so-called Euro-pudding *The Disappearance of Finbar* is impressive in parts for the way it replays both Jarmusch and Kaurismäki. Kevin Rockett is surely right to conclude that the younger directors are more formally conservative than the generation that launched Irish film-making twenty years ago. The films of Joe Comerford, Bob Quinn, Pat Murphy and some of the early films of Cathal Black are influenced by the avant-garde, both in its political and formal guises, but in the 1990s, these strategies do not seem appropriate to a generation of young film-makers so totally immersed in American culture. To their eternal credit, though, many of these younger directors show no sign of attempting merely to ape the dominant American mode and if this results in a little uncertainty about style and narrative it is the result of trying to work through difference critically – trying to live with Hollywood rather than trying to mimic it.

Chapter 10
Urban Ireland's Rural Landscape

We have seen how Irish cultural nationalism was constructed, among other things, on an opposition between the country and the city. In its clearest form this opposition posited the traditional Gaelic purity of Ireland's western seaboard and islands against the corruption of Irish identity epitomised by the city of Dublin, the 'strumpet city' that had prostituted itself to foreign cultural influence (McLoone, 1984). The further away from Dublin, the closer one got to the real Ireland, as long as this journey did not involve a north-easterly direction where Belfast might loom into view. The predominance of the myth of the west, given its classic cinematic expression in *Man of Aran* and *The Quiet Man*, has endured into the new millennium, despite the rapid modernisation of the economy that has characterised Ireland in the last forty years. Part of the reason for this, as we saw in relation to tourism in Ireland, is that contemporary Ireland has begun to fully realise its potential as a rural utopia, to be sold as a commodity to a world market. In one sense, this is perfectly understandable. Given the devastation wrecked by the Famine and a century of debilitating emigration, rural Ireland, especially the western seaboard, is one of the most under-populated areas of Europe. It might seem particularly crass to package the results of yesterday's misery into a commodity in the present but in marketing terms it seems eminently sensible. The success of the tourist industry in this regard has been an important contributory factor in recent economic success (Barrett, 1997) and it is tourist dollars and marks that allow so many people in Ireland to continue to live in rural communities.

In addition, as we have seen in the case of inward investment in cinema, Irish locations are attractive for foreign producers. Indeed, the Screen Commission, using the tax incentives, is designed precisely to sell Ireland as a film set. It is in this regard, that Bob Quinn has described Ireland as a 'backlot of Hollywood' (Quinn, 1999). However, the Kalem films of the 1910s show that there is nothing new in this. Given the relative advantage that Ireland enjoys in this regard it is hardly surprising that it should try to take advantage of its landscape, in particular, for attracting foreign capital of all kinds. The attractions of Irish locations (together with government subsidies) were instrumental in persuading Mel Gibson and his producers to relocate *Braveheart* (1994) from its

Scottish setting to Ireland. The 'timelessness' of this landscape thus allowed contemporary Ireland to double as medieval Scotland. A hard-edged economic logic lies behind Ireland's romantic evocations of its own landscape. In many ways, then, it would appear that the myth of rural Ireland that sustained cultural nationalism is no longer believed in by the Irish themselves (if, indeed, it ever was outside the imaginations of a small but influential coterie of urban intellectuals and poets). However, the situation is more complex than this might suggest.

In contemporary Ireland, this classical opposition between the country and the city seems increasingly problematic. As Fintan O'Toole has argued, it is debatable whether it makes sense any more to talk about rural and urban Ireland as distinct societies. O'Toole quotes directly from sociological research by Curtin, Haase and Tovey:

> Factors such as media access, especially television, travel, tourism, and the growing diversification of consumer products have contributed to the incorporation of the rural population into the global economy and society ... the populations of urban and rural areas are coming increasingly to resemble each other. (quoted in O'Toole, 1997, p. 16)

The classical opposition was a more complex one anyway. As Raymond Williams has argued:

> It is significant that the common image of the country is now an image of the past, and the common image of the city an image of the future. That leaves, if we isolate them, an undefined present. The pull of the idea of the country is towards old ways, human ways, natural ways. The pull of the idea of the city is towards progress, modernisation, development. In what is then a tension, the present experienced as tension, we use the contrast of the country and the city to ratify an unresolved division and conflict of impulses, which it might be better to face in its own terms. (Williams, 1985, p. 297)

This 'present tension' or 'undefined present', as Williams puts it, is even more significant when the country rather than the city has been linked inextricably with a sense of cultural or national identity. This is even more the case when we recall that the country and the city both have their negative images. The city may stand for the future and may indeed represent modernity and progress. However, it can also mean alienation, exploitation, poverty, pollution of body and mind, immorality and selfish individualism. On the other hand, the country may indeed represent the past and suggest old ways, more human ways and more natural ways. However, it can also represent deadening conformity, insularity, social and political conservatism, narrow intolerance and a lack of personal freedom. The present crisis in Ireland stems in large measure from the fact that the conflicting images of country and city, in all their contradictory complexity, still operate. The more attractive images of rural life, even if they are now packaged for tourists, still command a deep unconscious allegiance and operate in tandem with the more negative images of the city. The overweening importance of the myth of rural Ireland has been a factor that has inhibited the growth of a social realist tradition in Irish culture. This tradition in Britain, for example, had its roots in the documentary movement of the 1930s (mentioned in Chapter Two) and had a basically ameliorative agenda. To begin to sort out social problems, these had to be recognised, filmed and shown in the first place. In a country like Ireland, so committed to a romantic rural identity, there was always the likelihood that to show urban reality was to confirm rural prejudice. The problem, therefore, with representing the city in Irish cinema is that there has not been a realist tradition which it can then tap into. One of the present tensions for Irish cinema is finding an aesthetic capable of rendering the city experience in all its complexity without falling into the trap of rural prejudice.

It is hardly surprising, then, that more recently there has been an attempt to provide the kind of social realist images of the city that are so characteristic of British culture. Fintan O'Toole instances the four-part Roddy Doyle television series *The Family* (1994) as an example of this trend (O'Toole, 1999). As we have seen, the earliest short films made in the 1970s did, almost for the first time in Irish culture, begin the process of representing urban experience. A number of Joe Comerford's early shorts dealt with aspects of city life – *Emtigon* (1972), about alienation and a form of primitive 'stalking', and *Withdrawal* (1974), about drug addiction. His 1978 film *Down the Corner* was an important landmark in indigenous cinema in that it put the urban working class on the screen *as workers* and as the redundant victims of a harsh economic system. Kieran Hickey looked at the hypocrisies of middle-class Dublin life through a focus on the marriages and the frustrations of two upwardly mobile couples in *Criminal Conversation* (1980). Cathal Black's important short *Our Boys* (1981) painted a prescient picture of urban education and his 1984 feature *Pigs* used the declining grandeur of Georgian Dublin to good effect in a portrait of the city's marginal and outcast squatters. Despite all these, the early cinema was more noted for its revisionist images of rural Ireland or for its interesting reworking of history than for its treatment of urban society. In many ways, Joe Lee and Frank Deasy's *The Courier* (1987) demonstrates the problems that filming the city in Ireland brings and remains a salutary example of a kind of aesthetic conundrum.

The Courier was a film poorly received at the time and one that is still referred to as a marker for how badly things can go wrong (O'Connor, 1997). In retrospect, it can now be seen as a brave failure that marked an important stage in the development of recent cinema, especially for what it shows about the conventions of American genre cinema. The film is, of course, severely disabled by poor casting in the two central roles (Pettitt, 1997, p. 258). However, it attempts to employ the Hollywood thriller form to explore the gangland world of Dublin's heroin trade, an ambitious attempt both formally and in terms of content. Incredibly, nothing like this had been tried before and the directors had little to draw on as exemplars or, indeed, few personnel in Ireland with the experience of working with these genre conventions. Comerford at the same time was playing with the car-chase convention in his rural-based *Reefer and the Model* and playing the conventions for comic effect. *The Courier* is deadly earnest and when its generic elements do not work, they look cumbersome and absurd. This is why the film evokes the response it does today. In fact it attempts a marriage of different genres that we can now see was unwise. The motivation for the film was not, it is fair to say, merely a commercial one. It set out with the kind of ameliorative agenda that we associate with documentary film-making – the desire to represent that which has largely lain outside cultural expression, the desire to expose and change. To achieve this, the film-makers adopted the thriller format. The film, then, is really a slice of social realism masquerading as a thriller and the conventions of both pull against each other to further disable the film. What the film seems to prove is that Dublin is not amenable to the conventions of the American urban thriller (neither is London for that matter, and British cinema has also had difficulties translating the pace and the iconography of the thriller into its own milieu).

Since *The Courier* the Dublin drug scene has largely remained untouched. It remains a background issue in John Boorman's version of the life of Dublin criminal Martin Cahill, *The General* (1998). In one scene, the activities of concerned anti-drug parents groups are portrayed as a blatant political move by republicans to undermine the hold that Cahill has on the local working-class community. Cahill himself (Brendan Gleeson) is presented as a charismatic and likeable rogue rather than as a calculating and sometimes brutal gang warlord, a Robin Hood character with a clearly developed sense of class-consciousness and community morality. Cahill's disdain for urban drug culture, either as a recreational activity or as a source of criminal activity, reinforces his essential, if unconventional morality, and the film's portrait of the urban criminal world is studiously neutral compared to *The Courier*'s social concern. Cahill is moved to violence by only two issues – the suspected treachery of one of his own gang and his repugnance at the child abuse of another. The kind of wider social critique that was at least attempted in *The Courier* is largely absent from *The General* and the urban milieu that the film recreates is strangely dislocated from the actual urban climate of either deprived or 'boomtown' Dublin. This sense of dislocation is rendered aesthetically in the studied black and white cinematography that Boorman utilises, giving the whole film the look of cinematic history rather than of contemporary urban life.

Fintan Connolly's low-budget *Flick* (1999) returns to the drug world of contemporary Dublin and though it is a very different kind of film, nonetheless, it interestingly displays some of the same problems as *The Courier*. The film is a character study of middle-class Jack Flinter (David Murray), dope-smoker and dealer. He and his partner, Des, smuggle a large consignment of dope into Dublin and find themselves accordingly drawn into the underworld of Dublin's drug bosses. The problem with the film is that the generic thriller/cop plot does not work when it finally kicks in, detracting from the engrossing character study that had been centre stage until then. In fact the camera seems at times almost mesmerised by David Murray's presence, holding him in view as he does his drug deliveries and following him through the streets and the clubs, pubs and halls of contemporary Dublin. There is a certain studied stylishness in these scenes and as Jack is sucked further into a mire of his own making, the film begins to resemble a study in urban angst – the alienation and nihilism of a life dedicated to a nocturnal hedonism. The genre mix here is studied European angst with frantic American action and the first works much better than the second.

The city emerged in Irish cinema most publicly with the success of *My Left Foot* in 1989, although the story is centred on the struggles of Christy Brown to overcome personal handicaps rather on urban living in itself. The most consistent vision of urban Ireland has been in the adaptations of Roddy Doyle's work, each marking a difference in generic approach. Alan Parker's commercially successful contemporary rock-musical *The Commitments* (1991) is a Hollywood film in all its essential elements and as such is required to present aspects of Ireland that are 'recognisable' to the Hollywood audience. The result is a set of urban and Irish clichés that were absent in Doyle's original work (O'Toole, 1999, pp. 36–7). Stephen Frears' more modestly budgeted *The Snapper* (1993) and *The Van* (1996) were both essentially television films funded by the BBC. *The Snapper* is the more enjoyable, presenting a form of 'socialist/feminist' imaginary in the story of Sharon Curley's unplanned pregnancy and the impact it has on her family, and especially on her father, Dessie. There is, inevitably, a element of wishful thinking in the manner in which Dessie becomes involved in his daughter's pregnancy and in the general air of good-natured solidarity within the family that the film proposes. However, this is the point of Doyle's work. The urban working class is changing because society is changing and it is welcome that in the Doyle adaptations there is no collapse into a kind of working class nostalgia evidenced in *Agnes Browne* (1999). As O'Toole has shown, in Doyle's

Urban and Irish clichés:
tradition and modernity in
The Commitments

work, there is a reimagining and a reinvention of working-class life, not a collapse into either realist miserabilism or empty nostalgia for a past that never
existed. Colm Meaney plays the family patriarch in all three films, a man in the
process of reimagining himself. It is, at heart, as O'Toole puts it, the story of a
man escaping stereotypes (O'Toole, 1999, p. 37). By extension, the quality of the
Doyle adaptations is that they offer views of the Irish working class that similarly evade cliché. These are both aspirational and inspirational depictions that
attempt to push representation forward, to imagine a more harmonious and
restructured future – to dare to imagine differently.

As Raymond Williams has again pointed out, the experience of the city has
now been long enough a part of social history, even in Ireland, to allow for a
nostalgic response to the perceived problems of the present (Williams, 1985,
p. 297). Thus we are beginning to see films of urban nostalgia – in a documentary like Sé Merry Doyle's *Alive, Alive O! – A Requiem for Dublin* (1999) or
in the organic working-class community conjured up in *Agnes Browne*. It is significant that this is happening at a time when the cinematic image of the city
in Ireland has still not established a discernible pattern.

We have identified a number of ways in which the city has been imagined in recent Irish cinema and noted how these link to social changes in the wider society. The same kind of reimagining has happened in relation to the Irish country as well and given the importance of rural imagination to the construction of Irish national identity it is hardly surprising that images of landscape should form a key part of the underlying crisis over identity. What is ironic about landscape is that, although essentially a natural phenomenon, it enters into everyday consciousness as a cultural signifier, an aspect of what might be called 'banal nationalism'. This is the commonplace, everyday, material experience of nationhood and national identity which people live with (and through which they live their sense of collective identity). As Billig has termed it, banal nationalism is 'the ideological habits which enable the established nations of the West to be reproduced' (Billig, 1995, p. 6). In an interesting attempt to pursue this notion of the everyday 'banality' of the experience of nation-ness, Catherine Palmer has looked at three aspects of material culture – the body, food and the landscape. Her conclusions are that these three areas demonstrate how 'nation-ness is not just a feature of specifically identifiable national events, it is not just something that comes to the fore in times of uncertainty and danger such as wars and conflicts'. Rather, in the daily lived experience, national imagination is maintained by 'the habits and routines of people's lives; the physical relationships between individuals, choices and patterns of consumption and utilization of the natural landscape' (Palmer, 1998, p. 195). By considering the use of landscape in various national imaginings – English, Jewish, Canadian – she argues that landscape is not a passive marker of a nation's identity, it can evoke feelings, generate emotions and provide causes. 'Here nation-ness is experienced through the intermingling of a variety of different identities that represent regional, national and global perspectives of the "life-world" ' (Palmer, 1998, p. 196). In her discussion of Israeli identity she argues that landscape is also a central mechanism in the differentiation of 'us' and 'them'. In this way, defence of landscape 'is a defence of the culture and the State from "pollution" by outsiders' (Palmer, 1998, p. 194). Finally, she also notes a tendency to equate landscape with the character of the people (so that Norwegians, for example, are seen as a brave and hardy people of the mountains). She fails, here, to differentiate those characteristics that grew up internally as part of a national imagining and those which may have been part of another national imagining (in its own process of differentiation) and were then imposed from the outside.

Nonetheless, we have noted many of these themes in relation to landscape within cultural nationalism in Ireland. As Palmer has argued, landscape is used as part of the everyday exchange of 'banal nationalism', an important part of the process of imagining the nation. In this case, then, in contemporary indigenous cinema, something extremely interesting has been happening to this key marker of Ireland's identity. As we will see, this is encapsulated in one extraordinary image in *The Butcher Boy*, in which Neil Jordan literally blows apart the romanticism of the Irish landscape. We have also noted the way in which *This is My Father* plays with landscape. A reconfiguring of Irish landscape is a theme in the films of Joe Comerford and Bob Quinn, both of whom have chosen to work largely in the west of Ireland and have attempted to lay bare the accretions of myth and cultural significance which the west has held in Irish consciousness. Thus, in *Reefer and the Model* (1988) and *High Boot Benny* (1993), Comerford, with an almost postmodern playfulness, subjects the landscape to an encounter with an array of miscreants and social outcasts – aimless drifters, cynical politicos, the wretched and the dispossessed – seemingly devised for their perversity to the role models of Catholic nationalism. In *Reefer and the Model* there is a studiously perverse symbol of Mother Ireland herself in the pregnant, ex-drug addict, ex-prostitute character of Theresa (Carol Scanlon), who is later referred to as 'The Model'. Comerford opens the film with shots of the west of Ireland landscape but cuts immediately to a low-angle shot of Theresa's mini-skirted legs, the suggested sexuality offering a particularly telling intrusion into the myths that surround the west. In particular, *High Boot Benny*'s minimalist, bleak, windswept landscapes are in stark contrast to traditional views of rural Ireland.

In *Hush-a-Bye Baby* (1989), Margo Harkin's harrowing account of the pressures felt by a pregnant teenager in Catholic Derry, there is an interesting cinematic reflection on rural Ireland as a refuge from urban pressures. The protagonist, Goretti Friel, goes to the Donegal Gaeltacht (Irish-speaking area) to escape the encircling oppression of her home town and the beautiful scenery she encounters there is reminiscent of the rural utopia of John Ford's *The Quiet Man*. However, unlike Ford's hero, Sean Thornton, the rural retreat provides Goretti with no peace of mind and the pressures continue to mount. In one beautifully realised scene, the pregnant teenager sits on a beach, depressed and worried. The camera begins a slow track in on her anxious face, its encroaching movement intercut by shots of the waves lapping over the stones on the beach. The contrast between the supposed recuperative powers of nature and the emotional crisis faced by Goretti is stark and moving. The beautiful landscapes and seascapes of Ireland are stripped of their romantic connotations, as Goretti's emotional turmoil becomes more acute.

In Paddy Breathnach's *I Went Down* (1997) an urban gangland thriller spills over into the elemental boglands and woods of rural Ireland, culminating in a series of cross and double-crosses that is reminiscent of the Coen Brothers' *Miller's Crossing* (1990). The landscape here is resonant with the dirty deeds of contemporary urban humanity rather than heroic deeds of ancient history or the beauty of a bountiful nature.

One of the more interesting visual reworkings of the Irish landscape, how-ever, is in Thaddeus O'Sullivan's *December Bride* (1989). The film is set in turn-of-the-century Ireland, filmed on location in and around Strangford Lough, near Belfast, and concerns the scandalous relationship between a young woman, Sarah, and the two unmarried brothers she keeps house for, Frank and Hamilton Echlin. Since this unconventional relationship takes place within a close-knit Presbyterian community, O'Sullivan's use of the landscape already challenges conventional portrayals which associate such rural beauty with Catholic, nationalist Ireland. However, on occasions throughout the film, O'Sullivan interjects a series of painterly compositions which draw further attention to the landscape and the manner in which it is populated. Typically in these shots a character is framed in a sombre sunset against the darkening skyline, beating furiously on a Lambeg drum, which echoes off the hills around him. These shots are open to a number of interpretations. The drumming, both seen and heard, can be read as the defiant sounds of human culture, imposing itself on the sublime beauty of nature, asserting the stubborn presence of humanity in a romantic composition that traditionally has elided its presence, both visually and aurally. It can also be read as the recalcitrant sounds of Ulster Protestants, imposing their presence and beating out a reminder of their his-torical triumph over this land, over these hills, over the wilderness of nature. From the point of view of Catholic, nationalist Ireland, of course, these drums represent the strident militancy of sectarian politics – an image that contrasts the beautiful with the socially threatening.

It is tempting, however, to see these shots as an ironic play with the traditions of representation that have dominated the image of rural Ireland for many years and which have been central to a nationalist sensibility since the literary revival and beyond. Thus, the insertion of Orange drums and a devout Pres-byterian community into the Irish landscape is a reminder that the industrial workers of Belfast are only part of the Protestant story and that the romantic nationalism of Catholic Ireland is only part of the story of Irish landscape.

It is equally tempting to see in *December Bride* another ironic reference to the canon of Irish romantic imagery, this time in the form of the cinema's most famous and most enduring representation, *The Quiet Man*. This can be seen in the sequence in which Frank, having been ostracised by his devout community because of his scandalous relationship, attempts to re-establish contacts with his neighbours at the Twelfth of July celebrations. The scenes are shot outdoors on the shores of the lough, their flat, sandy beaches and low, undulating sand-dunes recalling the horse-race locations in Ford's film. This time, though, an assembly of bowler-hatted Orangemen, sombre farmers and a strident orator replace Ford's gallery of Irish stereotypes. The communal farce of the horse race is replaced by the earnest marching and the banners of the Orange parade.

The allusion to *The Quiet Man* goes further than this, however. Just as the horse-race in the Ford film contains a bizarre courtship ritual, so too does the communal celebrations of the Presbyterians in *December Bride*. In *The Quiet Man*, the young women of Innisfree put up their bonnets on poles at the finishing line, the winner of the horse-race having the choice of whose bonnet to collect and whose favours to pursue. In *December Bride*, the young women put up their shawls, which are then laid on the ground equidistant from the young men seeking their favours. At a given signal, the men charge for the shawls from opposite sides, the winner being the one who emerges from the ensuing scrum with the shawl held aloft. In *The Quiet Man*, Mary Kate has to be cajoled into putting up her bonnet and similarly, in *December Bride*, Molly, the young woman who has taken Frank's fancy, has also to be coaxed into putting up her shawl.

The sequences diverge from this point on, of course. In the Ford film, the bonnet sequence, typical of the general atmosphere of play and comic deceit which dominates the film, is an elaborate ruse that has been designed by the community to bring the lovers together. In O'Sullivan's film, Frank's success in the shawl ritual eventually leads to his crippling injuries and his final withdrawal from the community. But the similarities, both in setting and in narrative progression, are striking enough to alert the audience (especially the audience familiar with *The Quiet Man*) to the fact that a wholly different people

Reconfiguring Irish landscape and family: Protestant community in *December Bride*

have wandered into a recognisably Irish film. The aesthetic, political and ideo-logical implications are profound. To this extent as well, despite the 'televisual' genesis of *December Bride*, it is one of the most intensely *cinematic* of recent Irish films – not just because of its careful and studied cinematography, but because its complex themes are presented visually as well as narratively and because its wonderful cinematography is itself engaged in a debate precisely about the cinema's traditional representation of Ireland and the Irish. And in peopling a recognisably Irish landscape with a Northern Protestant com-munity, ultimately the film challenges sedimented assumptions about both.

Not all contemporary films, however, are engaged in this kind of interesting reassessment of traditional romantic imagery. The dominant mode still recurs, whether in the guise of a big-budget Hollywood epic like *Far and Away* ((1992) or more modest films like Peter Chelsom's *Hear My Song* (1989), John Irvin's *Widow's Peak* (1993) or in the traditional whimsicality of *Waking Ned* (1999). And disappointingly, given his track record in making politically astute, revi-sionist films in the USA, this is also a major problem with John Sayles' *The Secret of Roan Inish* (1995). The contrasts established by Sayles are almost per-versely traditional. One character even offers the lament that the 'west is our past and the east our future'. However, the narrative can only be resolved by the islanders turning west again to make contact with the magical and enchanted world of tradition. The film thus works to restore a primitive balance to the lives of the displaced islanders of Roan Inish, establishing a simplistic view of Irish modernity that would do credit to the wilder imaginings of nineteenth century cultural nationalism. The same trajectory is evident in Mike Newell's *Into the West* (1992). The sadly deficient city life that Papa Riley (Gabriel Byrne) imposes on his two sons is shown to be clearly unnatural to the spirit of his traveller roots. The narrative then follows his journey from urban malaise to reaffirmation of his roots in the recuperative embrace of the west of Ireland. Both these films feature the staple (for Irish films) incomplete family and it is only in the west and in rejecting the alienating confines of the city that the malaise afflicting the two families can be eased. All these films were made with the American audience in mind rather than an Irish one. *Into the West* is the work of two quintessential Dubliners, writer Jim Sheridan and co-producer and star Gabriel Byrne. We can assume that they also had the American and not the Irish audience in mind. As metaphors for the nation these two films offer excep-tionally traditional remedies to an old problem and mobilise the ancient myths of Ireland for an essentially regressive ideology. In terms of Raymond Williams' 'undefined present', in Ireland, the pull to the west still carries a considerable ideological charge.

What then is the nature of this undefined present that images of country and city in Ireland allude to? Williams locates it in the way in which a society generally responds to social change and upheaval. Crucial to this is a general feeling of loss that links it to the perception that harmony has given way to disharmony. We have noted that this is not confined to perceptions of rural life but that even former patterns of urban living can assume the appearance of greater harmony. Certainly, he cautions that this is often nothing more than the adult's perceptions of childhood, but there is a real crisis nonetheless. What is at issue, he argues, is a growth and alteration of consciousness, an alteration of perception and relationship.

> What was once close, absorbing, accepted, familiar, internally experienced becomes separate, distinguishable, critical, changing, externally observed … we live in a world in which the dominant mode of production and social relationships teaches, impresses, offers to make normal, even rigid, modes of detached, external perception and action: modes of using and consuming rather than accepting and enjoying people and things. (Williams, 1985, pp. 297–8)

In the forward rush towards European modernity so much of what it meant to be Irish for previous generations has been challenged, changed and forgotten. So many of the institutions of belonging, including the idea of the nation itself, have come under pressure from capitalist modernity. In this ferment and change conflicting and contradictory tendencies manifest themselves in society and in culture. The cinematic images of urban and rural Ireland show the nature of these contradictions and express in their different ways the desire for what Williams has called 'experiences of directness, connection, mutuality and sharing' (ibid.).

In other words, in the way in which recent cinema has dealt with Ireland's urban and rural identities we can locate a contradictory impulse. Some films attempt to imagine differently, to reconfigure a new sense of collective identity which is adequate to the needs of contemporary, affluent Ireland or to construct alternative families that prefigure a new, more inclusive sense of nation-ness. On the other hand, though, Irish cinema also displays a strong pull towards a more harmonious and more organic past, to rescue some sense of community from this mythic past for a contemporary existence perceived to be drifting towards fragmentation and individualism. To this extent, Irish cinema is a cultural reflection of the contradictory impulses identified in the largely theoretical debates we considered in Chapter Four. The 'present tension', as Williams dubs it, is about the fate of collective identity and communal responsibility in the global marketplace and images of country and city, no less than conflicting interpretations of the past, are at the heart of this tension.

Chapter 11
The Abused Child of History:
Neil Jordan's *The Butcher Boy* (1997)

The opening credits to Neil Jordan's *The Butcher Boy* are played against a background of comic book art illustrating heroes and action scenes across a range of different genres. In many ways, these scenes represent later manifestations of the kind of popular culture that was the particular concern of Irish-Ireland cultural nationalists and which was the focus of campaigns by Maud Gonne's Daughters of Erin and the Vigilance Committees. What Jordan suggests is that by the time of the film's setting – the early 1960s – these images and the imaginative universe that they conjure up had sunk deeply into the consciousness of the young Irish, much as they had elsewhere. The different campaigns to exclude them from Irish culture had failed and the film uses their ubiquitous presence to explore the consciousness of one boy for whom they represent an alternative to the grim reality that he faces.

The Butcher Boy is an adaptation of Pat McCabe's highly praised and controversial novel of the same name. Set in small-town Ireland of the early 1960s, the film traces the descent into violence and madness of twelve-year-old Francie Brady, the victim of a dysfunctional family and an uncaring and abusive environment. Francie starts out as a witty, loveable rogue whose happiness is built around his friendship with Joe Purcell. Both boys live in a fantasy world of adventure and derring-do, fuelled by the images and characters introduced into their lives by the advent of television. As Francie's home life deteriorates, he begins to focus all his frustrations on his neighbours, the Nugent family, who have lately returned from a period of living in England with attitudes and pretensions which Francie finds threatening to his own world. He comes to regard Mrs Nugent in particular as the source of all his troubles.

He teases and torments the Nugents with a series of hilarious and, to begin with, relatively harmless pranks. His home and community ties continue to break down, however, and he slowly begins to lose his grip on reality. His hitherto benign fantasy world is charged with extraordinary hallucinations and wild imaginings, a mixture of both home-grown and foreign influences that cohere into a vision that is at once logical and yet deeply disturbing (visions of a profane Virgin Mary, fantasies of nuclear holocaust). When he loses the friendship of Joe to the Nugent's prissy son Philip, his final hope of happiness is removed and he exacts a terrible and bloody revenge on the boy's reviled mother.

In the film Jordan has gone to great lengths to capture the beauty of the Irish countryside and to recreate the picturesque quality of the small rural village in which the action is set. He does this, however, in a slightly heightened and stylised manner, and the resulting visual splendour functions as an ironic counterpoint to the increasingly psychotic behaviour of the central character (played impressively by Eamonn Owens). Indeed what the audience sees is actually interpreted and 'explained' by Francie's sometimes hilarious, sometimes deeply disturbing, interior monologue and the combination here of the familiar and the increasingly bizarre, between what is seen and what is heard, gives the film an entirely unsettling feel.

Two images in particular stand out. In one striking sequence, Jordan frames a panoramic view of Ireland's natural beauty – green hills and valley and an azure blue lake – a shot which resembles a postcard from the John Hinde collection (nature ever so slightly airbrushed and embellished). This is a familiar image of a romanticised and stylised rural Ireland (the kind of image which has dominated cinematic representations of Ireland for decades) but as the shot is held, the lake suddenly erupts in the atomic mushroom of a nuclear explosion, shattering both nature and its slightly exaggerated cultural representation. It is an entirely unexpected sequence and its absurd, surreal quality is typical of the film as a whole. In a subsequent scene, Jordan recreates the small town in the aftermath of a nuclear explosion, devastated and barren, scattered with the charred heads of pigs and populated now by mutant humans with the heads of insects.

These are images that (literally) shatter audience expectations of Irish rural imagery and offer the most subversive representations of Ireland that the cinema has yet produced. These are also, however, sequences rich in significance and suggestion.

On a purely narrative level the nuclear explosion presages Francie's own explosion into murderous violence. It is a symbol of the inner turmoil he is suffering, as one tragedy after another befalls him (his mother's suicide, the death of his alcoholic father, incarceration in a reform school, sexual abuse at the hands of a priest and, most disturbingly for Francie, the loss of his best friend Joe to his enemies, the Nugent family). This inner world is the central concern of the film and the voiceover monologue allows the audience no escape from the unhinged logic of the boy's mind. This warped logic and the dark humour of the monologue gains its strength from the popular cultural references that Francie has absorbed from American film and television and from British comics. The atomic bomb sequences are Francie's sci-fi hallucinations and, caught between the film's stylised cinematography and Francie's unhinged monologue, the audience is denied the comfort of the familiar or the 'real' (or indeed the aesthetic comfort of realism itself).

Neil Jordan's considerable achievement in the film is to have found a cinematic way of rendering the first-person monologue of the original novel, co-scripting with the author Pat McCabe. Francie Brady's is a hilarious, haunting, disturbing and finally ineffably sad voice that narrates a grisly narrative with the wide-eyed innocence of a child. The nearest equivalent in literature is William Faulkner's Benjy in *The Sound and the Fury*, though here Benjy's 'tale told by an idiot' is grounded and explained by three other accounts of the same events. In McCabe's novel, the reader has nothing but Francie's voice as a guide through the events and if there are times when we become aware of a strange displacement in Francie's account, a kind of fatal misrecognition on his behalf, we are nonetheless denied an anchoring or validating other voice, a reality against which to compare Francie's narrative.

To achieve this cinematically, Jordan employs three techniques. First, he retains in Francie's dialogue most of the richness of his idiomatic speech as written up originally by McCabe. Second, he employs the device of a voiceover narration, spoken by the older Francie, which similarly retains the idioms and striking language of the original and which again disturbs the audience by being both strange and displaced while at the same time utterly logical in its own terms. Finally, Jordan chooses to visualise much of Francie's hallucinations and grotesque imaginings so that the film achieves a kind of insane magic realism that offers no point of reference for the bewildered viewer. Francie Brady is the only interpreter we have access to.

In this regard, the structure of the film provides an interesting contrast to the way in which Alan Parker in *Angela's Ashes* has chosen to render the authorial voice of Frank McCourt in the original novel. In Chapter Eight, we discussed the problem confronting the film. In *Angela's Ashes* the relationship between the voiceover narration and Parker's lush visuals of what the voice narrates works to render impotent the ironic anger of the novel. The film becomes merely a literal transcription on to the screen of the novel's events and leaves the audience with no leavening focus for anger or resistance. The film, in other words, is much more resigned than the novel. In *The Butcher Boy*, the visuals and the voiceover (narrated by Stephen Rea as the older Francie) works as a parallel discourse to what we see, opening out a complex world of fevered imagination laced with humorously inappropriate speculation and explanation. The film captures perfectly both the logic and humour of the authorial voice and yet also visualises its increasingly outlandish imaginings to devastating effect.

It could be argued, therefore, that the centrality of Francie's voice privileges the individual psychology of the disturbed mind above the socio-cultural context that produces it. The film thus works as an exploration of humanist themes – childhood neglect and abuse leading to psychosis – rather than as a 'state-of-the-nation' piece on contemporary Ireland. Many commentators have approached the film in this way and in interviews Jordan himself has talked at length about the nature of childhood and the psychopathology of the abused and neglected child. Jordan was perhaps unlucky with the timing of the film's US release, in this regard, coinciding as it did with the Jonesboro killings and the subsequent 'moral panic' in the American media about violence among schoolchildren. The debates engendered by the Jonesboro killings may well have influenced the film's release schedule in the US – they certainly influenced its critical reception.

The insistence here, however, is on reading the film more politically (and in its Irish context). This is not to deny the considerable strengths of other readings – the importance of the film, after all, lies precisely in its complexity and ambiguity. The way in which Francie's voice, for example, generates sympathy despite his psychosis implicates the audience in the ensuing tragedy in profoundly interesting ways.

However, the nuclear explosion is at the very least suggested by the 'real' world outside the imaginings of Francie's mind, the world of international affairs. There are constant references to the Cuban missile crisis throughout the film (the setting is small-town Ireland in 1962) and while these certainly provide further stimuli for Francie's idiosyncratic understanding of the world of adults, they nonetheless anchor the film (and thus Francie's inner psychosis) in a particular historical moment and in a wider political arena. Significantly, when Francie breaks into the home of his neighbour Mrs Nugent for the first time, Jordan has him watching on television the 'duck and cover' information films of the time which form the absurd centrepiece to Kevin Rafferty's 1982 compilation of bomb-related footage, *The Atomic Café*. In Pat McCabe's original novel, Francie watches an episode of *Voyage to the Bottom of the Sea*, which is more plausible (were it not for the pedantic detail that Irwin Allen's piece of comic-book kitsch did not actually begin its television run until 1964). While Jordan has certainly retained the importance of popular cultural reference points for Francie's interpretation of the world, he has given slightly more weight in his film adaptation to the political fears and anxieties of the time, occasioned by the Cuban crisis, and this is an important detail.

These atomic references also suggest another important, if entirely local, development in the Ireland of 1962, the inauguration of the country's national television service (now RTÉ). On its opening night (31 December), the inaugural address was given by the President, Eamon de Valera, who, in talking about the power of television, intoned rather ominously, 'Like atomic energy, it can be used for incalculable good but it can also do irreparable harm'. If the actual bomb goes off only in Francie's head, its metaphoric equivalent, the cultural explosion of de Valera's imagining, went off in Ireland in the early 1960s with the beginnings of a process of modernisation which continues at a more advanced level today (discussed in detail in Chapter Four). What the film asks the audience to consider is whether this process has done incalculable good or irreparable harm and offers in return neither an answer to the question nor a privileged discourse on it. Television and its images, of course, feature strongly in Francie's imagination.

The historic references are worth stressing. As with McCabe's original novel, Jordan's version of *The Butcher Boy* is a complex working through of the effects of modernisation in Ireland, a disturbing, ambiguous and challenging exploration of the clash between tradition and modernity and the impact of a largely American popular culture. It is important to fix the historic moment for another, ironic reason, for the film is ultimately not about this historical moment *per se*, but about how it is remembered and interpreted in the present. There is nothing in *The Butcher Boy* that would allow for empty 'heritage' nostalgia, not even its careful evocation of small-town rural life. Rather it is a profoundly contemporary film and is most interesting for the ways in which it intervenes in the contemporary cultural debate in Ireland that we considered in Chapter Four.

Jordan's previous film, 1996's *Michael Collins*, stirred the sometimes acrimonious nature of these debates as no other cultural artefact has in recent years. *Michael Collins* was an enormously popular film in Ireland, and remains second only to *Titanic* in the all-time box-office list, some comfort at least to the director for its relatively poor performance at the American box office. However, it generated a huge amount of press debate as well (in both Ireland and Britain) and was at the centre of controversy among cultural and political commentators in both countries. The film, of course, deals with another key historical moment (and a major historical figure) in Irish history and the debate centred on Jordan's interpretation of these, the veracity of his version of Collins and its significance for contemporary Ireland. (It has to be said that he was similarly unlucky with the release of *Michael Collins*. The first IRA ceasefire ended during the film's post-production and the levels of violence in Northern Ireland that coincided with the film's subsequent release did much to fuel the controversies.)

These debates centred, inevitably, around the kind of revisionist and anti-revisionist opinion in Ireland that we outlined in Chapter Four, both exuding a tendency to ignore the kind of complexities and contradictions that *The Butcher Boy* illustrates. The broad revisionist camp, as we have seen, is committed to the modernisation process and the kind of liberalisation of Irish society and culture that this inevitably entails. For such critics, Jordan's interpretation of Collins was dangerously close to a validation of the worst aspects of Irish nationalism and its violent republican past (and present), an atavistic celebration of an Ireland thankfully now long gone, radically transformed from its inward-looking nationalism by acquiring a modern, secular European identity. Collins' role in creating the stiflingly conservative Catholic Ireland of recent memory, for example, is absent, and he emerges from the film as a courageous, if sadly misunderstood, hero in the naive Hollywood mould.

In opposition, the equally broad anti-revisionist camp argued the importance of the film precisely because it did confront Ireland's violent past (however painful) and drew attention again to the anti-imperialist struggle that brought the modern Irish state into being in the first place, a necessary corrective to the collective amnesia proposed by the revisionists. If the film did have a contemporary relevance then it was to point to the parallels with Northern Ireland today, urging recognition that the violence there is political and needs to be confronted as a political rather than as a criminal problem. Implicit in much of the anti-revisionist rhetoric was the argument that the film and the controversy that surrounded it were a timely reminder that to ditch what is unique about the past (again however painful) is to run the risk of ditching also what is unique about the present and thus to capitulate tamely to the globalising and homogenising tendencies of the modernisation process.

This account of cultural debates in Ireland provides a context for considering the complexities of *The Butcher Boy*, for if the *Michael Collins* debate was largely generated outside of and about the film, these cultural themes are central to the meanings of *The Butcher Boy* itself. Is this a revisionist or an anti-revisionist film, according to Irish definitions of these terms? What does the film say about the way in which contemporary Ireland talks about its recent past or about its place in the global culture of the present? How we might begin to answer these questions depends on how we interpret the voice of Francie Brady and how we might read the metaphor of the abused child. To bring together this central motif with the wider socio-cultural context it is useful to discuss briefly the role of Sinéad O'Connor in the film and the set of references she brings to its overall structure.

O'Connor is best known in the USA for tearing up a picture of the Pope on prime-time television and her casting here as the Virgin Mary might suggest a degree of calculation on Jordan's part. There is no doubt that O'Connor's role was seen by some Catholics as provocative and insulting. Jordan has defended his decision on purely cinematic grounds. For him, O'Connor's bone structure and other facial qualities are reminiscent of the statues of the Virgin Mary that have dominated the public and private spaces of Catholic Ireland for over a century and the superbly cinematic nature of her brief appearances vindicate Jordan's decision. But O'Connor's public persona in Ireland is a little more complicated than perhaps it is in the USA.

She has made very public claims about being abused as a child (hotly disputed by members of her family) and she has taken a very public stance against child-abuse in general. Her music over the last few years has been dominated by the themes of mothering and childhood and in both her public pronouncements and in her music she has likened Ireland to an abused child. In her 1994 album *Universal Mother* there is a rap track called ' "Famine" ' (the quotation marks are important, indicating the track's theme that there never was a Famine, only a politically inspired destruction of the Irish people), in which she makes this analogy explicit. 'See we're like a child that's been battered', she argues and continues later in the track, 'I see the Irish as a race/ like a child that got itself bashed in the face'. Between the verses she sings snatches of the Beatles' 'Eleanor Rigby' ('Ah, look at all the lonely people/ Where do they all belong?').

It has to be said that this rap bears a passing resemblance to Francie Brady's monologue – disjointed and confused, slightly off-kilter in its historical references – but like Francie's as well it has its own internal logic, arguing that, as with all childhood traumas, Ireland's needs to be remembered and confronted if the country is to mature and move on. O'Connor is explicit about the nature of this childhood trauma. In particular, she locates it in the horrors of the Famine and the subsequent devastation and dispersal of the Irish population through starvation and emigration (all the lonely people whose sense of belonging is now being reclaimed by the Irish at home). In many ways, too, the song is contradictory and ambiguous, lambasting the patriarchal and abusive power of the Catholic church in Ireland and yet also chiding contemporary Ireland for ignoring its cultural heritage in the onward rush to embrace consumer modernity. What is interesting about O'Connor's work and her persona overall is that it suggests ways in which we can begin to understand the seeming obsession of Irish cinema with dysfunctional or incomplete families and especially with the interweaving themes of oedipal anxiety, child-abuse and incest, of which *The Butcher Boy* is the most complex example.

Clearly for O'Connor, as for many Irish directors who have broached the topic, child-abuse is both real and metaphorical. It is real in that the scandals and controversies of the 1990s have revealed the extent to which child-abuse was a factor in religious institutions in the recent past. More worrying, perhaps, is the horrifying thought of what the situation may have been in the distant past when it could have been more easily concealed. (For O'Connor, it is also real, of course, to the extent to which she herself has been a victim.) It is metaphorical in the sense that it symbolises the great abuse that the Irish people

The Abused Child of History:
Eamonn Owens in *The
Butcher Boy*

suffered, from colonialism generally but from the Famine and emigration in particular. This is suggestive indeed. The Famine hovers in Irish consciousness as a great tragedy that, like childhood trauma, has been suppressed and remains strangely unacknowledged. As Chris Morash has put it, the relative paucity of historical writing on the Famine is variously explained as a case of collective neurotic repression or as proof of the failure of revisionist historiography (Morash, 1995, p. 78). Thus O'Connor's 'abused child of history' is played out in countless ways in Irish culture, and like real-life controversies it involves a complex dialectic between accusations of suppression and hysteria on one side and 'false memory syndrome' on the other.

Francie Brady is the epitome of the abused child of Irish history, suffering through no fault of his own the degradations and neglect, abuse and exploitation that are the result of processes over which he has no control. He can only respond to the situations that he encounters, and if this response becomes increasingly unhinged and psychotic, it does so in direct proportion to the psychosis that is all around him. In this way, *The Butcher Boy* provides plenty of ammunition for both a revisionist and an anti-revisionist reading of Ireland's trauma. On one hand, Francie's psychosis is the product of the narrow Catholic society into which he was born, a culture riven by poverty, complacency, hypocrisy and neglect and encased in an unfeeling and empty nationalist rhetoric – precisely those social ills that modernisation and liberalisation set out to cure. In a deeper sense, though, following the metaphor of the family of the nation, the psychosis may lie further back, in the trauma of colonial oppression, Famine and emigration, which together have sapped the family of all its support mechanisms, leaving it disfigured and dysfunctional and prone to further dissipation. Francie's psychosis can also be seen as the result of the excesses of modernisation, personified in Mrs Nugent's pretentious airs and graces and her economic and social upward-mobility (significantly, traits which she picked up while living in England). The mismatch between modernity and traditional culture is epitomised in Francie's absorption of the language and images of American popular culture. As his world slowly unravels, the certainties and the security it once offered have been removed and his only option is to clutch uncritically at the discourses of a foreign popular culture, removed from the sources and roots that give them meaning. Denied his own rootedness and sense of belonging, he drifts off into a wholly idiosyncratic mental state that may contain its own internal logic but is ultimately murderously and violently negative. *The Butcher Boy*, therefore, seems to offer conflicting versions of Francie's dilemma and contrasting views of Ireland's recent history. Is it a revisionist or an anti-revisionist film? The answer inevitably is that it is both and neither at the same time, a wholly original exploration of these themes that challenges the familiar contours of both arguments.

One of the ironies about the cultural debates in Ireland, as we have seen, is that the broad revisionist/anti-revisionist camps referred to here are themselves intensely contradictory. Both have their neo-Marxist left and their conservative right wings, a situation on both sides that produces strange-bedfellows in the heat of political debate. Thus, the tragedy of Francie Brady can be appropriated by conservative economic modernisers as an indictment of the backward and superstitious Ireland of de Valera's 'frugal self-sufficiency' while at the same time endorsing a more neo-Marxist commitment to social and economic modernity and the wholesale radicalisation of the Irish economy.

Similarly, from the anti-revisionist right, Francie's confused voice can be read as an indictment of the destruction of traditional Catholic and rural values which modernisation has brought about and from the left as an attack on the uncritical acceptance in Ireland of (global) consumer capitalist values. Indeed in the post-colonial discourses favoured by many anti-revisionist critics on the left, one of the crucial questions is, following Spivak, 'can the subaltern speak?' (Spivak, 1993). Luke Gibbons, among others, has argued that the missing dis-

course in Irish culture is, in fact, the voice of rural Ireland, spoken for and traduced in the past by the nationalist (and urban) bourgeoisie and in
contemporary Ireland by the new liberal (again urban) revisionist consensus
(Gibbons, 1996). Rural Ireland represents for Gibbons, as we have seen, the suppressed 'radical memory' of the Irish, and in this regard Francie Brady can be
read as an attempt to 'voice' that which has gone unspoken, to render in
metaphorical terms the great hurt of the Irish people.

If this is so, however, it is the confused voice of the Irish subaltern, the voice
of rural Ireland caught in the cusp between two types of tradition and conflicting notions of modernity – between the formative, yet stifling aspects of
rootedness and the liberating, yet empty cosmopolitanism of *transcendence*. His
personal tragedy is intensely contradictory, testament to the essentially dialectical nature of his problem. As a metaphor for Ireland (the abused child of
history) the film offers neither nostalgia nor sentimentality, nor does it endorse
the certainties and complacency of the revisionist/anti-revisionist debates.
Francie's voice offers the audience no fixed point from which to assess his problem, the film inviting the audience to confront the complexities for itself.

In Francie Brady, Jordan and writer McCabe have, in a sense, conjured up an
Irish Caliban – amiable, likeable but deeply disturbed and driven to monstrous
acts by the injustices and abuse heaped upon him. Through the voice of this
Caliban, the film offers a certain logic and even justification for Francie's disturbed behaviour. Caliban, in all his glorious contradictions, was, of course, the
creation of a colonial imagination. Shakespeare's *The Tempest* was first performed in 1611 as England's colonial ambitions were expanding and the
colonisation of Ireland was being consolidated. The play rehearses, in the confrontations between Caliban and Prospero, some of the native/settler tensions
implicit in a process of cultural denigration that inevitably followed such con-
quest. Shakespeare describes Caliban as a 'savage and deformed slave' though it
is clear that until Prospero took over his island and told him otherwise, Caliban had a higher regard for himself and felt 'mine own king'. In his own way,
Francie Brady is a child of both colonial and neo-colonial cultural oppression.
As Caliban says of Prospero, 'You taught me language; and my profit on 't /Is,
I know how to curse' (Act 1, Scene ii, line 363). Francie, in other words, suffers
from a crisis of identity – at one minute speaking in the rich and idiomatic voice
of the native and yet confusedly mimicking the voice of the Anglo-American
coloniser. And yet, the film also invites the Irish audience, through a process of
identification with Francie's unsettling narrative, to ape Prospero's half-guilty
admission: 'This thing of darkness I acknowledge mine.' In this way, Francie is
a thoroughly Irish creation, born of a cultural imagining that suppressed
human warmth and blighted youthful optimism with the dead hand of
Catholic conformity.

In many ways, then, *The Butcher Boy* encapsulates the themes that we have located in recent Irish cinema in general. The film is concerned with the problem of reconciling the traumatic past of Irish history, both colonial and nationalist, with the realities and contradictions of its affluent present. Like so many recent films, it employs the metaphor of the dysfunctional or incomplete family to probe the psychosis of the nation. Like so many other Irish films, it is concerned with a moment of profound change, when an older order is fading and a newer order has not yet fully materialised. Thus the old and the new, the past and the future, coexist uneasily in an unsettled present. Although it addresses ultimately a political condition, it is a metaphorical rather than a political film, a characteristic we have noted already in much recent cinema. However, visually, *The Butcher Boy* lays assault to the dominant paradigms of cinematic Ireland and especially to the representation of landscape and rural life that continue to emanate from the Hollywood and the British industries. It is a film rich in a visual imagination which surprises, shocks and disturbs the audience and in the process reimagines Ireland in a profoundly challenging manner. In this regard, it is the film which most perfectly articulates the concatenation of forces that shape contemporary Ireland.

Bibliography

Achebe, Chinua (1990) 'The Song of Ourselves' in *New Statesman and Society*, 9 February

Adams, Michael (1968) *Censorship: The Irish Experience* (Alabama: University of Alabama Press)

Anderson, Benedict (1983) *Imagined Communities: Reflections on the Origin and Spread of Nationalism* (London: Verso)

Aniagolu, Chichi (1997) 'Being Black in Ireland' in Ethel Crowley and Jim MacLaughlin (eds) *Under the Belly of the Tiger: Class, Race, Identity and Culture in the Global Ireland* (Dublin: Irish Reporter Publications), pp. 43–52

Barrett, Alan and Fergal Trace (1998) 'Who is Coming Back? The Educational Profile of Returning Migrants in the 1990s', *Irish Banking Review*, Summer, pp. 38–51

Barrett, Sean (1997) 'Policy Changes, Output Growth and Investment in Irish Tourism 1986–96', *Irish Banking Review*, Autumn, pp. 39–48

Barry, Frank (ed.) (1999) *Understanding Ireland's Economic Growth* (London: Macmillan)

Barsam, Richard (1988) *The Vision of Robert Flaherty: The Artist as Myth and Filmmaker* (Bloomington and Indiana: Indiana University Press)

Barthes, Roland (1957/73) *Mythologies* (St. Albans: Granada)

Barton, Ruth (1997) 'From history to heritage: Some recent developments in Irish Cinema', *The Irish Review*, 21, Autumn/Winter, pp. 41–56.

Barton, Ruth (1999) 'Feisty Colleens and Faithful Sons: Gender in Irish Cinema', *Cinéaste*, xxiv, (2/3) (Contemporary Irish cinema supplement), pp. 40–45

Berger, John (1972) *Ways of Seeing* (Harmondsworth: Penguin)

Billig, Michael (1995) *Banal Nationalism* (London: Sage)

Black, Cathal (1996) Interview, *Film West*, 24 (Spring), pp. 18–22

Black, Gregory D. (1997) *The Catholic Crusade Against the Movies, 1940–1975* (Cambridge: Cambridge University Press)

Brown, Terence (1981) *Ireland: A Social and Cultural History* (London: Fontana)

Burke, Marina (1995) *Telling Tales*, Film Ireland, 48, August/September, pp. 24–5

Butler, David (1993/4) 'High Boot Benny', *Film Ireland*, December/January, pp. 30–32

Caherty, Thérèse et al. (eds) (1992) *Is Ireland a Third World Country?* (Belfast: Beyond the Pale Publications)

Calder-Marshall, Arthur (1963) *The Innocent Eye: The Life of Robert J. Flaherty* (London: W. H. Allen)

Chanan, Michael (1997) 'The Changing Geography of Third Cinema', *Screen*, 38 (4) (Winter), pp. 372–88

Collins, Michael (1922/1968) *The Path to Freedom* (Dublin, Mercier)

Coombes, Annie E. (1991) 'Ethnography and National and Cultural Identities' in Susan Hiller (ed.), *The Myth of Primitiveness* (London: Routledge), pp. 189–214

Coulter, Carol (1992) 'Where in the World?' in Thérèse Caherty et al. (eds) *Is Ireland a Third World Country?* (Belfast: Beyond the Pale Publications), pp. 3–14

Coulter, Carol (1998) 'Feminism and Nationalism in Ireland' in David Miller (ed.) *Rethinking Northern Ireland* (Harlow: Addison Wesley Longman), pp. 160–78

Crowley, Ethel and Jim MacLaughlin (eds) (1997) *Under the Belly of the Tiger: Class, Race, Identity and Culture in the Global Ireland* (Dublin: Irish Reporter Publications)

Cullen, Paul (1997) 'The 1997 Border Campaign: Refugees, Asylum and Race on the Borders' in Ethel Crowley and Jim MacLaughlin (eds) *Under the Belly of the Tiger: Class, Race, Identity and Culture in the Global Ireland* (Dublin: Irish Reporter Publications), pp. 101–8

Curran, Joseph M. (1989) *Hibernian Green on the Silver Screen: The Irish and American Movies* (Westport, Conn.: Greenwood)

Curtis Jr., L. P. (1968) *Anglo-Saxons and the Celts: A Study of Anti-Irish Prejudice in Victorian England* (Bridgeport, Conn.: Conference on British Studies)

Curtis Jr., L. P. (1971/1997) *Apes and Angels* (Newton Abbot: David and Charles)

Curtis, Liz (1984) *Nothing But the Same Old Story: The Roots of Anti-Irish Racism* (London: Information on Ireland)

Darby, John (1983) *Dressed to Kill: Cartoonists and the Northern Ireland Conflict* (Belfast: Appletree)

Deane, Seamus (ed.) (1991) *The Field Day Anthology of Irish Writing* (Derry: Field Day Publications), 3 volumes

Deane, Seamus (1992) 'Canon Fodder: Literary Mythologies in Ireland' in J. Lundy and A. Mac Póilin (eds) *Styles of Belonging: The Cultural Identities of Ulster* (Belfast: Lagan Press), pp. 22–32

Dunne, Tom (1992) 'New Histories: Beyond "Revisionism"', *The Irish Review*, 12 (Spring/Summer), pp. 1–12

Durkan, Joseph, D. Fitz Gerald and C. Harmon (1999) 'Education and Growth in the Irish Economy' in Frank Barry (ed.) *Understanding Ireland's Economic Growth* (London: Macmillan)

Eagleton, Terry (1995) *Heathcliff and the Great Hunger: Studies in Irish Culture* (London, Verso)

Eagleton, Terry (1998) *Crazy John and the Bishop and Other Essays on Irish Culture* (Cork: Cork University Press)

Economic and Social Research Institute (ESRI) (1999) *Medium Term Review* (Dublin: ESRI)

Edge, Sarah (1998) 'Representing Gender and National Identity' in David Miller (ed.) *Rethinking Northern Ireland* (Harlow: Addison Wesley Longman), pp. 211–27

Eijsbouts, W. T. (1999) 'Law, Limit, Life: Reflections on the Irish legal system as a sensory organism', *The Irish Review*, 24 (Autumn), pp. 1–8

Elsaesser, Thomas (1988) *New German Cinema* (London: BFI)

Empire (1994a) 'Oh Dear … An American punter sues Universal Pictures over the "hyped-up" *In the Name of the Father*', 59 (April), p. 9

Empire (1994b) *The Empire Guide to the Hottest Sex Scenes in the Movies*, 65 (November) (free booklet)

Espinosa, Julio García (1993) 'The double morality of cinema', *Vertigo*, 2 (Summer/Autumn), pp. 12–16

Fanning, Ronan (1983) *Independent Ireland* (Dublin: Helicon)

Film Base News (1989), 15 (November/ December), p. 1 (Statement of Aims)

Fisher, Desmond (1978) *Broadcasting in Ireland* (London: Routledge and Kegan Paul)

Frampton, Kenneth (1985) 'Towards a Critical Regionalism: Six Points for an Architecture of Resistance' in Hal Foster (ed.) *Postmodern Culture* (London: Pluto Press), pp. 16–30

French, Brandon (1978) *On the Verge of Revolt: Women in American Films of the Fifties* (New York: Frederick Ungar)

Gellner, Ernest (1983) *Nations and Nationalism* (Oxford: Blackwell)

Gibbons, Luke (1987) 'Romanticism in Ruins: Developments in Recent Irish Cinema', *The Irish Review*, 2, pp. 59–63

Gibbons, Luke (1988a) 'Romanticism, Realism and Irish Cinema' in Kevin Rockett, Luke Gibbons and John Hill, *Cinema and Ireland* (London: Routledge), pp. 194–257

Gibbons, Luke (1988b) 'Coming out of Hibernation? The Myth of Modernity in Irish Culture' in Richard Kearney (ed.) *Across the Frontiers: Ireland in the 1990s* (Dublin: Wolfhound Press), pp. 205–18

Gibbons, Luke (1990) 'Fragments in Pictures – an interview with Thaddeus O'Sullivan', *Film Base News*, November/December, pp. 8–12

Gibbons, Luke (1991) 'Challenging the Canon: Revisionism and Cultural Criticism' in Seamus Deane (ed.) *The Field Day Anthology of Irish Writing* (Derry: Field Day), 3, pp. 561–8

Gibbons, Luke (1992) 'On the Beach', *Artforum*, October, p. 13

Gibbons, Luke (1996) *Transformations in Irish Culture* (Cork: Cork University Press in association with Field Day)

Goldring, Maurice (1975/1982) *Faith of our Fathers: The Formation of Irish Nationalist Ideology 1890–1920* (Dublin: Repsol)

Graham, C. (1994) ' "Liminal Spaces": Post-Colonial Theories and Irish Culture', *The Irish Review*, 16 (Autumn/Winter), pp. 29–43

Hailes, Anne (1998) 'It's "Cool" to be Irish', *The Irish News*, 22 April, p. 11

Harkin, Margo (1991) 'Broadcasting in a Divided Community', panel discussion, in Martin McLoone (ed.) *Culture, Identity and Broadcasting in Ireland: Local Issues, Global Perspectives* (Belfast: Institute of Irish Studies), pp. 110–16

Higgins, Michael D. (1995) Public interview at the National Film Theatre, London, October

Hill, John (1988) 'Images of Violence' in Kevin Rockett, Luke Gibbons and John Hill, *Cinema and Ireland* (London: Routledge), pp. 147–93

Hill, John (1990) '*The Quiet Man*' in Nicholas Thomas (ed.) *International Dictionary of Films and Film-makers – 1: Films* (Chicago and London: St James Press), pp. 732–3

Hill, John (1991) 'Hidden Agenda: Politics and the Thriller', *Circa*, 57 (May/June), pp. 36–41

Hill, John (1996) '*Some Mother's Son*', Review article, *Cinéaste*, xxiii (1), pp. 44–5

Hill, John (1999a) *British Cinema in the 1980s* (Oxford: Oxford University Press)

Hill, John (1999b) ' "The Past is Always There in the Present": *Fools of Fortune* and the Heritage Movie' in James MacKillop (ed.) *Contemporary Irish Cinema* (Syracuse, NY: Syracuse University Press), pp. 29–39

Hill, John (1999c) 'Film Production in Northern Ireland – A Brief History', *Green Screen* – Special supplement on the contemporary Irish film industry, *Fortnight*, 379 (June), pp. 5–7

Hill, John and Martin McLoone (1996) *Big Picture, Small Screen: The Relations Between Film and Television* (Luton: John Libbey/University of Luton Press)

Hobsbawm, E. J. (1990) *Nations and Nationalism since 1780: Programme, Myth, Reality* (Cambridge: Cambridge University Press)

Hutchinson, John (1987) *The Dynamics of Cultural Nationalism* (London: Allen & Unwin)

Hyde, Douglas (1892/1986) 'The Necessity for De-Anglicising Ireland' in Douglas Hyde, *Language, Lore and Lyrics* (Dublin: Irish Academic Press), pp. 153–70

Hyndman, David (1995) 'Broadcasters Call the Shots?', *Film West*, 20 (Spring), p. 7

Ignatiev, Noel (1995) *How the Irish Became White* (London: Routledge)

Inglis, Tom (1987) *Moral Monopoly: The Catholic Church in Modern Irish Society* (Dublin: Gill and Macmillan)

Johnston, Claire (1981) '*Maeve*', *Screen*, 22 (4), pp. 54–71 (Review article and interview)

Jones, Harri Pritchard (1974) *Wales Ireland: A TV Contrast* (Dublin: Conradh na Gaeilge)

Jordan, Neil (1996) *Michael Collins: Film Diary and Screenplay* (London: Vintage)

Kaplan, E. Anne (1978) *Women in Film Noir* (London: BFI)

Kedourie, Elie (1960) *Nationalism* (London: Hutchinson)

Kennedy, Liam (1992/3) 'Modern Ireland: Post-Colonial Society or Post-Colonial Pretensions?', *The Irish Review*, 13 (Winter), pp. 107–21

King, Philip (1991) (producer) *Bringing It All Back Home* (Hummingbird Production for BBC in association with RTÉ). A five-part documentary series on the influence and development of Irish music

Kirkland, Richard (1999) 'Gender, Nation, Excess: Reading *Hush-a-Bye Baby*' in Scott Brewster et al. (eds) *Ireland in Proximity: History, Gender, Space* (London: Routledge), pp. 109–21

Knobel, Dale T. (1986) *Paddy and the Republic: Ethnicity and Nationality in Antebellum America* (Middletown, Conn.: Wesleyan University Press)

Lee, J. J. (1989) *Ireland 1912–1985: Politics and Society* (Cambridge: Cambridge University Press)

Linehan, Hugh (1999) 'Myth, Mammon and Mediocrity: The Trouble with Recent Irish Cinema', *Cinéaste*, xxiv, (2/3) (Contemporary Irish cinema supplement), pp. 46–9

Lourdeaux, Lee (1990) *Italian and Irish Filmmakers in America* (Philadelphia: Temple University Press)

Lyons, F. S. L. (1971) *Ireland Since the Famine* (London: Fontana)

Lyons, F. S. L. (1979) *Culture and Anarchy in Ireland* (Oxford: Oxford University Press)

MacLaughlin, Jim (1997) 'Ireland in the Global Economy: An End to a Distinct Nation' in Ethel Crowley and Jim Mac Laughlin (eds) *Under the Belly of the Tiger: Class, Race, Identity and Culture in the Global Ireland* (Dublin: Irish Reporter Publications), pp. 1–22

MacLaughlin, Jim (1999) 'The "New" Intelligentsia and the Reconstruction of the Irish Nation', *The Irish Review*, 24 (Autumn), p. 65

MacKillop, James (1999) 'The Quiet Man Speaks' in James MacKillop (ed.) *Contemporary Irish Cinema* (Syracuse, NY: Syracuse University Press), pp. 169–81

McBride, Joseph and Michael Wilmington (1974) *John Ford* (London: Secker and Warburg)

McCafferty, Nell (1985) *A Woman to Blame* (Dublin: Attic Press)

McCann, Eamon (1988) 'Drama Out of a Crisis', *Broadcast*, 19 September, pp. 17–18

McCourt, Frank (1996) *Angela's Ashes* (New York: Scribner)

McIlroy, Brian (1998) *Shooting to Kill: Film-making and the "Troubles" in Northern Ireland* (Trowbridge: Flicks)

McLaughlin, Noel and Martin McLoone (2000) 'Hybridity and National Musics: The Case of Irish Rock Music', *Popular Music*, 19 (2), pp. 181–99

McLoone, Martin (1984) 'Strumpet City – The Urban Working Class on Television' in Martin McLoone and John MacMahon (eds), *Television and Irish Society: 21 Years of Irish Television* (Dublin: RTÉ and Irish Film Institute), pp. 53–88

McLoone, Martin (1988) 'ACNI-Culture – A Blurred Vision', *Circa*, 39 (April/ May), pp. 17–21

McLoone, Martin (1991a) 'Inventions and Re-imaginings: Some Thoughts on Identity and Broadcasting in Ireland' in Martin McLoone (ed.) *Culture, Identity and Broadcasting in Ireland* (Belfast: Institute of Irish Studies), pp. 2–31

McLoone, Martin (1991b) 'Spirit of the Festival', *Circa*, 56 (March/April), pp. 34–5

McLoone, Martin (1993) 'The Commitments – The NIO anti-terrorism ads', *Fortnight*, 321 (October), pp. 34–6

McLoone, Martin (1994) 'National Cinema and Cultural Identity: Ireland and Europe', in John Hill, Martin McLoone and Paul Hainsworth (eds) *Border Crossing: Film in Ireland, Britain and Europe* (Belfast, London: Institute of Irish Studies, BFI), pp. 146–73

McLoone, Martin (1996) 'Boxed In? The Aesthetics of Film and Television' in John Hill and Martin McLoone, *Big Picture, Small Screen: The Relations Between Film and Television* (Luton: John Libbey /University of Luton Press), pp. 76–106

McLoone, Martin (1999) 'December Bride: A Landscape Peopled Differently' in James MacKillop (ed.) *Contemporary Irish Cinema: From* The Quiet Man *to* Dancing at Lughnasa (Syracuse: Syracuse University Press)

McLoone, Martin (2000) 'Music Hall Dope and British Propaganda? Cultural Identity and Early Broadcasting in Ireland', *Historical Journal of Film, Radio and Television*, 20/3, pp. 301–15

McLoone, Martin and John MacMahon (eds) (1984) *Television and Irish Society: 21 Years of Irish Television* (Dublin: RT´ and Irish Film Institute)

McNee, Gerry (1990) *In the Footsteps of* The Quiet Man (Edinburgh: Mainstream Publishing)

McQuillan, Deirdre (1994) *Mary Robinson: A President in Progress* (Dublin: Gill and Macmillan)

McSwiney, Séamus (1996) 'From Hollywood Barracks to Hollywood Boulevard', Interview with Terry George, *Film West*, 25 (Summer), pp. 10–17

McWhiney, Grady (1988) *Cracker Culture: Celtic Ways in the Old South* (Tuscaloosa: University of Alabama Press)

Mansfield, Michael (1994) 'Jurassic Justice', *Sight and Sound*, 4 (3), p. 7

Morash, Chris (1995) 'Spectres of the Famine', *The Irish Review*, 17/18 (Winter), pp. 74–9

Mullen, Pat (1934) *Man of Aran* (London: Faber and Faber)

Mulvey, Laura (1975) 'Visual Pleasure and Narrative Cinema', *Screen*, 16 (2), pp. 6–18

Murphy, Clíona (1992) 'Women's History, Feminist History, or Gender History?', *The Irish Review*, 12 (Spring/Summer), pp. 21–6

Murphy, Tim (1997) 'Immigrants and Refugees: The Irish Legal Context' in Ethel Crowley and Jim MacLaughlin (eds) *Under the Belly of the Tiger: Class, Race, Identity and Culture in the Global Ireland* (Dublin: Irish Reporter Publications), pp. 95–100

Murphy, William T. (1978) *Robert Flaherty: A Guide to References and Sources* (Boston, Mass: G. K. Hall & Co.)

Nairn, Tom (1977) *The Break-up of Britain: Crisis and Neo-Nationalism* (London: New Left Books)

O'Brien, Conor Cruise (1972) *States of Ireland* (London: Hutchinson)

O Caóllaí, Maolsheachlainn (1974) *Open Broadcasting: A Recipe for Extinction* (Dublin: Conradh na Gaeilge)

O Caóllaí, Maolsheachlainn (1975a) *Open Broadcasting: An Alternative* (Dublin: Conradh na Gaeilge)

O Caóllaí, Maolsheachlainn (1975b) *Broadcasting and the Growth of a Culture* (Dublin: Conradh na Gaeilge)

O Caóllaí, Maolsheachlainn (1979) *Tiarnas Cultúir: Craolachán in Èirinn* (Dublin: Conradh na Gaeilge)

O'Connor, Nuala, (1991) *Bringing It All Back Home: The Influence of Irish Music* (London: BBC Books)

O'Connor, Derek (1997) 'Irish Trash Classics – The Courier', *Film West*, 29, p. 10

O'Dowd, Liam (1992) 'State Legitimacy and Nationalism in Ireland' in P. Clancy, M. Kelly, J. Wiatr and R. Zoltanieckie (eds) *Ireland and Poland: Comparative Perspectives* (Dublin: Department of Sociology, UCD)

Ó'Gráda, Cormac (1997) *A Rocky Road: The Irish Economy Since the 1920s* (Manchester: Manchester University Press)

Irish Film

Irish Film: *The Emergence of a Contemporary Cinema* will be published by Indiana University Press on April 23, 2001. Oscars for Daniel Day Lewis and Brenda Fricker for their roles in <u>My Left Foot</u> (1989) and Neil Jordan's original screenplay Oscar for <u>The Crying Game</u> (1992) are examples of the international recognition that the growing body of Irish cinema has attained in recent years. **Irish Film** explores the dominant images of the Irish found in British and American cinema and considers the ways in which recent Irish-made films might be said to be a response to them. The book offers detailed readings of a wide range of key films, including <u>The Butcher Boy</u> (1998), <u>Patriot Games</u> (1993), and <u>Angela's Ashes</u> (2000). It discusses the full range of Irish cinematic production, from the low-budget work of indigenous filmmakers like Comerford and Breathnach, to the bigger Hollywood productions like Ron Howard's Far and Away (1992), and the "second" cinema of a number of Irish directors such as Neil Jordan and Jim Sheridan, where medium-sized budgets permitted greater creative control.

". . . This book, therefore, is about contemporary Ireland and the cinema which it both produces and inspires. It adopts a broad strategy that considers cinema in a wider cultural, social and historical context. It is concerned to look at the way in which Irish society has had an impact on the cinema as well as the way in which the cinema has reflected back on Irish society. Especially of interest is the legacy of emigration and the broadening definitions of Irishness that a renewed interest in this has helped to promote. Such definitions, the book argues, are imagined and constantly reimagined in the cultural arena, subject to wider economic and social forces. One key site for such a process is the cinema and diasporic definitions of Irishness especially have played a key role in the development of cinematic genres and stereotypes in the cinema in general. The diasporic imagination, however, has always existed in a complicated relationship to the native and a key theme in the book is the way in which these have interacted down the years. Crucial in this regard is the nature of the native imagining that came to dominate culture and society in Ireland itself in the twentieth century. . ."

—from the Introduction

About the Author:
Martin McLoone is Senior Lecturer in Media Studies, University of Ulster at Coleraine.

INDIANA UNIVERSITY PRESS

601 North Morton Street
Bloomington, Indiana
47404-3797

812-855-4203
Fax: 812-855-8507

Book Information:
Irish Film: *The Emergence of a Contemporary Cinema*
by **Martin McLoone**
British Film Institute
240 pages, illus., bibl., index, 6 x 9 1/4
Cloth; ISBN: 0-85170-792-0; Price: $65.00 / Paper; ISBN: 0-85170-793-9 Price: $27.95
To be distributed <u>April 23, 2001</u> by Indiana University Press
Available at bookstores or by calling 1-800-842-6796
Release Date: April 9, 2001

O'Neill, Liam (1987) 'The Making of *Frankie and Johnny*', *Film Base News* (now *Film Ireland*), 3 (September/October), pp. 4–5

O'Toole, Fintan (1997) *The Ex-Isle of Erin: Images of Global Ireland* (Dublin: New Ireland Books)

O'Toole, Fintan (1999) 'Working-Class Dublin on Screen: The Roddy Doyle Films', *Cinéaste*, xxiv, (2/3) (Contemporary Irish cinema supplement), pp. 36–9

Paisley, Ian R. K. (1959) *The 59 Revival* (Belfast: Free Presbyterian Church)

Palmer, Catherine (1998) 'From Theory to Practice: Experiencing the Nation in Everyday Life', *Journal of Material Culture*, 3/2, pp. 175–99

Pettitt, Lance (1997) 'Pigs and Provos, Prostitutes and Prejudice: Gay Representation in Irish Film, 1984–1995' in Éibhear Walshe (ed.) *Sex, Nation and Dissent in Irish Writing* (Cork: Cork University Press), pp. 252–84

Pickard, Roy (1980) *The Award Movies* (London: Frederick Muller Ltd.)

Pines, Jim and Paul Willemen (1989) (eds) *Questions of Third Cinema* (London: BFI)

Place, Janey (1979) *The Non-Western Films of John Ford* (Secaucus, NJ: Citadel Press)

Pramaggiore, Maria (1998) 'The Celtic Blue Note: Jazz in Neil Jordan's "Night in Tunisia", *Angel* and *The Miracle*', *Screen*, 39 (3) (Autumn), pp. 272–88

Quinn, Bob (1999), 'Irish Cinema at the Crossroads: A Filmmakers' Symposium', *Cinéaste*, xxiv (2/3) (Contemporary Irish cinema supplement), p. 73

Robertson, Roland (1992) *Globalization: Social Theory and Global Culture* (London: Sage)

Rockett, Kevin (1980) *Film and Ireland: A Chronicle* (London: A Sense of Ireland) (Booklet)

Rockett, Kevin (1988) 'History, Politics and Irish Cinema' in Kevin Rockett, Luke Gibbons and John Hill, *Cinema and Ireland* (London: Routledge), pp. 3–146

Rockett, Kevin (1991) 'Aspects of the Los Angelesation of Ireland', *Irish Communications Review*, 1, pp. 18–23

Rockett, Kevin (1994) 'Culture, Industry and Irish Cinema' in John Hill, Martin McLoone and Paul Hainsworth (eds) *Border Crossing: Film in Ireland, Britain and Europe* (Belfast, London: Institute of Irish Studies, BFI), pp. 126–39

Rockett, Kevin (1996) *The Irish Filmography* (Dublin: Red Mountain Press)

Rockett, Kevin (1999) 'Irish Cinema: The National in the International', *Cinéaste*, xxiv (2–3) (Contemporary Irish cinema supplement), pp. 23–5

Rockett, Kevin, Luke Gibbons and John Hill (1988) *Cinema and Ireland* (London: Routledge)

Roddick, Nick (2000) 'Quality Street' (Review of *Angela's Ashes*), *Sight and Sound*, 10 (1), pp. 40–41

Said, Edward W. (1978) *Orientalism: Western Perceptions of the Orient* (Harmondsworth: Penguin)

Said, Edward W. (1988) *Nationalism, Colonialism and Literature: Yeats and Decolonization* (Derry: Field Day)

Schiller, Herbert I. (1978) *New Modes of Cultural Domination* (Text of a Lecture given to Conradh na Gaeilge, 2 September 1975) (Dublin: Conradh na Gaeilge)

Sight and Sound (1996) 'Purity' (editorial), *Sight and Sound*, 6 (10) (October), p. 3

Slater, Eamonn (1993) 'Contested Terrain: Differing Interpretations of Co. Wicklow's Landscape', *Irish Journal of Sociology*, 3, pp. 23–55

Solanas, Fernando and Octavio Gettino (sic) (1969/1976) 'Towards a Third Cinema' in Bill Nicholls (ed.) *Movies and Methods* (Berkeley: University of California Press), pp. 44–64

Sontag, Susan (1975) 'Fascinating Fascism' in Bill Nicholls (ed.) *Movies and Methods* (Berkeley: University of California Press), pp. 31–43

Stoneman, Rod (1995) 'Creativity,
Continuity, Cinema …', *Review and
Annual Report 1994* (Galway: Bord
Scannán na hÉireann/The Irish Film
Board), pp. 3–5

Spivak, Gayatri Chakravorty (1993) 'Can the
Subaltern Speak?' in P. Williams and L.
Chrisman (eds) *Colonial Discourse and
Post-Colonial Theory: A Reader* (Hemel
Hempstead: Harvester Wheatsheaf),
pp. 66–111

Sullivan, Megan (1998) 'Orla Walsh's *The
Visit* [1992]: Incarceration and Feminist
Cinema in Northern Ireland', *New
Hibernia Review/Iris Éireannach Nua*, 2
(2) (Samhradh/ Summer), pp. 85–99

Sweeney, Paul (1998) *The Celtic Tiger:
Ireland's Economic Miracle Explained*
(Dublin: Oak Tree Press)

Taylor, Richard (1995) 'Response to David
Hyndman's Letter', *Film West*, 21
(Summer), p. 7

Tobin, Fergal (1984) *The Best of Decades:
Ireland in the 1960s* (Dublin: Gill and
Macmillan)

Walsh, Orla (1998) Letters, *Film Ireland*, 65
(June/July), p. 44

Webster, Duncan (1989) *Looka Yonder: The
Imaginary America of Populist Culture*
(London: Routledge)

Whyte, John (1971) *Church and State in
Modern Ireland 1923–70* (Dublin: Gill
and Macmillan)

Willemen, Paul (1989) 'The Third Cinema
Question: Notes and Reflections' in Jim
Pines and Paul Willemen (eds) *Questions
of Third Cinema* (London: BFI), pp. 1–29

Williams, Raymond (1985) *The Country and
the City* (London: Hogarth Press)

Wollen, Peter (1972) *Signs and Meanings in
the Cinema* (London: Secker and
Warburg)

List of Illustrations

Whilst considerable effort has been made to identify correctly the copyright holders this has not been possible in all cases. We apologise for any apparent negligence and any omissions or corrections brought to our attention will be remedied in any future editions.

Frontispiece: *Fifth Province* Ocean Films/Strawberry Vale/British Screen; **Introduction:** *I Could Read the Sky* Arts Council of England/Irish Film Board/Channel Four/British Film Institute; *The Disappearance of Finbar* © First City Features Ltd/Samson Films Ltd/Victoria Film AB: **Chapter 1:** *The Butcher Boy* © Geffen Pictures; *Angela's Ashes* © Universal City Studios/Polygram Holdings, Inc./Paramount Pictures; **Chapter 2:** *Man of Aran* Gainsborough Pictures/Gaumont-British Picture Corporation; *The Quiet Man* Republic Pictures Corporation; **Chapter 3:** *JAK* Cartoon © Patrick Jackson; *Blown Away* Trilogy Entertainment Group/UIP; *In the Name of the Father* Hell's Kitchen/Universal Pictures; *Resurrection Man* © Polygram Films (UK) Ltd/Polygram Filmed Entertainment; **Chapter 4:** *Hush-A-Bye Baby* Derry Films & Video Collective; **Chapter 5:** *Down the Corner* Ballyfermot Community Arts Film Workshop/Arts Council of Ireland/Radio-Telefís Éireann; **Chapter 6:** *Maeve* British Film Institute Production Board/Radio-Telefís Éireann; **Chapter 7:** *Blessed Fruit* Roisín Rua Films; **Chapter 8:** *A Love Divided* Parallel Film Productions/Radio-Telefís Éireann/Bord Scannàn na hÉireann/BBC Films; *Last of the High Kings* First Independent/Miramax Films/ Parallel Film Productions Ltd; *The Last Bus Home* Bandit Films/Irish Screen/Bord Scannàn na hÉireann; *Agnes Browne* Hell's Kitchen/Good Machine/October Films/UIP; **Chapter 9:** *This Is My Father* Buena Vista International (Ireland)/Filmline International Inc./Hummingbird Communications Ltd; **Chapter 10:** *The Commitments* First Film Company/Dirty Hands/Beacon Communications/20th Century-Fox; *December Bride* Little Bird/Film Four International/Central Independent Television/Ulster TV/British Screen; **Chapter 11:** *The Butcher Boy* © Geffen Pictures; **Jacket:** *The Butcher Boy* © Geffen Pictures

Index